THE EUCHARISTIC
JEREMY TAYL

The Most Reverend H. R. McAdoo, PhD, DD, STD was born in 1916 and educated at the Mountjoy School and Trinity College, Dublin. His career in the Church of Ireland began as Curate Assistant at Christ Church Cathedral, Waterford in 1939 and he was elected a Bishop in 1962 and Archbishop of Dublin and Primate of Ireland in 1977. He is the author of many distinguished articles and contributions and his best known publications are *The Structure of Caroline Moral Theology* (1949), *The Spirit of Anglicanism* (1968) and *Rome and the Anglicans* (1985, with J. C. Aveling and D. M. Loades). Recently he has contributed to *Authority in the Anglican Communion* (Toronto 1987) and *Christian Authority* (Oxford 1988).

He was a member of the Joint Preparatory Anglican/Roman Catholic Commission which produced the *Malta Report* (1968) and Co-Chairman of ARCIC I which produced the *Final Report* (1982).

The Eucharistic Theology of Jeremy Taylor Today

H. R. McADOO

THE CANTERBURY PRESS NORWICH

The Canterbury Press Norwich, St Mary's Works,
St Mary's Plain, Norwich, Norfolk NR3 3BH

The Canterbury Press Norwich is a publishing imprint
of Hymns Ancient & Modern Limited

Cover design by Richard Morgan

ISBN 1 85311 004 3

First published 1988

The Publishers and author extend a general acknowledgement of grateful
thanks to all persons, or their representatives, whose work has been referred
to or quoted in this text.

Photoset in Great Britain by
Rowland Phototypesetting Limited, Bury St Edmunds, Suffolk
and printed by St Edmundsbury Press Limited,
Bury St Edmunds, Suffolk

Contents

FOR LESLEY

Introduction

WHY SHOULD ANGLICANS TODAY READ A BOOK ABOUT JEREMY TAYLOR? It is a good question the answer to which lies not only in the man himself, a complex and attractive personality who suffered for his Church, but in the range and depth of his contribution to the spirit of Anglicanism. What Taylor gave in terms of spiritual and moral theology, of eucharistic theology and of the independent liberality of his thinking has been absorbed into the Anglican blood-stream. What we are as Anglicans is in part shaped by our community memory and by those figures which stand out with varying degrees of vividness in that memory. That which essentially constitutes the Church is the Word and Sacraments, the Book and the Bread used by the Spirit to build up in the baptised members of the household of apostolic faith a new quality of life in Christ. That which is formative and normative for the Church at all levels of its life is the gospel. Yet there is another element, time-conditioned but subtly pervasive, which goes to establish a distinctive identity for the Church in each of its local manifestations. It has to do with the manner and mode of a Church's reception, interpretation and proclamation of the faith 'once for all delivered'. It is about how in the course of its history a Church understands, expounds and lives that faith, for 'we have this treasure in earthen vessels'. Not only the style of the interpretation and presentation of the 'deposit of faith', but outstanding interpreters and presenters, live in the consciousness of the local Church. Both it and they become part of what the Church is in time and space, part of our community memory, an element in our identity. Anglicanism would not be what today we understand it to be without creative figures in our collective memory such as Cranmer, Jewel, Hooker, the Cambridge Platonists, Stillingfleet, Keble,

Pusey, Liddon and countless others who transmitted the Faith in the way that they did. Among them and in that memory which is more than simply historical record since it is also a sort of ecclesial consciousness, Jeremy Taylor occupies a place important in his own right but significant too for the development of Anglican theology in our time. To substantiate that claim and in particular to show the relevance of his eucharistic theology to the inter-Church dialogues and Agreements on that subject, so vital for Christian unity, is the objective of this study.

As to the man himself, we are dealing with a highly-qualified theological mind, an expert in the patristic tradition who, as his friend George Rust observed, 'had the acuteness of a school-man, the profoundness of a philosopher . . . and the piety of a saint'. More than that, Taylor's spirit was always independent and even individualist to the extent that, in spite of the contemporary popularity of many of his writings, he was not really trusted by powerful church-leaders such as Sheldon. Time and again, we are struck by the curiously 'modern' tone of his writings and by the way in which he anticipates later developments in theology and liturgy. There is a quality of liberality in his thought which we find congenial today, keeping company as it does with a serene confidence concerning the faith 'once for all delivered'.

Born in 1613 at Cambridge to Nathaniel and Mary Taylor, his father being a barber and churchwarden, Jeremy Taylor was a pupil at the Perse School and proceeded at the age of fifteen to Gonville and Caius College where eventually he received a junior Fellowship. He was duly ordained, and Rust, later Bishop of Dromore and a minor Cambridge Platonist, commented at this time on Taylor's 'florid and youthful beauty, and sweet and pleasant air'. Archbishop Laud heard of his eloquence and learning and sent for him. Some time later and on Laud's proposal he became a Fellow of All Souls, Oxford. His friendship there with Chillingworth would be one of the influences which combined with his High Church views to produce a theologian who remained very much his own man. In 1638 he was instituted rector of Uppingham and he was appointed a royal chaplain at Laud's instigation who also made him one of his own chaplains. In the same year he was married and the academic began to learn the skills of pastor and parish priest. At the same time he was proceeding with the writing of *Episcopacy Asserted*. The scene seemed set for a normal progression, with favourable omens, in the clerical life but the storm broke. Laud was impeached and the clergy became targets. Just at this time, Taylor's small son died and he himself, as a royal chaplain, joined the king at Nottingham. In the ensuing turmoil his whereabouts are not known though he was appointed to the parish of Overstone in the following year but it is not certain that he ever went there. We do know that he was taken prisoner at Cardigan Castle in 1645. Taylor had gone into Wales and now, being a priest whose living had been sequestered, he had set up a school at Newton Hall near Golden Grove in company with William Nicholson, also ejected from his Welsh parish, and with William Wyatt, an Oxford friend. It seems likely that when the war came to Wales, Taylor had joined again as an army chaplain and had been captured. At all events, he was released through the efforts of Lord Carbery and the co-operation of Colonel Laugharne whom he describes in *The Liberty of Prophesying* as 'a noble enemy'. Taylor then became private chaplain to the Carbery household and continued with his schoolmastering.

Thus began at Golden Grove a lengthy period of intense literary activity interrupted by a second period of imprisonment at Chepstow Castle. From time to time he visited London and became a friend of the diarist John Evelyn to whom he acted as spiritual adviser. The haven of Golden Grove gave Taylor the quiet and the time he needed for writing and it is to this period that belongs the greater part of his tremendous output. Domestic tragedies however marred his peace: his beloved wife died in 1651 and though later he married happily again three more of his children died. Anglicanism is indebted to the hospitality and seclusion of Golden Grove in Wales for much that has passed into its lifestream from books such as *Holy Living* and *Holy Dying*, *The Real Presence* and *Unum Necessarium*.

By 1657 we find Taylor now serving hidden congregations in London, a dangerous and illegal ministry, and once again being put in gaol, his release this time being obtained through the efforts of the influential Evelyn. Still he was writing and casting his net wide to include his major work on moral theology, *Ductor Dubitantium*, published in the year of the Restoration, and preceded by his liturgically remarkable

Collection of Offices in 1658. Sadly, in the same year another son died, though three of his daughters outlived him, one of them to marry Francis Marsh, later Archbishop of Dublin, temporarily driven from his see at the accession of James II.

Wales sheltered Taylor for the best part of twenty years and there he produced the books which we shall be considering. At the Restoration he hoped for an English bishopric but the most outstanding theological writer and one of the most admired preachers of the seventeenth-century English Church was mistrusted by the ecclesiastical powers-that-be because of his independence and liberality of mind. He was instead nominated Bishop of Down and Connor and shortly afterwards Vice-Chancellor of the University of Dublin. So it was in the other part of 'the Celtic fringe' that Taylor completed his ministry. Commenting on the episcopal appointments made between 1660 and 1663, I. M. Green writes that 'obscurity is perhaps the best word to describe the origins and background' of many of them, amongst whom he mentions Taylor's friend Nicholson, nominated to Gloucester. Most of them, he says, had published nothing at all and he thinks that they may have been compromise candidates between High and Low: 'But their elevation is the more striking in that at the Restoration there was no shortage of more senior, experienced men or of men who had done more for their ailing mother the Church of England in previous years'.[1]

Before leaving England Taylor sent *The Worthy Communicant* to the publisher. His episcopate in Ireland was troubled by controversy and he had virtually to reconstitute Dublin University. During this period his son Edward died. When in Ireland, he wrote his *Dissuasive*, his *Rules and Advices* for his clergy and a treatise on *Confirmation*. His astonishing industry and intellectual vitality remained with him to the end when in August 1667 he died at the age of fifty-four of a fever caught when sick-visiting. In the same month died his remaining son, Charles.

Such a bare outline of a life beset with uncertainty and scarred by much personal loss in times of national upheaval conveys but a hint of the man himself and little of the importance of his work. We glimpse him through his friend George Rust and in the diary of John Evelyn and in their exchange of letters. Yet one has not begun to see the man or the theologian until one begins to realise the depth of his religion and the seriousness and practicality of his life of prayer and sacrament the end of which (to quote himself) is 'for wonder and euchar-ist'. One who knew him and had worked with him spoke of 'his great humility . . . notwithstanding his stupendous parts and learning . . . his humility was coupled with extraordinary piety . . . his solemn hours of prayer took up a considerable portion of his life'. The result was not a formidable prelate or a remote and ascetic scholar but a pastor 'of easy access' who 'knew how to counsel and to advise', a man 'of great candour and ingenuity . . . who . . . charmed his hearer'. Rust can hardly be accused of hagiography seeing that his hearers knew Jeremy Taylor as well as he did. The picture is confirmed by John Evelyn who never missed an opportunity of hearing Taylor preach, often receiving the blessed sacrament from him and, from 1655, 'using him thenceforward as my ghostly father'. He heard his friend preaching on 'being a worthy communicant' and Taylor baptised Evelyn's fourth son 'officiating in the withdrawing-room at Says-Court' because of the times. Evelyn himself had had the experience of being at church in London when soldiers surrounded the chapel and 'held their muskets against us as we came up to receive the Sacred Elements as if they would have shot us at the Altar'.

Later generations have not hesitated to call Taylor a genius and Coleridge reckoned him with Shakespeare, Bacon and Milton as the four great geniuses of English literature 'four-square, each against each'. This is one of the qualities which has helped to ensure Taylor's place in the community memory. It is captured in the opening sentence of what must long remain the standard modern *Life*, C. J. Stranks's *The Life and Writings of Jeremy Taylor* (1952): 'It is not often that a great divine is also a great man of letters'. The attractiveness of the man comes through for his mind is multifaceted, richly stored and sharply analytical. He is not only one of the most able of Anglican theologians but he is possessed of a vein of true lyricism so that, on occasion, he is a poet writing prose.

That Taylor could write as he did is a bonus but it is the content of his writing which reveals him as one of the most intelligent and original minds among Anglican theologians of the seventeenth century. Essentially, he is a man of paradox, his roots going deep into the tradition stemming from the early centuries. Yet at the same time one is frequently made aware of an individual component deriving from a quality of liberality in his theological stance and from his independent spirit. This is specially to be noticed in the curiously modern insights occurring from time to time in his doctrinal expositions and in the style of his reasoning. It is observable also in what one may call his modern use of antiquity, for, together with his obvious veneration for the Fathers there goes an approach to their writings which is critical in the modern sense. There is paradox too in the fact that though he was steeped in patristics and the schoolmen he controverted Roman Catholic theology, both popular and Tridentine. Yet he evolved a eucharistic theology which passed into the Anglican doctrinal awareness so that Taylor may be reckoned as a precursor whose work made possible for Anglicans the Windsor Agreement on Eucharistic Doctrine of ARCIC I in 1971. The paradox which runs deep in his theological make-up has its parallel in his affinities. By association with his patron Laud and others, by his sense of the rich continuity of the Catholic heritage and by his knowledge and love of liturgy, his affinity is Laudian. A visitor to Uppingham Vicarage observed a small altar and crucifix in his study. His doctrine of the Church and of the Ministry and of the Sacraments is unmistakably a high doctrine and he stressed the apostolic succession when preaching at his own consecration as bishop. Nevertheless, by association with William Chillingworth, by his sense of toleration and by his unyielding emphasis on reason in theology, Taylor is also in company with members of the Oxford school of rational theologians. The group which gathered round Lucius Cary, Lord Falkland, at Great Tew in Oxfordshire included such men as Morley, Waller, Hales, Chillingworth and Gilbert Sheldon, later to become Archbishop of Canterbury, who with Henry Hammond was to be one of the Laudian leaders of the Church of England under persecution. Thus, Sheldon, like Taylor, shared this dual spiritual and intellectual inheritance. Temperamentally very different, Sheldon and Taylor maintained an uneven friendship through the difficult years but when Sheldon came to power and influence at the Restoration the mistrust of Taylor's liberality which he had twice shown previously revealed itself decisively. Taylor's friendship with Henry More, the Cambridge Platonist whose keen moral sensitivity would not allow him to 'swallow down that hard doctrine concerning Fate or Calvinistick Predestination', was of the same temper and calibre as his Great Tew associations. The Erasmian view with its emphasis on practical ethics rather than on abstract speculation had its influence not only on More and on the Great Tew circle but on Taylor himself although I would contend that in his case it was transformed into moral/ascetic theology, a very different matter. It is significant for assessing the influences on Taylor to note that among More's small circle of friends was George Rust, of the same Cambridge Platonist persuasion, who became Dean of Connor and subsequently Taylor's successor in the See of Dromore. He was Taylor's friend too and preached his funeral sermon.

The fact is that Taylor had affinities but no party. He cannot be conveniently labelled and he remains, from start to finish, his own man. This makes him a fascinating, even an exciting, figure but his worth and value are solidly based on profound learning and a keen perception of the human condition. Taylor continues typically Anglican in that the three-fold appeal to scripture, antiquity and reason, is not only implicit in all his writings but is explicitly declared as his theological method both in eucharistic and moral theology. In its purpose and application the appeal is both faith-guarding and identity-affirming. The thrust of it is that Scripture is rightly interpreted only within the community while at the same time it continuously controls and guides that interpretation. Tradition is evaluated by its consonancy with the original *depositum fidei* and therefore the appeal to antiquity refuses Roman innovations as creating rather than obeying tradition. It thus reflects Anglican consciousness of being pre-ultramontane Catholicism. The appeal has nothing to do with ecclesial antiquarianism but is designed to affirm identity with the Primitive Church in terms of a living continuity of faith and order. William Payne's is a characteristic seventeenth-century expression of this conviction and one with which Jeremy Taylor would be in complete agreement: 'Let the Scripture, therefore, as sensed by the Primitive Church, and not by the private judgment of any particular man, be allowed and agreed by us to be the Rule of our Faith; and let that be accounted the true Church, whose Faith and Doctrine is most conformable and agreeable with the Primitive.' Yet Taylor is not a type-cast Anglican and suffered in his personal career through being theologically suspect to some of his influential contemporaries. The further one penetrates his thinking the more he resists easy classification. His liberality and modernity are conspicuous in his handling of the perennial faith and reason debate and in his refusal to accept the current Augustinianism in the question of original sin, a line of thought which quickly got him into trouble. All the while, he will maintain that he is in step with the Early Church and the Anglican formularies, yet he is open and candid in his claim that here a latitude of interpretation exists but in order to the purpose of ascertaining the truth, the only criterion by which he desires his views to be judged.

Remarkable too is what one can only describe as the anticipatory quality which from time to time makes itself felt in Taylor's thought. This is particularly noteworthy in his moral theology.[2] He is the leading figure in the group of Anglican seventeenth-century writers who saw the need for a moral theology which would be a theology of new life in Christ, both traditional and reforming in its structure and quite different from the old juristic science which was a theology of legalist interpretation rather than a science of Christian living. Taylor and colleagues like Sanderson were determined to restate the goal and to redefine the nature of moral theology. This they achieved by making moral and ascetic theology one science concerned with our life in, with, and through Christ. In other words, they re-sited moral theology within the kerygmatic totality of the gospel and rooted it in the New Testament concepts of faith and love. Its subject is not so much the penitent at the tribunal as the Christian in the Church.

What is remarkable is that when one compares this in detail with the results of the quiet revolution which has gone on in Roman Catholic and Anglican moral theology during the latter part of the twentieth century, one finds that almost all its major elements have been anticipated by the earlier Anglican group in which the work of Jeremy Taylor is outstanding. Nor was he a theorist only but a much sought-after counsellor and spiritual adviser, skilled in casuistry as Rust tells us.

In liturgy too, there are instances of Taylor's anticipation both of the teaching of the present liturgical revival and of features of its practical application. One has to bear in mind that Taylor was not only a student of the early liturgies but was himself a composer of liturgy.

Modern studies of Taylor have dealt with these and other aspects of his work.[3] So far as I can discover, however, no full-length evaluation of his eucharistic theology exists. It seemed to me that this was a gap to be filled, all the more noticeable in view of the strongly sacramentalist quality of Taylor's religion. As theologian, devotional writer and moralist, it is not possible fully to evaluate and appreciate him without giving its due weight to this essential element in his understanding of the Christian faith and how it works. It is in the modest hope of adding fresh touches to the as yet unfinished theological portrait of a richly complex figure that the present study is offered. The only book containing an assessment of Taylor's eucharistic teaching is C. W. Dugmore's *Eucharistic Doctrine in England from Hooker to Waterland* (1942). This was the Norrisian Prize Essay in the University of Cambridge for the year 1940. Being a survey of works spread over nearly two centuries, it naturally treats that of Taylor as one among others, though an important one. Inevitably, all the writers cannot be treated in full and in depth, though Dugmore's estimate of Taylor is always to be treated with respect.

One thinks of Taylor's eucharistic theology in terms both of its setting and its substance. Basically, of course, the substance of Taylor's eucharistic theology is his Church's teaching seen in the light of and in continuity with the theology of the Early Church as he understood it. At the same time allowance has to be made for an individual component which stems, as I have been suggesting, from a quality of liberality in his theological stance and from the independence and originality of his spirit. The substance, then, is what he has received from the great tradition, digested and made his own before being transmitted. As to the setting of Taylor's eucharistic theology, I would wish to convey something more than the idea of the general ambience of his views in relation to the eucharistic theology of his own times and that of the continuing tradition. Clearly both are involved but there is more to the 'setting' than this. Taylor's theology of the eucharist appears to me to be thoroughly embedded in his moral/ascetic theology just as the latter reflects both the methodology of his wider theological concerns and their conclusions about man's salvation in the purposes of a God who is love. For this reason, the opening chapter attempts to catch an impression of his approach to certain important areas of doctrine and theology because his handling of theology is all of one piece. What he thinks about faith and reason, for example, bears not only on that debate but has implications for how one does all theology. His conclusions on original sin have to do not only with the long-continuing controversy on the subject: they impinge on doctrine and on how you depict human personality and the practicalities of Christian living and on the understanding of sacramentality and on the economy of grace.

What I am hoping to convey concerning the setting of Taylor's eucharistic theology is something like three ever-moving concentric circles. The outer circle is the eucharistic theology of the tradition as this has developed down to Taylor's day. The second circle is Taylor's exposition of eucharistic theology as expounded in the context of his own general theological position. The inner circle is his moral/ascetic theology which is all about the life of Christ continuing in the lives of the members of His mystical Body through the Spirit whose accustomed instruments are the Word and Sacraments. This is the immediate setting of his theology of the eucharist and at the still centre of the circles is Taylor's constantly-emphasised, life-transforming concept, 'Christ, who is our life'.

Today, with the exception of *Holy Living* and *Holy Dying*, most of his works are not easily accessible unless the reader is within reach of the fifteen-volume edition of R. Heber (1828) or the ten-volume revision by C. P. Eden (1850). For this practical reason and also because Taylor's thought and expression can often be very nuanced, it has been advisable and necessary to quote him freely. Moreover, because he is in truth 'a great man of letters', often using inimitable language and striking imagery, to summarise rather than to quote is to risk being guilty of a kind of literary vandalism and of theological misprision, failure to appreciate the precise value of the point being made.

Jeremy Taylor, like every man, belonged to his own times —dangerous and discouraging years through which he did not pass unscathed. Yet one has the feeling on occasion that he belongs to other times too when a flash of what I have ventured to call 'modernity' seems to make him our contemporary also. This book attempts to evaluate his work not only in itself and in its theological and historical context but in respect of its relevance to and frequent consonance with modern developments in eucharistic theology and in the quest for an ecumenical convergence. There is an anticipatory quality in his handling of theological questions, in the content and structure of his moral theology, and in aspects of his eucharistic theology and liturgical compositions, which makes Taylor stand out among the precursors whose life and work have contributed to the creation of the spirit of Anglicanism.

I am indebted to my friend, the Master of Peterhouse, the Reverend Dr. Henry Chadwick, who generously gave time to reading the typescript and made some valuable suggestions on which I have acted.

H. R. McAdoo

Notes

1. *The Re-Establishment of the Church of England 1660–1663* (1978), by I. M. Green, pp. 89–96.
2. See *The Anglican Moral Choice* (1983), Ch. 2, pp. 33–62, H. R. McAdoo 'Anglican Moral Theology in the Seventeenth Century: An Anticipation'.
3. For a list of these, see Chp. I, n. 3.

1 Taylor's Theology: Modernity and the Use of Antiquity

Jeremy Taylor was cast in too large a mould to belong exclusively to any century, even his own. So it seemed to his friend and contemporary, George Rust: 'Indeed, it was a rare mixture and a single instance, hardly to be found in an age . . . but that which made his wit and judgment so considerable, was the largeness and freedom of his spirit'.[1] So it seems also to us, for subsequent centuries including our own have been aware of Taylor. As theologian, moral theologian and devotional writer, as prose stylist, his influence has been as deep as it has been wide. Paul Elmen has demonstrated in a study showing the number of editions of Taylor's works in the seventeenth, eighteenth and nineteenth centuries that Taylor's fame has been durable.[2] The twentieth century has shown an equal awareness, for Taylor's many-sided contribution to Anglicanism has featured in a number of books during the last three decades.[3] The range of his work has helped to ensure a continuing interest in Jeremy Taylor. His importance as a devotional writer, his pioneer work as a moral theologian, his general theological writings ranging from the doctrine of original sin to the quest for Christian unity, combine with the openness and freshness of his mind to make one aspect or another of his work attractive to one generation after another. This quality of attractiveness, which must be part of the explanation of his continuing fame, comes through in his writings just as it did for his contemporaries: 'His soul was made up of harmony; and he never spake, but he charmed his hearer, not only with the clearness of his reason, but all his words, and his very tone and cadences, were strangely musical'.[4] The liveliness of his mind, the vividness of his style, the rich imagery and the essentially poetical quality of his prose, the wisdom with which he assessed the human experience, all come through in the variety of subjects on which he wrote. His was not simply a theological learning for, as Rust said, 'he was a rare humanist, and hugely versed in all the polite parts of learning'.[5] C. J. Stranks confirms the contemporary assessment: 'It is not often that a great divine is also a great man of letters, but when such a combination occurs as it does in Jeremy Taylor the interest is doubled. Students of pure literature have as much to do with research into his life and mind as theologians'.[6] The circumstances of his life, too, have helped to create for later generations a sympathetic figure, a candid, devout and courageous man of ten talents who loved and served his Church at no little cost to himself, living with uncertainty as his one sure companion during the Commonwealth. Taylor suffered for his Church's sake at the hand of its enemies and he suffered at the hands of its friends for what they considered to be his unorthodox views in one specific field.

As we set about evaluating his eucharistic theology, it is borne in upon us that, unlike the specialisation with which we are familiar today, no branch of theology can claim Jeremy Taylor exclusively. Further, there are throughout his varied work an interlocking of themes and an underlying unity of thought, so that one must first see his eucharistic theology in the context of his general theology. We shall find throughout, I believe, a vein of moral/ascetic theology and a vein of sacramental theology, which merge and undergird all that he writes, whether it be the *Life of Christ*, *The Liberty of Prophesying*, the devotional works or the sermons, apart altogether from books specifically about the eucharist or about moral theology. All the time and explicitly in all the subjects which he treats Taylor's methodology is that which has created and creates the spirit of Anglicanism, the appeal to Scripture, to antiquity and to reason. This is the basis of how he does theology. It provides the structure of *The Real Presence of Christ in the Blessed Sacrament* and the form of the *Dissuasive*, as it does in his early booklet *On the Reverence due to the Altar*. The preface to the *Ductor Dubitantium* formally sets it out as his approach: 'I have begun an institution of moral theology . . . (and) . . . I affirm nothing but upon grounds of Scripture, or universal tradition or right reason . . .'.[7] The same threefold appeal runs through the argument of *The Liberty of Prophesying*.

To see Taylor in the round as a theologian is a necessary first step to entering into and understanding his eucharistic theology. It is more than just a matter of setting the context, for his theological position is the sacramental theology of one whose over-riding concern as a moral/ascetic theologian is with the Christian life seen as the life of Christ continuing in the lives of the members of his mystical body, the Church. This is the living, existential ambience of all that he has to write about the eucharist of which he says 'Nothing else but the actual enjoying of heaven is above it'. Despite the diversity of the subjects treated over a wide range of faith and order and of the whole area of moral and devotional theology, there is this unifying quality in all Taylor's work. He is undoubtedly a whole man, his theology and his piety integrated by his unswerving Anglicanism. Nevertheless, Taylor is not a copybook Anglican or a hide-bound theologian. His constant appeal to the Primitive Church, his knowledge and love of the Fathers ('his great acquaintance with the fathers' says Rust[8]), are of the essence of Taylor's method but part and parcel of it too is a liberality, even a modernity, which prevents him from being pigeon-holed or type-cast. In a sense, this Catholicism with freedom is the inevitable expression of the Anglican appeal to reason and to Scripture and the Primitive Church. It has been a recurring theme in the Lambeth Conferences and it is part of being an Anglican from Hooker to our own time,[9] but in Taylor's case there is an individuality in the situation, a many-sidedness which may account for his work never being at any stage quite out of the Church's mind and which has at times this strangely modern quality. Taylor was a Laudian by sympathy and not just because Laud brought him into the forefront as a young priest. But he also read and valued Grotius and Episcopius. He was a friend of Chillingworth and More, and like the latter, he knew both Plato and Descartes, and by that preference alone a fresh element found a place in his outlook. However, because of his Laudian affiliations, his sense of the continuity of the Church in history, and his liturgical feeling, neither of which was shared to any marked degree by the Cambridge Platonists although Chillingworth had something of both, Taylor remains, more typically than they did, an example of theological method in its wholeness.

With some hesitancy I have been hinting at a quality of what I called modernity in Taylor, chiefly for want of a more suitable and more nuanced word to convey an essential but elusive element in his theological make-up. It is a quality in his thought more easily felt and experienced than described. Clearly, he was one who was alive to and sensitive to his own times, but that would not make him modern for *our* present. Equally, (to be anachronistic) he is no modernist, subordinating tradition to harmonise it with current concepts and fashions. Yet there is in his thought, and frequently expressed, *a certain quality which is congenial with the way we think nowadays* and which makes us feel, for a passing moment, that somehow Jeremy Taylor is our contemporary too. Perhaps Alec Vidler's 'liberality' comes nearest to catching this aspect of a man who was at the same time thoroughly at home in the Fathers and a firm upholder of the appeal to tradition. It is, writes Vidler, 'the opposite not of conservative, but of fanatical or bigoted or intransigent. It points to the *esprit large* and away from the *idée fixe*'.[10] One remembers that Rust spoke of Taylor's 'largeness and freedom of spirit', so this may be what we are seeking to capture. Just because his style is so much his own and his range is so wide (from *Episcopacy Asserted* through *The Liberty of Prophesying*, the *Unum Necessarium* to *Holy Living*, to mention some of the variety of subjects) the true distinctiveness of Taylor can easily be overlooked. He embraced the full extent of the Anglican appeal to Scripture and to antiquity, though his reading of the Fathers was far from uncritical and his use of them was as being confirmatory of Scripture: 'for when the Fathers appeal to tradition . . . it is such a tradition as delivers the fundamental points of Christianity, which were also recorded in Scripture'.[11] Undoubtedly, he was influenced here by Daillé's book, to which Taylor refers his readers,[12] *Du Vrai Usage des Pères* (1632), and with which his friends of the Great Tew group were familiar.[13] This connection with Chillingworth and Hales is surely a part-source of his liberality but it must be borne in mind that in regarding patristic evidence as corroborative or complementary, Taylor was running true to type as far as seventeenth-century Anglicanism's use of the appeal to antiquity was concerned, for tradition was not seen as an independent source of doctrine ranking in any degree with Scripture. Archbishop Laud was speaking for a whole Church when he wrote: 'though they do materially, yet they do not equally confirm the authority either of other. For Scripture doth infallibly confirm the authority of Church traditions truly so called: but tradition doth but morally and probably confirm the authority of Scripture'.[14] The appeal to antiquity aimed rather at establishing identity of doctrine with the Primitive Church. This, and not the establishing of tradition and the writings of the Fathers as a separate and independent source of received doctrine, was the objective. This position had been well set out by Taylor's patron, in his *Conference*.[15] Taylor expressed this appeal to Scripture and antiquity with a liberality of viewpoint and a sensitive understanding of the nature and function of reason. To this he added a wide reading in later poets, philosophers and other writers. Part of his distinctiveness lay in the way in which he kept this theological and intellectual element in contact with the emphasis on the development of the human person through the means of grace and the experience of the individual within the continuing life of the Church. He has a deep concern for the truth of things and a desire for a theology which is relevant and helpful to those whose calling it is 'to grow in grace and in the knowledge of Our Lord Jesus Christ'.[16]

I suggested that there are moments as we turn the pages of his massive output when Taylor seems to be thinking and speaking in terms that are strangely congenial to our times, and I ventured very hesitantly to use the term 'modern' to describe this impression which seems to me to derive from this quality of liberality (*not* liberalism) in his thought. His is a complex mind rich with the Catholic inheritance yet, like his friend John Hales (also Laud's chaplain) ready to use more 'maybes and peradventures', more 'old men's modesty'.[17] At the Synod of Dort, Hales heard Episcopius speaking on John 3.16 and 'There I bid John Calvin good night'. Significantly it was in the controversial area of the doctrine of original sin that Taylor got into trouble and both he and Hales spoke movingly of the goodness and love of God. The concern of both for generosity and toleration is clear and it is here that we can discern that liberality which makes us feel that we are listening in part to contemporaries: 'Let it not offend any that I have made Christianity rather an inn to receive all than a private house to receive some few'.[18] All the time, one must remember, Taylor is speaking and even speculating from a firm centre of faith, the Catholic inheritance, but from within a tradition which, while not ashamed to adore, is not afraid to reason. How far the Anglican understanding of reason and the Anglican acceptance of the *hapax* of Jude, v. 3, 'the faith once for all delivered', limits this liberality is matter for an essay on the relation of individual freedom to corporate faith.[19] But one dare not stereotype the seventeenth-century outlook when even Laud himself (caricatured by some later journalistic historians as a reactionary of the first water) could assert: 'There is a *latitude* in faith especially in reference to different men's salvation: but to set a bound to this, and strictly to define it—Just thus far you must believe in every particular, or incur damnation—is no work for my pen . . . for though the foundation be one and the same in all, yet a 'latitude' there is, and a large one too, when you come to consider, not the foundation common to all, but things necessary to many particular men's salvation . . . for the gifts of God, both ordinary and extraordinary, to particular men are so various . . . nor will I ever take upon me to express that tenet or opinion, *the denial of the foundation only excepted*, which may shut any Christian, the meanest, out of heaven'.[20] So, Laud's *protégé* is not so far from his patron and the word 'latitude' is something of a proleptic gesture since the chief of the Latitudinarians, Stillingfleet, in his *Rational Account* (1664) would later vindicate the argument of Laud's *Conference* in all respects thus demonstrating the remarkable unity of Anglican theological method in the seventeenth century. 'Grace' writes Laud 'is never placed but in a reasonable creature'.[21]

Yet when all necessary *caveats* have been entered there is still in Taylor's writings as well as his inherited and shared Anglican attitude a distinctive quality over and above this healthy respect for reason stemming originally from Hooker's *Ecclesiastical Polity*. It is a liberality not altogether of his own times, something special to Taylor, and I think that I would settle for the concept common to Vidler and to Rust—the *esprit large*, 'the largeness of his spirit'.

Something of this, I believe, can be seen in his discussion of the relationship of faith and reason and in his handling of the original sin controversy. Nor does it seem to me to be far-fetched to signalise elements in his thinking about the eucharist which match emphases stressed, or perhaps one should say rediscovered, in modern eucharistic agreements. One is not trying to claim that Taylor was not a man of his century or that he was in all respects theologically ahead of his time. But it is the fact that, in common with his Anglican fellow moral theologians he anticipated most of the changes which the last three decades have brought about in today's Roman Catholic and Anglican moral theology, the quiet revolution which has changed a juristic science dominated by canon law and the tribunal-concept into an instrument of moral/ascetic theology such as was forged by the seventeenth-century Anglicans.[22]

Bearing in mind then that our's is a climate in which questioning and pragmatism, unbelief and agnosticism are common and run deep in an empiricist culture, and that the seventeenth century was capable of combining acceptance and questioning in a different way and degree because the climate was basically one of belief, how does Taylor face the *impasse* when, in his own words, 'reason and revelation seem to disagree'? Can he afford an agnosticism about this or that because his acceptance of fundamental doctrines, his conviction of their relevance to life, his sacramental piety and practical devotion, form a living centre for his thought? Some years ago, in the *New Reformation*, John Robinson, writing about this same *impasse*, maintained that 'there is an agnosticism which releases', while holding that the function of fundamental doctrines is to be held on to as 'limiting concepts' for they are safeguards of an existential relationship of man 'to God in Christ'. Given the differing climates in which theology worked then and now, Taylor's approach is not dissimilar. I believe (and this is what underlies my feeling about what I discern as a strain of liberality in Taylor) that his is no museum-piece theology, for an essential orthodoxy and a near-modernity surface constantly in the writings of a man who recognised that there are question marks.[23] There is discernible in Taylor a candid acknowledgment that all the answers are not forthcoming. Then 'if we cannot quit our reason or satisfy it, let us carry ourselves with modesty'.[24] Yet in fairness it must be asserted that his orthodoxy, his acceptance of 'the revelation' (a favourite term) controls his thinking, but within the parameters of the *hapax* he goes deep as he endeavours to show that 'it is reason that carries me to objects of faith, and faith is my reason so disposed, so used, so instructed'.[25]

Fundamentally, he is wrestling with the question put by Austin Farrer: 'Can reasonable minds still think theologically? How much, if so, of the traditional pattern must they discard?'[26] Taylor is coming at it from the other end, that of refuting the attitudes of the obscurantist or the enthusiast or the authoritarian, but basically he too is seeking an accommodation between faith and reason which will not compromise the faith once for all revealed but perceives 'that into the greatest mysteriousness of our religion, and the deepest articles of faith, we enter by our reason'.[27] Farrer wrote 'Faith implies genuine persuasion; and persuasion is not genuine unless it comes from the thing which persuades us. It cannot be got going by stoking up the furnaces of the will'.[28] This persuasion can only come initially through reason, notes Taylor: 'If I find that all things satisfy my reason, I believe him saying that God said so; and then *pistis* or faith enters'.[29]

How does Taylor handle the question? Basically, he seems to be suggesting that the antithesis between faith and reason is really not such a clear-cut distinction and there is the implication that a rehabilitated natural theology may be the way in. He tries to come at the problem by degrees and as his argument progresses we are made aware by turns of Taylor's uncompromising adherence to the *hapax* and of the occasional near-modernity of his thought.[30] For some people, he says, the solution of the *impasse* is simply to jettison what they cannot explain. When 'some articles which are said to be of faith, cannot be made to appear consonant to their reason, they stick to this, and let that go'. Others go to the opposite extreme, and while agreeing that reason is the proper guide in human affairs, deny that it can be of use in religion: 'Here we are to believe, not to dispute'. In his view both sides have 'fair pretences, which when we have examined, we may find what part of truth each side aims at, and join them both in practice'.[31] The compromise Taylor proposes here was largely unacceptable to many of his contemporaries, and he is critical of the current approaches by way of a magisterial authority or a subjective individualism or a 'system of divinity' his description of which is reminiscent of John Robinson's 'debate between a closed circle of mandarins within the agreed terms of their system'.[32]

These three approaches are, in Taylor's view, totally in-
admissible: 'so do these men allow us to be Christians and
disciples, if we will lay aside our reason, which is that guard of
our souls . . .'.[33]

To make it possible for men 'to see before they can believe',
to see the reality of the Incarnation, is the primary task of the
Church and theology today according to Robinson.[34] Taylor
is on the same track but in his diagnosis reason has a harder,
sharper outline: 'There are some things in reason which are
certainly true, and some things which reason does infallibly
condemn . . . and St. John's argument was certain, "That
which we have seen with our eyes and heard with our ears, and
which our hands have handled of the Word of life, that we
preach", *that is, we are to believe what we see* and hear and
feel; and as this is true in the whole of religion, so it is true in
every article of it'.[35] What is true for me must be true for all
men. There must be an internal balance between what is given
and what is appropriated by reason and experience. As he
strives to clear the ground, certain basic elements surface in
Taylor's thinking on the subject. In the course of his setting-
out of the problem and his analysis of it one encounters both
his scholastic method and his *esprit large*, and our assessment
of the value and method of his argument ranges from dis-
appointment to a sense of recognition that at times he is
speaking *our* language. We can, I think, uncover several of his
working principles the first of which is that faith includes
reason and continues on from it, demanding an extra step but
never requiring something which is against reason: 'For it is to
be considered, whatsoever is above our understanding, is not
against it: *supra and secundum may consist together in several
degrees*'. How optimistic is this? Or is it in fact a realistic
deduction in all the circumstances? Farrer writes 'The readiness to accept that "more" will be faith, or the effect of faith'.
Farrer's initial persuasion leading to faith and Taylor's reason
leading us into 'such proportions of faith' as it can are very
close. Taylor says there are three ways of knowing which are at
work in every science, noesis, dianoesis and pistis. By these
terms he means knowing through the recognition of self-
evident principles, knowing through deduction or inference
from those principles, and knowing through assenting to the
testimony or affirmation of others. Reason enters into the

analysis of any subject by principles proper to the enquiry: 'it does not prove a geometrical proposition by moral philosophy, so neither does it prove a revelation by a natural argument, but into one and the other it enters by principles proper to the inquisition; *and faith and reason are not opposed at all.* Faith and natural reason are several things, and arithmetical and moral reasons are as differing, but it is reason that carries me to objects of faith, and faith is my reason so disposed, so used, so instructed'. The consequence is this 'that into the greatest mysteriousness of our religion, and the deepest articles of faith, we enter by our reason: not that we can prove every one of them by natural reason: for to say that, were as vain, as to say we ought to prove them by arithmetic or rules of music; *but* whosoever believes wisely and not by chance, enters into his faith by the hand of reason; that is, he hath causes and reasons why he believes. *He indeed that hath reasons insufficient and incompetent, believes indeed not wisely, but for some reason or other he does it*'.[36] This looks like Farrer's initial persuasion—if we are persuaded, some element of faith is there. This faith, Taylor holds, is 'an act or habit of the understanding consenting to certain propositions for the authority of the speaker'. It is just as much an act of the reason 'as to assent to a proposition for a reason drawn from the nature of things'. This is to speak of faith 'formally in its proper and natural capacity'.[37]

What of faith 'taken materially' and as 'a habit infused by God, and by God's Holy Spirit'? Then, says Taylor, 'there is something more in it than thus: for so, faith is a vital principle, a magazine of secret truths, which we could never have found out by natural reason ... by all secular experiences and conversations with the world'.[38] This is *Saving Belief*, to use the title of Farrer's book and both he and Taylor speak in terms of a transcendent God who revealed Himself in His Son and to whose love men respond with the trust of sons. Was it not Scott Holland who said long ago that this sort of faith was the exercise of our sonship? 'Now here is the close and secret of the question' says Taylor '*whether or no faith, in this sense, and materially taken, be contrary to our worldly or natural reason ... or ... are not our reasons, which we rightly follow in natural philosophy, in metaphysics, in other arts and sciences, sometimes contrary to faith?* And if they be, whether shall be followed? Or can it, in any sense, *be an article of faith, if it be contrary to right reason?*[39] His reflections by way of answer reveal that mixture of acceptance and questioning which is more a feature of Taylor's time than ours. Human reason is not 'the affirmative or positive measure . . . of articles and mysteries of faith'. This is so because many of them depend on the free grace of God and man's part is to 'admire the secret, and adoring the wisdom, and expecting till the curtain be drawn'. To say that a thing is not so and has no existence, because we cannot see the reasons for it is unreasonable. Taylor distinguishes between the mysterious in Christian faith—what is uncomprehended rather than incomprehensible ('not to be comprehended by our dark and less instructed reason, but yet not impossible to be believed')—and what he calls human appendages to dogma.

Why does God, who hates evil, 'permit evil for good ends'? How to explain that God foreknows what I should do at any time 'and yet it is free to me at that time . . . to do or not to do, that thing'? Who can explain reasonably the rôle and the fate of Judas? 'Well may we wonder that God should wash a soul with water, and with bread and wine nourish us up to immortality.' These things are part of Christian believing and since our reason cannot tell us why or how therefore 'our reason is not the positive measure of mysteries'. This is not as unyielding as it sounds when one recalls what he has to say about reason leading us on to faith, Farrer's initial persuasion, and both the liberality and the *hapax* keep company (if on strict terms) in his conclusion: 'The result is this—every thing that is above our understanding, is not therefore to be suspected or disbelieved; neither is any thing to be admitted that is against Scripture, though it be agreeable to right reason, *until all information is brought in*, by which the sentence is to be made'.[40] There is however another consequence to this approach for although right reason is *not* the *positive* measure of any article of faith 'yet it is the *negative* measure of every one. So that, whatsoever is contradictory to right reason, is at no hand to be admitted as a mystery of faith'.[41] This we might call Taylor's second working principle and he will even affirm as its consequence that if anything be claimed as the doctrine of Scripture 'and confessed to be against right reason, it is certainly not the doctrine of Scripture, because it cannot be true, and yet be against what is true'.[42] Here the argument is dependent on another of Taylor's guidelines that 'as God is one, so truth is one'. This concept, which no doubt owes something to the Cambridge Platonists, he spells out as being basic: 'Now the measure and the limit of this, is that very thing which is the reason of this, and all the preceding discourse—one truth cannot be against another:—if therefore your opinion or interpretation be against a truth, it is false and no part of faith. A commandment cannot be against a revelation, a privilege cannot be against a promise, a threatening cannot mean against an article, a right cannot be against a duty; for all reason, and all right, and all truth, and all faith, and all commandments, are from God, and therefore partake of his unity and simplicity'.[43] From within the household of faith this may be convincing but for those on the fringe he will carry reason in religion as high as he dares, asserting that although 'natural reason cannot teach us the things of God . . . yet it is false to say that reason cannot; for *reason illuminated* can perceive the things of God'.[44] We meet this concept of 'an aided reason' in John Jewel who, according to John E. Booty, 'made much use of reason in solving the problem of authority' though his appeal to Scripture and to the Primitive Church was every bit as strong as Taylor's.[45] It is in fact the point in seventeenth-century theology where reason and faith are brought closest together—grace, 'the aids of God's spirit', being in Taylor's view, the reconciler. Like many today he claims that humility and piety are the best dispositions for understanding the faith but he is wholly himself in the aside that when disputing with an unbeliever 'a good reason will sooner convince him than a humble thought!'[46]

But what about the obedience of the understanding? Is this the medieval in Taylor getting the upper hand or, at least, the ascendancy of the current climate of belief in his mind? Even here Taylor does not disappoint us and we glimpse again his *esprit large* as he writes 'that we must submit our understanding to God, is very true, but that is only when God speaks. But because we heard him not, and are only told that God did speak, our reason must examine whether it be fit to believe them that tell us so'.[47] This, of course, opens the whole debate and he makes clear the limitations of intellectual obedience as he understands it: 'We must judge and discern the sayings of

God, from the pretences of men, and how that can be done without using our reason in the inquiries of religion, is not yet discovered'.

We may not, for example, submit our understanding to man 'unless he hath authority from reason or religion to command our conformity'. Things which claim the support of reason and have acquired a fictitious authority 'make no part of our religion'.[48] Taylor makes no bones about recommending suspended judgment in certain circumstances and he rejects any ultimate compulsion of the understanding: 'When reason and revelation seem to disagree, let us so order ourselves, that so long as we believe this to be a revelation, no pretence or reason may change our belief from it: if right or sufficient reason can persuade us that this is not a revelation—well and good; but if reason leaves us in the actual persuasion that it is so, we must force our reason to comply with this, since no reason does force us to quit this wholly; and if we cannot quit our reason or satisfy it, let us carry ourselves with modesty, and confess the revelation, though with profession of our ignorance and unskilfulness to reconcile the two litigants'.[49]

Reason itself, says Taylor, is not fallible but ratiocination, the reasoning process, is and 'so are the pretences of revelation subject to abuse; and *what are we now the nearer? . . .* then and always our reason (such as it is) must lead us into such *proportions of faith* as they can: according as our reason or motives are, so ordinarily is the *degree of our faith'*.[50] This may well serve as Taylor's *envoi* on the subject. He has not resolved the problems of faith and reason. Neither for that matter has Farrer nor Thomas Aquinas but he has brought us (surprisingly) as far as Farrer brings us in answering his own question as to whether reasonable minds can think theologically, and in much of Taylor's answering his idiom is not strange to us today. His phrase 'Beyond this we can do no more' strikes a responsive chord.[51]

II

It is when we turn to Jeremy Taylor's writing on original sin that we see in clearest outline his liberality and 'the largeness and freedom of his spirit'. Here perhaps more than anywhere else in his extensive output is revealed that quality for which I have been seeking a more nuanced description. The *Unum Necessarium* is a moral theologian's book on the doctrine and practice of repentance written not only from the theological but also from the devotional angle and so is typical of that moral/ascetic theology of the Anglican school the goal of which was well set out by Taylor's older contemporary and fellow moral theologian, Robert Sanderson: 'But when all is done, positive and practique Divinity is it must bring us to Heaven: that is it must poise our judgments, settle our consciences, direct our lives, mortify our corruptions, increase our graces, strengthen our comforts, save our souls . . . there is no study to this, none so well worth the labour as this'.[52] This was the view of the science shared by Taylor, and *Unum Necessarium* together with *Ductor Dubitantium* form part of his declared project of providing an Anglican synthesis of moral theology for the clergy who had no choice but to consult Roman Catholic manuals for dealing with cases of conscience. Sanderson's work had influenced Taylor's views on conscience but when *Unum Necessarium* appeared the older man shared the general alarm concerning the doctrine of original sin there expounded. That Taylor expected controversy is clear and his friend John Evelyn the diarist (to whom he acted as 'my ghostly father') refers in a letter to the *Further Explication* which was being prepared by the author in defence of *Unum Necessarium*. The controversy however soon grew in proportions while Taylor was a prisoner in Chepstow Castle and while there he was in correspondence with John Warner, bishop of Rochester. Taylor did not budge from his position and in the epistle dedicatory to Warner prefixed to the *Further Explication* he insists that he would rather die than 'willingly give occasion or countenance to a schism in the Church of England'. He is convinced that his views are loyally Anglican, substantiated by the appeal to Scripture, to the Fathers and to reason, and he concludes the dedication with the words 'so my doctrine I humbly submit to my holy mother the Church of England'. Into the history of the controversy there is no need to enter here and it has been discussed in detail elsewhere.[53] What concerns us is the light thrown on Taylor's theological method and on his mind and spirit by his handling of the subject which undoubtedly damaged his contemporary reputation through its opposition to the then dominant Augustinian school of theology. The relevant writings are Chapter VI of the *Unum Necessarium*, to which was added as Chapter VII in later editions, *A Further Explication of the Doctrine of Original Sin*. The date of publication was 1655 and in the following year he published *Deus Justificatus* which demonstrated that he remained totally unconvinced by the arguments advanced against his views in the controversy.

It is relatively easy to exhibit a largeness and freedom of spirit in congenial surroundings and discussions. This becomes much more difficult during a controversy in which not only the truth of the question but one's personal repute and standing are involved. Taylor comes through the test with this quality unimpaired.

Whatever we may mean nowadays by 'original sin' it is as well to recall that the term is not found in Scripture. Tertullian in *De Anima* has 'vitium originis' but it was Augustine who gave common currency to the term 'peccatum originale'. Generally speaking, the Fathers held a reasonably optimistic view of human nature, seeing original sin in terms of a deprivation, whereas with St. Augustine in his conflict with Pelagius the view emerged, and after him gained ground, that it was really a depravation. Some of the Reformers took this a step further and asserted the total depravation of human nature. Articles IX and X reflect both the earlier and the later controversies and Taylor's attempt to show the consonance of his teaching with the intention and exposition of the Articles is interesting. Nevertheless, like the Thirty-Nine Articles and like all his contemporaries, he accepted the historicity of Adam and of the Fall. However, his freedom of spirit and, above all, his certainty that God is love, obliged Taylor to refute the current doctrines which he held could not be substantiated from Scripture, the early Fathers and reason. Furthermore, his liberality obliged him to, at the very least, an agnosticism concerning much that was currently affirmed about the graces and gifts of original righteousness: 'That Adam had any more strengths than we have, and greater powers of nature, and by his fall lost them to himself and us, being part of the question, *ought not to be pretended, till it be proved*. Adam was a man, as his sons are, and no more; and God gave him strength to do his duty; and God is as just and loving to us as to him'.[54]

Stranks is just in his assessment made from our contemporary standpoint, that 'Taylor had time on his side. Long before the theory of evolution made theologians approach the problem of evil from a different angle, men were beginning more and more to revolt from a doctrine which, as Taylor truly said, fastened on God cruelties from which a human being of moderate standards would recoil with horror'.[55] None of this, of course, detracts from the very difficult position in which he found himself. Suspected of heresy and obliged to keep protesting his loyalty to his Church's position, the absence of any note of stridency in his book is worthy of comment. That his loyalty was in question hurt him is clear but he only allows himself the clinical comment 'my friends also take exceptions; and there are some objections made, and blows given me'.[56]

As to his handling of the whole subject, 'I find' wrote Taylor to the Dowager Countess of Devonshire 'that men are angry at my ingenuity and openness of discourse'.[57] This indeed is self-revealing and is characteristic of his methodology as it declares itself in the course of his investigation: 'I am tied to no man's private opinion any more than he is to mine; if he will bring Scripture and right reason from any topic he may govern me and persuade me, *else I am free*, as he is'.[58] It is precisely this absence of freedom, of liberality, which bedevils the question in Taylor's view and leads to errors and an unworthy idea of God: 'If men would give themselves *freedom of judgment*, and speak what they think most reasonable, they would speak honour of God's mercy, and not impose such fierce and unintelligible things'.[59] Far too many of those engaged in the controversy 'put fetters and bars upon their own understanding by an importune regard to the great names of dead men'.[60] For himself 'I must go after truth wherever it is'.[61] Considering the fierce dogmatism of some of his contemporaries there is an almost wistful modernity in Taylor's reflection that 'infinite opinions there are in matters of religion, and most men are confident, and most are deceived in many things, and all in some; and those few that are not confident, have only reason enough to suspect their own reason'.[62] It is like an echo of his friend Hales but Taylor is too thorough and constructive a theologian merely to indulge in generalities and he approaches the problem with the intention of dealing with it openly and systematically. This he does by submitting the propositions and their implications to testing by the criteria of Scripture, antiquity and reason.

Straight away he sets out his procedure and his method. 'In the meditation of these sad stories, I shall separate the certain from the uncertain, that which is revealed from that which is presumed, that which is reasonable from that which makes too bold reflections upon God's honour and the reputation of his justice and his goodness. *I shall do it in the words of the Apostle*, from whence men commonly dispute this question.'[63] Accordingly, Taylor analyses *Romans 5: 12* and other passages and affirms 'Having now explicated those words of St. Paul, which, by being misunderstood, have caused strange devices in this article, we may now, *without prejudice*, examine what *really* was the effect of Adam's sin and what evil descended on his posterity'.[64] Against the various assertions of contemporary Augustinianism his conclusion is, that far from being sin for which men must repent and that which makes us heirs of damnation, original sin is in us only as 'a contagion' which infects the race with mortality and concupiscence, 'and this is the whole state of original sin so far as is fairly warrantable'.[65] Nor has it impaired man's freedom of choice nor created in his nature a determinism of sinning: 'Adam had liberty of choice and chose ill and so do we'.[66] The Fall left mankind 'in pure naturals', but 'mere nature brings not to hell, but choice'.[67] Taylor's insistence is that all these propositions are not just un-Scriptural but are totally against reason: 'Could we prevent the sin of Adam? Could we hinder it? *Were we ever asked?*'[68] This comes like a breath of fresh air in the hot-house atmosphere of much of the contemporary controversy. At the same time, Taylor rejects Pelagianism and his positive theme is always that 'Man being left in this state of pure naturals could not by his own strength arrive to a supernatural end'. We must not canonise our suppositions about original righteousness and the one certainty is man's need for grace: 'What gifts and graces, or supernatural endowments God gave to Adam in his state of innocence, we know not . . . but after his fall, *we find no sign of anything but a common man*. And therefore as it was with him so it is with us; our nature cannot go to heaven without the helps of divine grace'.[69] Taylor is basically a moral/ascetic theologian with a strongly sacramental and practical piety and it is this as much as his reverent understanding of the Divine attributes which infuses a vast simplicity of common sense concerning the human situation into his thought. The artificiality which appears to be suggesting that God 'hath cured us of an evil which we never had' has nothing to do with reality—'I understand not that'. The reality for the Christian is Christ who 'came to bring us grace and life and spirit'. To be human is to inherit mortality, infirmity, inclinations to evil—'born under sin, that is, under such inclinations to it'—but 'let what will happen to us, it is not true that we are guilty of what we never did'.[70] Taylor's Catholic inheritance in theology and his experience as a spiritual director blow away the cobwebs of sublapsarianism and supralapsarianism as he writes 'from this state Christ came to redeem us all by his grace and by his Spirit, by his life and by his death, by his doctrine and by his sacraments, by his promises and by his revelations, by his resurrection and by his ascension, by his interceding for us and judging of us' and 'these glorious things' are enough 'to merit from us all our services and all our love'.[71]

Taylor's liberality dictates the quality and content of his general remarks on the subject: 'Thus everyone talks of original sin and agree that there is such a thing, but what it is they agree not, and therefore in such infinite variety he were of a strange imperious spirit that would confine others to his particular fancy'. He continues, setting out his own position; 'for my own part, now that I have shown what the doctrine of the purest ages was, what uncertainty there is of late in the question, what great consent there is in some of the main parts of what I affirm, and that in the contrary particulars men cannot agree, I shall not be ashamed to profess what company I now keep in my opinion of the article; no worse men than Zwinglius, Stapulensis, the great Erasmus, and the incomparable Hugo Grotius'.[72] Earlier he has noted that 'but two things are affirmed to be the constituent parts of original sin, the want of original righteousness, and concupiscence, and neither of these can be a sin in us, but a punishment and a consequent of Adam's sin they may be'. There are disputes both among Roman Catholics and among Protestants as to the finer points involved here and 'The effect of these is this, that it is not certain among the churches that either one or the other is formally our sin, or inherent in us; and we cannot affirm either without crossing a great part of Christendom in their affirmative'.[73] Taylor's conclusion on the basis of applying the first of the three criteria is that 'We find nothing else in Scripture, expressed to be the effect of Adam's sin: *and beyond this, without authority, we must not go*. Other things are said, but I find no warrant for them in that sense they are usually supposed—*and some of them in no sense at all*'.[74]

This same liberality (is it question-begging to call it a kind of modernity?) can be felt both in his use of the appeal to antiquity and in his reconciliation of his views with Article IX. As he looks to the Fathers one discerns this modernity in the use of antiquity which he learned from Daillé and which is also a feature of the Great Tew circle. Taylor sets great store by agreement with the primitive Church's writers but he cannot regard them and their expositions as ultimates or decisive in themselves: 'they that are dead some ages before we were born, have a reverence due to them, yet more is due to truth that shall never die; and God is not wanting to our industry any more than to theirs; but blesses every age with the understanding of his truths'.[75] He spells out his position in a situation and atmosphere in which to quote St. Augustine or Calvin was sometimes virtually a conversation-stopper and in which Taylor observes that 'every man that is angry in this question calls his enemy Pelagian'.[76] He writes 'I have a great reverence for antiquity, yet it is the prime antiquity of the Church, the ages of martyrs and holiness that I mean; and I am sure that in them my opinion hath much more warrant than the contrary'. As to renowned theologians of later times he is rather more critical but in any *ancients versus moderns* debate it must always be reason which tips the scales; 'but for the descending ages, I give that veneration to the great names of them that went before us which themselves gave to their predecessors; I honour their memory, I read their books, I imitate their piety, I examine their arguments; for therefore they did write them, and where the reasons of the moderns and their's seem equal, I turn the balance on the elder side and follow them; but *where a scruple or a grain of reason is evidently in the other balance, I must follow that*'.[77]

As he puts the current doctrines of original sin to the test of agreement with antiquity, Taylor follows up his own precepts both in the weight he gives to the many patristic sources supporting his interpretation and in his criticism of the views of St. Augustine and his modern followers: 'Having therefore turned to all the ways of reason and Scripture, I at last apply myself to examine how it was affirmed by the first and best antiquity'. He rejects the accusation of novelty levelled at his own doctrine, rather 'reckoning new that is but renewed'. Roundly he declares that 'the usual affirmations of original sin are a popular error; yet I will make it appear that it is no catholic doctrine'.[78] He summarises his own view that original sin 'hath left us in pure naturals' and standing in the need of grace; but it is a stain, not a sin or an inherent evil. Neither does it destroy man's liberty nor 'introduce a natural necessity of sinning'. His belief in the loving goodness of God, and his own love of children make repugnant to him the belief of some that unbaptized children are condemned to eternal punishment. Having set out his case, Taylor continues 'And now how consonant my explication of the article is to the first and best antiquity . . . will appear by the following authorities'.[79] He then goes on to give extracts from a dozen or so patristic authors in support of his own exposition and concludes 'I think I have said enough to vindicate my sentence from novelty'.[80] That the appeal to antiquity vindicates his position as against 'the usual propositions which are variously taught nowadays' seems thus clear to Taylor but even here his liberality and intellectual independence do not desert him. The following extract may serve to indicate what is implied by the phrase, his modernity in the use of antiquity: 'I consent to antiquity and the schoolmen's opinion thus far; that the destitution or loss of God's sight are the effects of original sin, that is, by Adam's sin we were left so as that we cannot by it go to heaven. *But here I differ*: whereas they say this may be a final event, I find no warrant for that; and think it only to be an intermedial event; that is, though Adam's sin left us there, yet God did not leave us there; but instantly gave us Christ as a remedy.'[81]

He continues in the same vein and one notices, as in the faith and reason discussion, Taylor's willingness, uncharacteristic of most Churches and of much theology in that period, to say 'I do not know'. He writes 'now what in particular shall be the state of unbaptized infants, so dying, I do not profess to know or teach, because God hath kept it a secret; I only know that he is a gracious Father, and from his goodness, nothing but goodness is to be expected; and that is, since neither Scripture nor any father till about St. Austin's time did teach that poor babes could die, not only for Adam's sin, but twice and for ever, I can never think that I do my duty to God if I think or speak any thing of him that seems unjust or so much against his goodness.'[82]

The great Augustine's theology is like a watershed down either slope of which flow the streams of what would later become characteristic Protestant and Catholic affirmations of faith. As Taylor confronts one aspect of this theology we are made aware of his 'largeness and freedom of spirit' taking form as a criticism of antiquity, for, like Daillé, he is not prepared to regard even Augustine's views as in any way determinative. Not to put too fine a point on it, says Taylor, St. Augustine was wrong: 'But St. Austin gave it complement and authority by his fierce disputing against the Pelagians . . . indeed their error was a great one . . . but . . . error is no good confuter of error . . . his zeal against a certain error made him take in auxiliaries from an uncertain or less discerned one and caused him to say many things which all antiquity before him disowned and which the following ages took up upon his account.'[83] This is straight talk but there is more to follow for on the subject of repentance relative to original sin he says bluntly 'St. Austin was indeed a fierce patron of this device and one of the chief inventors and finishers of it'.[84] He is fair, but only just: 'It was well said of St. Austin in this thing, though he said many others in it less certain . . . the article we all confess; but the manner of explicating it is not an apple of knowledge but of contention'.[85] He quotes six or seven early writers to show that 'the fathers before St. Austin generally maintained the doctrine of man's liberty remaining after the fall, the consequents of which are incompossible and inconsistent with the present doctrines of original sin'.[86] Taylor cannot resist taking a thrust at 'St. Austin's harsh and fierce opinion' and comments that 'St. Austin sometimes calls as good men as himself by the name of Pelagians'.[87] As we recall the question whether reasonable minds can still think theologically and how much of the traditional pattern they must discard in the process, Taylor's use of antiquity is interesting and illustrative of the spirit of Anglicanism. Scripture is the touchstone and the witness of antiquity is confirmatory but, in his own words, reason is the judge and so the *esprit large* rather than the *idée fixe* sets the tone of his theology.

III

This quickly surfaces also in Taylor's denial that his teaching is contrary to the Thirty-nine Articles. Significantly, he entitles this section 'An exposition of the ninth Article of the Church of England concerning original sin: *according to Scripture and Reason*'. This is the touchstone. He refers to it again and again and it constitutes the working principle which, together with Taylor's 'openness of discourse' (his own self-description) acts as a standard of assay. Though he resents the charge of doctrinal disloyalty what really matters is the truth of his exposition: 'it is pretended and talked of that my doctrine of original sin is against the ninth Article of the Church of England; and that my attempt to reconcile them was ineffective, Now *although this be nothing to the truth or falsehood of my doctrine*, yet it is much concerning the reputation of it.'[88] He submits the key sentences of the Article to a careful analysis and his integrity and openness are apparent in his conclusion that 'all I can do is to expound the article and make it appear that not only the words of it are capable of a fair construction but also that it is reasonable they should be expounded *so as to agree with Scripture and reason*, and as may best glorify God, and that they require it'. His honesty and 'largeness and freedom of spirit' and his view of the Articles as formularies of peace keep close company as he writes 'I will not pretend to believe that those doctors who first framed the article did all of them mean as I mean; I am not sure they did or that they did not—but this I am sure, that they framed the words with much caution and prudence, and so as might abstain from grieving the contrary minds of differing men'. There is an endearing quality about Taylor's openness and he strives to support his own insistence on freedom and latitude by stressing that the Articles are not like a Continental Confession of Faith but are of the nature of a peace formula: 'It is not unusual for churches, in matters of difficulty, to frame their articles so as to serve the ends of peace, and yet *not to endanger truth or to destroy liberty of improving truth or a further reformation*. . . . To tie the article and our doctrine together is an excellent art of peace and a certain signification of obedience; and *yet is a security of truth and that just liberty of understanding*, which, because it is only God's subject is then sufficiently submitted to men when we consent in the same form of words.'[89]

In *Deus Justificatus* he returns to the same points in simpler language: 'It was very great prudence and piety to secure the peace of the church by as much *charitable latitude* as they could contrive . . . and therefore I have reason to take it ill if any man shall deny me liberty to use the benefit of the church's wisdom; for I am ready a thousand times to subscribe the article'. The charge of disloyalty still rankles but resentment is submerged by concern for truth and the complete conviction that Scripture and reason authenticate his teaching: 'I will not suffer myself to be supposed to be of a differing judgment from my dear mother which is the best church in the world. Indeed, Madam, I do not understand the words of the article as most men do; *but I understand them as they can be true*, and as they can very fairly signify, and as they agree with the word of God and right reason'.[90] How true it is that liberality is the opposite of intransigence and fanaticism and points to the *esprit large* is, I submit, illustrated in Taylor's handling of the controversial subject of original sin. Let him have the last word: 'Why such tragedies should be made of it, and other places of Scripture drawn by violence to give countenance to it, and all the systems of divinity of late made to lean upon this article, which yet was never thought to be fundamental or belonging to the foundation, was never put into the creed of any church, but is made the great support of new and strange propositions, even of the fearful decree of absolute reprobation, and yet was never consented in, or agreed upon what it was, or how it can be conveyed, and was (in the late and modern sense of it) as unknown to the primitive church . . . it is not easy to give a reasonable account.'[91] Taylor has replied to the 'moderns' of his own time with a more modern use of the appeal to antiquity.

Such is the mind and spirit and such is the theological method of Jeremy Taylor whose eucharistic thought is enclosed in his total theology. But to say this is not to say enough because no estimate is valid which does not also embed his theology in his piety. H. Trevor Hughes is surely right in the thesis of his book that Taylor's 'conception of piety had a marked and increasing influence on his whole theological outlook'.[92] George Rust, his friend, spoke of the time Taylor gave to prayer and commented 'His humility was coupled with an extraordinary piety'. There is in his piety a warmth and a devotion to the Sacred Humanity and yet he is no pietist. The warmth is balanced by a sinewy and practical view of the spiritual life inevitable in one who saw moral theology and the theology of the spiritual life as all of a piece, one science. To this Taylor made a major contribution fully endorsing Rust's comment on his great skill in 'casuistical divinity, and he was a rare conductor of souls and knew how to counsel and to advise; to solve difficulties, and determine cases, and quiet consciences'. As he is no pietist so he is no mere moralist: quite simply he is a moral/ascetical theologian in whose concept of the Christian life sacramentality is endemic. Constantly, as we shall see, he links 'I live, yet not I, but Christ lives in me' with the sacramental means of grace through which the Life of the risen Christ enters and transforms human lives. Surely in this he echoes Richard Hooker: 'Life being therefore proposed unto all men as their end, they which by baptism have laid the foundation and attained the first beginning of a new life have here their nourishment and food prescribed for continuance of life in them. Such as will live the life of God must eat the flesh and drink the blood of the Son of man, because this is a part of that diet which if we want we cannot live.'[93] Thus, a modern eucharistic agreement declares 'Its purpose is to transmit the life of the crucified and risen Christ to his body, the Church, so that its members may be more fully united with Christ and with one another'.[94] Here then is the point at which we begin to examine in the context of his total theological method the eucharistic doctrine of Jeremy Taylor who wrote: 'The sum is this: Christ's body, his flesh and blood, are therefore called our meat and drink, because by his incarnation and manifestation in the flesh he became life to us; so that it is mysterious indeed in the expression, but very proper and intelligible in the event, to say that we eat his flesh and drink his blood, since by these it is that we have and preserve life.'[95]

At the end of this survey the reader may feel inclined to ask to what purpose is this examination of Jeremy Taylor's general theology in a book purporting to be about the substance and the setting of his eucharistic theology. The answer lies as much in Taylor the man as in Taylor the theologian. To study his approach to these areas of theology is to attempt to understand the cast of his mind and the individuality which enters into his handling of theological questions, for his theology of the eucharist was not formulated and developed in some sort of intellectual vacuum but was part and parcel of Taylor's understanding of how the fruits of the Paschal Mystery grow and are effective in the members of the Body of Christ. The inherited richness of the tradition combines with the largeness of his spirit to produce a theology of the eucharist both orthodox and individual and deeply devotional.

Notes

1. *Funeral Sermon, Works* (Heber ed.), Vol. I, p. 20.
2. 'The Fame of Jeremy Taylor', *Anglican Theological Review*, vol. xliv, no. 4, p. 389.
3. Examples are: H. R. McAdoo, *The Structure of Caroline Moral Theology* (1948); C. J. Stranks, *The Life and Writings of Jeremy Taylor* (1952); T. Wood, *English casuistical divinity during the 17th century, with special reference to Jeremy Taylor* (1952); F. R. Bolton, *The Caroline Tradition of the Church of Ireland, with special reference to Jeremy Taylor* (1952); H. T. Hughes, *The Piety of Jeremy Taylor* (1960); H. R. McAdoo, *The Spirit of Anglicanism* (1965); C. A. Allison, *The Rise of Moralism* (1966); Harry Boone Porter, *Jeremy Taylor—Liturgist* (1979).
4. *Funeral Sermon*, loc. cit., p. 19.
5. ib. p. 21.
6. C. J. Stranks, *The Life and Writings of Jeremy Taylor* (1952), p. 9.
7. *Works* (ed. Heber, 1828), Vol. XI, p. 356.
8. *Funeral Sermon*, pp. 21–2.
9. One may compare Amand de Mendieta's experience after becoming an Anglican; 'There is no other Church in the Catholic tradition . . . which so passionately believes in spiritual freedom, and which so positively demands it from clergy and laity alike' (*Anglican Vision* by Emmanuel Amand de Mendieta, London 1971, p. 63). T. S. Eliot, also a convert to Anglicanism, wrote 'A Catholicism without the element of humanism and criticism would be a Catholicism of despair': *For Lancelot Andrewes* (London 1928), p. 160.
10. Alec R. Vidler, *Essays in Liberality* (London 1957), pp. 21–22.
11. *The Liberty of Prophesying*, Sect. V (8) and (11), Heber ed. Vol. 8, pp. 19, 24.
12. ib. Sect. VIII (4), ib. Vol. 8, p. 84.

13. For the interlocking of Laudians and the Tew Group, see H. R. McAdoo, *The Spirit of Anglicanism* (1965), p. 356.

14. William Laud, *A Relation of the Conference*.

15. For the Anglican appeal to antiquity, see H. R. McAdoo, *The Spirit of Anglicanism*, Chapters IX and X.

16. For a fuller examination of Taylor's theology, see H. R. McAdoo, *The Spirit of Anglicanism*, pp. 52–80.

17. *The Golden Remains of the Ever-Memorable Mr John Hales* (3rd impression), p. 7.

18. ib. p. 44: For an assessment of Hales see *The Spirit of Anglicanism*, pp. 15–21.

19. See Essay No. 3 (H. R. McAdoo) in *Authority in the Anglican Communion* (1987), ed. Stephen W. Sykes.

20. William Laud, *The Conference (1622) with Mr. Fisher the Jesuit* (1639), Ch. XIV.

21. *Conference*, Ch III.

22. See *The Anglican Moral Choice* (1983. ed. Paul Elmen), Ch. 2, 'Anglican Moral Theology in the Seventeenth Century: An Anticipation', by H. R. McAdoo.

23. For fuller details see H. R. McAdoo, 'Jeremy Taylor: An essay on the relationship of faith and reason', *Hermathena*, no. cvii, 1968.

24. *Ductor Dubitantium*, Rule III, (61), Heber ed. Vol. XI, p. 462.

25. *Ductor Dubitantium*, Rule III, (23), Heber ed. Vol. XI, p. 442.

26. Austin Farrer *Saving Belief* (1964), p. 5.

27. ib., Rule III (24), p. 442.

28. loc. cit., p. 14.

29. ib., Rule III (22), p. 441.

30. What follows on faith and reason is in part reproduced from my article in *Hermathena*, no. cvii, 1968.

31. ib. Rule III (8), p. 434.

32. *The New Reformation*, p. 22 and Taylor, Rule III, (17)–(19), pp. 437–9.

33. ib. Rule III (19), p. 439.

34. loc. cit., p. 37.

35. Rule III, (47), p. 453.

36. ib. Rule III (23)–(24), p. 442.

37. ib. Rule III (24), p. 442.

38. ib. Rule III (25), pp. 442–3.

39. ib. Rule III (26), p. 443.

40. ib. Rule III (31), p. 447.

41. ib. Rule III (33), p. 448.

42. ib. Rule III (35), p. 448.

43. Rule III, (49), p. 455.

44. Rule III, (56), p. 460.

45. *John Jewel as Apologist for the Church of England* (1963), pp. 139–140.

46. ib. Rule III, (57), p. 460.

47. ib. Rule III, (58), p. 461.

48. ib. Rule III, (59–60), p. 461.

49. ib. Rule III, (61), p. 462.

50. ib. Rule III, (64), pp. 462–3.

51. ib. Rule III, (63), p. 462.

52. *Complete Works* (ed. W. Jacobson, Oxford, 1884), Sermon 3 ad Clerum, Vol. II, p. 105. For the moral theology of the period see *The Structure of Caroline Moral Theology* (1949) by H. R. McAdoo and *Conscience: Dictator or Guide? A Study in Seventeenth-century English Protestant Moral Theology* (1967) by Kevin Kelly.

53. See C. J. Stranks, *The Life and Writings of Jeremy Taylor*, Ch. VII and H. R. McAdoo, *The Spirit of Anglicanism*, pp. 76–80.

54. *Unum Necessarium*, Ch. VI, (44), Heber ed. Vol. IX, p. 22.

55. *The Life and Writings of Jeremy Taylor* (1952), p. 161.

56. *Deus Justificatus*, Heber ed. Vol. IX, p. 330.

57. Introductory letter to *Deus Justificatus*.

58. *Deus Justificatus*, ib. Vol. IX, p. 363.

59. *Unum Necessarium*, ib. Ch. VII, (16), Vol. IX, p. 91.

60. *Deus Justificatus*, ib. Vol. IX, p. 331.

61. *Deus Justificatus*, ib. Vol. IX, p. 342.

62. *Unum Necessarium*, Ch. VI, Section VII, (82), ib. Vol. IX, p. 54.

63. ib. Ch. VI, Section I, (6), ib. Vol. IX, p. 2.

64. ib. Ch. VI, Section I, (18), Vol. IX, p. 9.

65. ib. Ch. VI, Section I, (22), Vol. IX, p. 12.

66. ib. Ch. VI, Section IV (67), Vol. IX, p. 40.

67. ib. Ch. VII, Section IV (16), Vol. IX, p. 89.

68. ib. Ch. VI, Section I (36), Vol. IX, p. 17.

69. ib. Ch. VI, Section I (3)–(4), Vol. IX, pp. 1–2.

70. ib. Ch. VII, Section II (12), Vol. IX, p. 84.

71. ib. *Deus Justificatus*, Vol. XI, pp. 339–340.

72. ib. Ch. VII, Section V (26), Vol. IX, p. 106.

73. ib. Ch. VII, Section II (10), Vol. IX, p. 81.

74. ib. Ch. VI, Section I (21), Vol. IX, p. 10.

75. *Deus Justificatus*, Vol. IX, p. 342.

76. *Unum Necessarium*, Ch. VII (23), Vol. IX, p. 103.

77. *Deus Justificatus*, Vol. IX, p. 341.

78. *Unum Necessarium*, Ch. VII, Section I (1), Vol. IX, p. 73.

79. ib. Ch. VII, Section V (18), Vol. IX, p. 94.

80. ib. Ch. VII (18)–(24), Vol. IX, pp. 95–103.

81. ib. Ch. VII, Section IV (16), Vol. IX, p. 92.

82. ib. Ch. VII, Section IV (16), Vol. IX, p. 92.

83. ib. Ch. VI, Section V (77), Vol. IX, p. 50.

84. ib. Ch. VI, Section VI (79), Vol. IX, p. 51.

85. ib. Ch. VII, Section I (1), Vol. IX, p. 73.

86. ib. Ch. VII, Section III (14), Vol. IX, p. 85.

87. ib. Ch. VII, Section IV (16), Vol. IX, pp. 90–91.

88. ib. Ch. VII, Section VI (27), Vol. IX, p. 107.

89. ib. Ch. VII, Section VI (27), Vol. IX, pp. 107–108.

90. *Deus Justificatus*, Vol. IX, p. 362.

91. *Unum Necessarium*, Ch. VII, Section VI (41), Vol. IX, p. 118.

92. H. Trevor Hughes, *The Piety of Jeremy Taylor* (1960), p. 153.

93. Richard Hooker, *The Laws of Ecclesiastical Polity*, V, lxvii, 1.
94. The Windsor Agreement of ARCIC I on *Eucharistic Doctrine* (6).
95. *The Worthy Communicant*, Ch. I, Section II (4), Vol. XV, p. 419.

II Beginning a Theology of the Eucharist

'The eucharist is the fulness of all the mysteriousness of our religion' wrote Jeremy Taylor in *Clerus Domini*; 'the great mystery of Christianity and the only remanent expression of Christ's sacrifice on earth.'[1] Elsewhere he goes further, 'Nothing else but the actual enjoying of heaven is above it'.[2] These and countless similar extracts from his various writings on the subject place Taylor firmly in the great tradition which from the beginning, as the Fathers testify, sees the eucharist as the Church's expression of itself, 'You are one bread, one body'. For Taylor, the Church is the eucharistic fellowship of the baptized united by the apostolic faith: 'They who were baptized . . . continued steadfastly in the apostles' doctrine and fellowship, in the breaking of bread and the prayers' (Acts 2:41–42). He sees the eucharist as proclaiming the Gospel and as being the channel of the new life, Christ's life transforming ours, so that 'If we have communicated worthily, we have given ourselves to Christ; we have given him all our liberty and our life . . . and in exchange have received him; and we may say with St. Paul "I live, but not I, but Christ liveth in me".'[3] Behind Taylor stretches the tradition back through the Reformation, the medieval period, the patristic writings, to the life of the Primitive Church and to the New Testament. The tradition expresses itself primarily through a richness and variety of devotion but also through a richness of theology exploring what it is that happens in the eucharistic action, the interplay of realism and symbolism, the nexus between the Cross and the eucharist, the nature of the life-giving presence, a change in the elements and a change in the worshipper. Ahead of Taylor lies the continuing tradition, enriched by the devotion and theology which has gone before, passing through a long period of entrenched and polemical positions on these aspects of eucharistic doctrine, and beginning now to emerge into an atmosphere of convergence and quest for what the formularies on both sides have been trying to say. The past few decades have seen the Churches officially and semi-officially seeking agreement and the fruits of this movement are seen in the eucharistic agreements of ARCIC I, of the Lima Report, of the Lutheran-Roman Catholic Statement and of the inter-confessional Group of Les Dombes. 'Shall I wish that men would give themselves more to meditate with silence what we have by the sacrament, and less to dispute of the manner How'[4]—so wrote Richard Hooker. The sentiment is unexceptionable but some meeting of minds there must be, at least on a basis of what ARCIC I called substantial agreement, described by J. M. R. Tillard as 'a search for what pertains to the essence, and according to which, in diverse forms, the two traditions live'.[5] The modern agreements have sought to get behind the polemics of the past and have consciously taken as their starting-point 'biblical teaching and the tradition of our common inheritance'. It is to these same sources that Jeremy Taylor turned and in an age more controversially minded, the effects of which he did not himself escape though because of his liberality they were less noticeable in his work than in that of many contemporaries.

If one were to attempt to simplify—a particularly perilous enterprise when treating of eucharistic theology—one would venture to signalize, among many others, three matters or questions of great moment. The handling of each at different periods and in a variety of forms and presentations during the long centuries of the tradition from the beginning to the present has marked crucial stages in the understanding of and therefore in the theology of the eucharist. As I see it, taken out of their many historical contexts and stripped of the incidental refinements created by such contexts, these three matters could be expressed in the form of two questions and a statement:

(1) Who, or what, is being sacrificed?
(2) Who, rather than what, is present?
(3) Christ present means Christ active.

All three lie behind the general question '*What happens at Holy Communion*'? As our investigation of Taylor's work proceeds, their apparent crudity and over-simplicity will, I hope, be enriched and deepened and given real substance. Yet *in one form or another* it seems to me that from the earliest Christian writings down to the modern eucharistic statements these three matters have been at the heart of men's efforts to understand and explain 'the eucharist which is the fulness of all the mysteriousness of our religion'. How Taylor's thought and teaching shape and form themselves in this context, and bearing in mind his use of and appeal to antiquity, is the subject-matter of this study.

Two preliminary points need to be made. The first is that we have become conditioned to looking at the doctrine of the eucharist under different headings such as Sacrifice, Presence and Communion. This is probably inevitable in the circumstances and the pattern is followed by the modern eucharistic statements. The reminder of G. W. H. Lampe is therefore not to be ignored that early Christian writing on the eucharist was not compartmentalised in this way: 'it does not lend itself to precise definition or to clear-cut theories about presence, sacrifice, consecration, and the relation of the sacramental act and of the visible elements to the reality which they signify. Early Christian belief about the eucharist is complex.'[6] There is more than a hint that Taylor was aware of this.[7] Nevertheless, the only effective way of evaluating his teaching will be to consider it under certain headings as these arise. Such headings will be, Mystery, Presence, Sacrifice, Representation, the Heavenly Altar, Anamnesis, Life, Sacramental signs, the Holy Spirit and Holy Communion. It is under these headings, to speak artificially, that the substance of his eucharistic theology is found.

The second preliminary point is one explanatory of procedure. The different books in which Taylor deals with one aspect or another of eucharistic teaching and practice are taken in order of publication. This establishes the chronology of his eucharistic theology and should shed light on any developments in his thought and on the weight which he attaches to certain of the themes characterised above as headings. We shall see that however the balance or emphasis is altered by the nature of any particular book and by the requirements necessitated by its objective, Taylor's methodology remains basically that of the appeal to Scripture, to antiquity and to reason. Constantly too we are reminded that for him the eucharist is always in context, that of the life of the Christian who in faith and repentance is called to holy living.

This brings us to the first work in the course of which he wrote about the eucharist and which is in fact the first work from his pen though, oddly, it was the last to be discovered. The manuscript was found in the library of Queen's College, Oxford, early in the nineteenth century, too late to be included in Heber's edition of the works but in time for the revision by Eden, having first been published separately in 1848. It seems to have been written when Taylor was a Fellow of All Souls College, a post which he owed to Archbishop Laud who had been much impressed by the young man's gifts.[8] Clearly, Laud discerned in him, and quite correctly, a High Churchman whose views were sympathetic with the Archbishop's policy. Taylor, as is evident throughout his works, loved order and dignity in worship and was deeply aware of the living continuity of faith and order coming from the Upper Room and from the Paschal Mystery and from the life of the early Church down to the Church of his own time. Yet, interestingly, it was at Oxford that he got to know William Chillingworth, also one of Laud's *protégés*. Here we may well find the partial source of Taylor's liberality as it was just at this time, as Stranks reminds us, that Chillingworth was at work on his great book *The Religion of Protestants*. For two reasons, however, the expression 'partial source' seems fair. In the first place—and acquaintances as well as his writings indicate this—the quality of liberality appears to be part of Taylor's temperament and make-up. Secondly, when looking at the seventeenth-century scene, one has to forget Pusey and Liddon and remember Gore when looking for modern parallels and terms of comparison. One cannot say that there is no such animal as a liberal High Churchman at this time, for even Taylor's patron, so conscious of his Church's Catholic inheritance, would still insist on a freedom and latitude for private men within the parameters of 'the faith once for all delivered'. Typically, Taylor was at this time deeply involved in the study of the Fathers and the Schoolmen but one recalls that *The Liberty of Prophesying* appeared as early as 1647. In other words, one resists the temptation to type-cast Taylor.

At all events, his first work to contain reflections on the meaning of the eucharist, entitled *On the Reverence due to the*

Altar, was clearly the work of a High Churchman. Really more
in the nature of a tract, C. W. Dugmore has written that it
'provided a far better *apologia* for the High Churchmen than
anything which Laud himself produced on the subject'.[9] In his
thorough and acute analysis of seventeenth-century Anglican
eucharistic doctrine he has outlined what he sees as the
dilemma of the High Churchmen unanimously rejecting transubstantiation but firmly committed to belief in the 'real
presence' and at a loss for a category in which to express it. My
only criticism of a masterly survey would be to suggest that
perhaps Dugmore has not allowed sufficiently for the possibility that the High Church stress on mystery and consequently
on agnosticism concerning the 'how' of the presence is a
deliberate stance. He speaks of 'intellectual bankruptcy' and of
theologians like Laud and Mountague taking 'refuge' at this
point in the idea of a *mysterium tremendum*. Could it not be,
however, that they did so because they held it to be impossible
and unacceptable to define as *de fide* what could not be
claimed as Scripturally revealed and authenticated? This was
the line taken by Lancelot Andrewes in the *Responsio*, his
reply to Cardinal Bellarmine: 'Christ said, "This is my Body".
He did not say, "This is my Body in this way". We are in
agreement with you as to the end; the whole controversy is as
to the method. . . . *and because there is no word, we rightly
make it not of faith*; we place it perhaps among the theories of
the Schools, but not among the articles of faith . . . we believe
no less than you that the presence is real. Concerning the
method of the presence, we define nothing rashly . . .'[10] That
was written in 1610 and over forty years later the same
approach is found in John Bramhall's *Answer to M. de la
Milletière*.[11] This is not quite the same as being desperately in
search of a category to express the mode of the eucharistic
presence. Rather is it a considered affirmation of the existence
of mystery and one recalls Taylor's description of what is
mysterious in religion as uncomprehended rather than incomprehensible and always to be distinguished from 'human
appendages' to dogma. Did he not also 'wonder that God
should. . . . with bread and wine nourish us up to immortality'? Nor is it special pleading to point out that this same strain
of recognising mystery in the matter of Christ's presence in the
eucharist and of refraining from defining the mode of that

presence has left discernible traces in some of the modern eucharistic agreements. For example, ARCIC I heads one of the sections of the Windsor Statement 'The Mystery of the Eucharist' and simply refers to 'his true presence, effectually signified by the bread and wine which, in this mystery, become his body and blood'.[12] The Lima Report reads 'Some are content merely to affirm this presence without seeking to explain it. Others consider it necessary to assert a change wrought by the Holy Spirit and Christ's words, in consequence of which there is no longer just ordinary bread and wine but the body and blood of Christ. Others again have developed an explanation of the real presence which, though not claiming to exhaust the significance of the mystery, seeks to protect it from damaging interpretations'.[13] When ARCIC I states that 'the bread and wine become the body and blood of Christ by the action of the Holy Spirit' it has not established any category in which the truth of the real presence is expressed other than an affirmation of the mystery of the Spirit's working in the sacrament.[14] Taylor said the same in the *Great Exemplar*: 'Whatsoever the Spirit can convey to the body of the Church, we may expect from this sacrament; for as the Spirit is the instrument of life and action, so the blood of Christ is the conveyance of his Spirit'.[15] Though Taylor has much to say on various aspects of the presence and sacrifice especially in his later works, as we shall see, he never retreats from the position that 'the sacraments are mysteries' and the eucharist 'the queen of the mysteries'.[16] Interestingly, the 1967 Lutheran/Catholic statement concludes that 'our conversations have persuaded us of both the legitimacy and the limits of theological efforts to explore the mystery of Christ's presence in the sacrament'. This hardly brings us further in the matter than the Laudian affirmations particularly as the conversationalists, echoing Lancelot Andrewes, conclude that 'there is agreement on the "that", the full reality of Christ's presence. What has been disputed is a particular way of stating the "how", the manner in which he becomes present'. They anticipate 'increasing convergence and deepened understanding of the eucharistic mystery'.[17]

In the tract *On the Reverence due to the Altar*, Jeremy Taylor's position would appear to be that of a High Churchman of the Laudian type and he treats his subject by way of appealing to Scripture, to the Fathers and the liturgies, and to reason. His theme is that the worship of God is both external and internal and that this external worship is 'specially . . . where He is most praesentiall'.[18] There is no need here to follow Taylor's argument in detail as he seeks support from Scripture and from numerous patristic writings. Part of his thesis is that holy places have what he terms a 'relative sanctity' and particularly 'where the Christian Altar is placed and our Sacrifice commemorated'.[19] He develops this idea in several places: 'Where God is present, there he is to be worshipped, and so according to the degree of his presence'.[20] Consequently, the altar 'being a place of the greatest sanctity, there ought to be the expressions of the greatest devotion'.[21] He returns to it again at the close with a warning that it is who and not what that is worshipped: 'Our worship is towards holy places but the adoration is intended to God . . . but there is a veneration or reverence to be given to holy things for *their relative sanctity*'. He quotes St. Chrysostom on honouring the altar because it receives the Lord's body, 'for its relation to the body of Christ'.[22] We find here too the first indication of Taylor's continuing stress on the eucharist as the channel of Christ's Life to ours when he quotes John Damascene on 'the life-bringing table'. Or as ARCIC I put it, 'its purpose is to transmit the life of the crucified and risen Christ to his body, the Church' and 'when this offering is met by faith, a lifegiving encounter results'.[23] This will be a major theme in the developing eucharistic theology of Jeremy Taylor.

It is in his summary of the eucharistic function of the altar that we have a setting-out in brief of the Laudian position which contains the germs of teaching which Taylor would later develop in detail concerning the presence, the *anamnesis* and sacrifice, and the mystery of the eucharist. The passage is worth quoting in full as being the point from which the young Fellow of All Souls' began his thinking and writing about the eucharist:

'The Altar or Holy Table is *sedes Corporis et Sanguinis Christi*. S. Chrysostom: hom: 21. in 2 Cor: *et alibi*. And if the Altars, and Arke and the Temple in the Law of Nature and Moses were Holy, because they were God's Memorialls, as I shewed above, then by the same reason shall the Altar be *huperagion*, highly Holy, because it is Christ's Memoriall, there we commemorate his Death, and passion in the dread-full, and mysterious way that *himself with greater mysterious-ness appointed* . . . doe this for my memoriall. Here are all the Christian Sacrifices presented. *Panem accepit, et calicem similiter et suum Sanguinem confessus est et novi Testamenti novam docuit oblationem, quam Ecclesia ab Apostolis acci-piens in Universo mundo offert Deo*, saith that Apostolicall man S. Irenaeus. Wee doe believe that Christ is there really present in the Sacrament, there is the body and bloud of Christ which are "verely, and indeed" taken and received by the faithfull, saith our Church in her Catechisme. Now if places become holy at the presence of an angell . . . and in the old Law, for God alwayes appeared by Angells, shall not the Christian Altar be most holy where is present the blessed Body and Bloud of the Sonne of God? But, what when the Sacrament is Gone? The relation is there still, and it is but a relative Sanctity we speake of . . .'[24] Having given numerous quota-tions from the Fathers and from the Greek and Latin liturgies in support of reverencing the altar 'for its relation to the body of Christ', Taylor concludes 'These witnesses are enough to make faith of the practise of the primitive church'.[25]

The booklet, structured on the threefold appeal with a heavy emphasis on the witness of antiquity, is a paradigm of Taylor's methodology in his maturer works. Slight though the amount of eucharistic material is, being incidental to the overall objec-tive of the tract, its interest is twofold. In the first place, it gives an indication of the writer's early stance on the presence and the sacrifice. Secondly, by its emphasis on the 'mysteriousness' of the eucharistic action it places Taylor's thinking in the context of the Laudian affirmation of mystery and rejection of transubstantiation.

In a sense, Lancelot Andrewes is a pre-Laudian, having been born eighteen years before the great Archbishop. Nevertheless they were bishops together for some five years. Andrewes asserts that none of the Fathers knew of any change of substance in the elements but they and 'we allow that the elements are changed'. Here is the mystery (the 'how' not being revealed); 'At the coming of the almighty power of the Word, the nature is changed so that what before was the mere element *now becomes a Divine Sacrament*, the substance nevertheless remaining what it was before . . . There is that

kind of union between the visible Sacrament and the invisible
reality (*rem*) of the Sacrament which there is between the
manhood and the Godhead of Christ . . .'[26] This mysterious
presence is a sacramental presence, a dynamic, indwelling
presence, and in a Christmas sermon Andrewes returns to the
same understanding of the mystery that in 'the Blessed Eucharist' there is 'a kind of hypostatical union of the sign and
the thing signified, so united together as are the two Natures of
Christ'.[27] This approach is surely as patient of a reasonable
setting out as is the doctrine of transubstantiation!

Herbert Thorndike, possibly the most sophisticated theologian among the Laudians, took the same line later in the
century tying together mystery and sacramentality as the mode
of Christ's presence. The Fathers, he claims, 'acknowledge the
elements to be changed, translated, and turned into the substance of Christ's Body and Blood; *though as in a sacrament,
that is, mystically*; yet, therefore, by virtue of the consecration,
not of his faith that receives'.[28] He gives a classic example of
this way of affirming the real presence when he writes: 'If a
man demand further, how I understand the Body and Blood of
Christ to be present "in", "with", or "under", the elements,
when I say they are "in", and "with", and "under", them, as
"in", and "with", and "under", *a sacrament mystically*; I
conceive I am excused of any further answer, and am not
obliged to declare *the manner of that which must be mystical*,
when I have said what I can say to declare it'.[29]

John Cosin, sequestrated and forced into exile, wrote his
Historia Transubstantiationis in Paris, and he clearly understands the real presence in the same way. Commenting on the
Pauline account of the institution, he writes: 'Hence it is most
evident that the bread and wine (which, according to St. Paul,
are the elements of the Holy Eucharist) are neither changed as
to their substance, nor vanished, nor reduced to nothing, but
are solemly consecrated by the Words of Christ, that by them
His Blessed Body and Blood may be communicated to us. And
further it appears from the same words, that the expression of
Christ and the Apostle is to be understood *in a Sacramental
and mystic sense*; and that no gross and carnal presence of
Body and Blood can be maintained by them.

And, though the word *Sacrament* be no where used in
Scripture to signify the Blessed Eucharist, yet the Christian

Church ever since its primitive ages hath given it that name, and always called the presence of Christ's Body and Blood therein mystic and Sacramental'.[30]

Cosin, like Taylor, is committed to the conviction that basically 'the sacraments are mysteries' and he would make his own the sentence of Durandus quoted by Bramhall in his *Answer to M. de la Milletière*, '*Motum sentimus, Modum nescimus, Praesentiam credimus*'. Bramhall, pointing out that Aquinas observed that how Christ is present can neither be perceived by sense nor by imagination, rejects those who 'anatomize mysteries' and 'determine supernatural not-revealed truths'. This is the reason 'Why we rest in the Words of Christ, This is my Body, leaving the manner to him that made the Sacrament'. Bramhall, as did Andrewes, rejects any attempt to classify an explanation of the 'how' as *de fide*: 'No genuine son of the Church of England did ever deny' a true Real Presence: 'Christ said, *This is my Body*; what he said, we do steadfastly believe. He said not, after this or that manner, *neque con, neque sub, neque trans*. And therefore we place it among the opinions of the schools, not among the Articles of our Faith'.[31] John Cosin is content with the same affirmation that 'we that are Protestant and Reformed according to the ancient Catholic Church do not search into the manner of it with perplexing inquiries; but, after the example of the primitive and purest Church of Christ, we leave it to the power and wisdom of Our Lord, yielding a full and unfeigned assent to His words'.[32]

All I am saying here is that the Laudian view of the real presence is a deliberately-taken position based on the mystery of the eucharist, the essential mystery of sacramentality. The conviction was well put by William Forbes, the first bishop of Edinburgh, 'that the Body and Blood of Christ are really and actually and substantially present and taken in the Eucharist, but in a way which the human mind cannot understand and much more beyond the power of man to express, which is known to God alone and is not revealed to us in the Scriptures, —a way indeed not by bodily or oral reception, but not only by the understanding and merely by faith, but in another way known, as has been said, to God alone, and to be left to his omnipotence . . . .'.[33]

Taylor, as will become evident, has a good deal to say in his later works on mystery and sacramentality. Whether he is able to clarify his position further will be a question. But for the young Laudian who wrote *On the Reverence due to the Altar* this is the theological ambience of his thinking about the eucharist. To change the imagery, the Laudian position fits like a glove at this stage of his development. It is fair to ask incidentally how that position in respect of the real presence differs from that of the Windsor Statement of ARCIC I; 'Thus, in considering the mystery of the eucharistic presence, we must recognize both the sacramental sign of Christ's presence and the personal relationship between Christ and the faithful which arises from that presence'.[34] As in the Windsor Statement, so in the *Elucidation* (1979), the Commission speaks of 'the mystery of the eucharist' and of 'Christ's sacramental presence'.[35] It takes from *Windsor* (6) the much-discussed phrase 'his true presence, effectually signified by the bread and wine which, *in this mystery, become* his body and blood,' and comments as follows; '*Becoming* does not here imply material change . . . It does not imply that Christ becomes present in the eucharist in the same manner that he was present in his earthly life. It does not imply that this *becoming* follows the physical laws of this world. What is here affirmed is *a sacramental presence* in which God uses realities of this world to convey the realities of the new creation: bread for this life becomes the bread of eternal life. Before the eucharistic prayer, to the question: 'What is that?' the believer answers: 'It is bread'. After the eucharistic prayer, to the same question he answers 'It is truly the body of Christ, the Bread of Life'.[36]

If the reader turns back to the extracts from Lancelot Andrewes and from John Cosin, by way of comparison, the identity of thought and exposition must surely be found to be striking. This is more than a fortuitous parallelism and furnishes a modern instance of the combined concepts of mystery and sacramentality which, I suggest, is, in the case of the Laudians, a deliberate and defensible position rather than a taking refuge in inexplicability.

If *The Psalter, or the Psalms of David* (1644), which contains some eucharistic prayers, is really the work of Jeremy Taylor then it belongs to this period of his development. At its first appearing, the author's name was given as Christopher Hatton. This was queried by Wood who took the view that it was the work of Taylor and his name was given as author when the eighth edition was published, after his death, in 1672. C. J. Stranks considers that Hatton would hardly have had 'the knowledge of early Church history, the lives of the Fathers, and liturgiology, which the preface claims, but of course Taylor was well acquainted with them all.' On the other hand, his opinion of the stylistic evidence is that it weighs against Taylor's authorship. These doubts would seem to one reader at least to have substance. Stranks's conclusion may well be as far as we can get: 'All the evidence points to this edition of the Psalter having been the work of Hatton, but that Taylor supplied the learning and touched up the whole. A story to that effect would be enough to make Wood set Taylor down as the author'.[37] It will, of course, be remembered that Hatton had been Taylor's patron and that *Episcopacy Asserted* had been dedicated to him, so the connection existed over a long period of time. Stranks does not refer to the half-dozen eucharistic prayers 'preparatory to the receiving of the blessed Sacrament' and it is perhaps worthy of comment that the first is an adaptation of a prayer of Aquinas and the last an adaptation of the *Salve Regina* addressed instead to the Redeemer.[38]

The 'Aquinas' prayer speaks of receiving 'Thy blessed body and blood in the mysterious sacrament'. The second prayer asks 'still to give thyself to me, to convey health, and grace, and life, and hopes of glory, in the most blessed sacrament. I adore thee, O most righteous Redeemer, that thou art pleased under the visible signs of bread and wine, to convey unto our souls thy holy body and blood, and all the benefits of thy bitter passion'. It concludes with a petition 'that I may be led through the paths of a good life'. The third prayer seeks both the spirit of devotion and the grace of holy living 'for his sake, who is both Sacrifice and Priest, the Master of the Feast and the Feast itself, even Jesus Christ'. The last prayer but one is addressed to the Father who 'offered life, and grace, and salvation to us, by the real exhibition of thy Son, Jesus Christ, in the sacrifice of his death upon the altar of the cross, and by commemoration of his bitter agonies in the holy sacrament; grant that that great and venerable sacrifice, *which we now commemorate sacramentally*, may procure of Thee for Thy whole Church mercy and great assistance in all trials'. A further petition requests 'that this blessed sacrament and sacrifice of commemoration, in virtue of that dreadful and proper sacrifice upon the cross, may obtain for me, and for us all who have communicated this day, pardon and peace'.

Questions of authorship apart, these prayers exhibit qualities and features common to Taylor and the Laudians, such as devotional realism, the stress on mystery in the eucharist, the nexus between the Church's eucharistic action and the one perfect Sacrifice of the Cross in terms of commemoration and memorial, and the benefits of this Sacrifice in the lives of those who, through the sacrament, 'may be firmly and indissolubly united to thy mystical body' (First Prayer). There is also an emphasis on devotion to the Sacred Humanity through a concentration on the Passion of Christ which is a recurring feature in Taylor's writings. All of these themes we shall find developing in Jeremy Taylor's later work.

Notes

1. *Clerus Domini*, Sect. V (1) and (5), Vol. XIV, pp. 452, 454.
2. *Christian Consolations*, Ch. V, Vol. I, p. 160. Heber accepts its ascription to Taylor but Stranks rejects it.
3. *The Worthy Communicant*, Ch. VII, Section I, (14); Vol. XV, p. 675.
4. *Ecclesiastical Polity*, V, lxvii, 3.
5. See 'Anglican/Roman Catholic Dialogue' in *One in Christ*, Vol. VIII, No. 3, 1972.
6. *Eucharistic Theology Then and Now* (1968), Essay 3 (G. W. H. Lampe) on 'The Eucharist in the Thought of the Early Church'.
7. See *The Real Presence and Spiritual of Christ in the Blessed Sacrament*, Section XII, Heber ed., Vol. X, pp. 60–68.
8. For Taylor's relationship with Laud, see C. J. Stranks, *The Life and Writings of Jeremy Taylor*, Ch. III.
9. C. W. Dugmore, *Eucharistic Doctrine in England from Hooker to Waterland* (1942), p. 92.
10. *Responsio ad apologiam Cardinalis Bellarmine*, Ch. I (1).
11. *Works* (L.A.C.T. ed.), Vol. I, pp. 7–8.
12. *The Final Report* (1982), pp. 12, 14.
13. *Baptism, Eucharist and Ministry* (1982), p. 13.
14. loc. cit., p. 16.
15. *The Great Exemplar*, Discourse XIX, (9), Vol. III, p. 300.
16. See the epistle dedicatory and the introduction to *The Worthy Communicant*, Vol. XV, pp. 397–402.
17. *Modern Eucharistic Agreement* (London 1973), p. 43.
18. *Works* (ed. Heber and Eden), Vol. V, p. 319.

19. ib., p. 322.
20. ib., p. 325.
21. ib., p. 327.
22. ib., p. 335.
23. *The Final Report*, p. 15.
24. loc. cit., p. 330.
25. ib., p. 334.
26. From his *Responsio*, quoted in *Anglicanism* (1935), ed. More and Cross.
27. Sermons of the Nativity, XVI, L.A.C.T. ed., Vol. I, p. 282.
28. *Works* (L.A.C.T. ed.), Vol. IV, p. 73.
29. ib., p. 35.
30. *Works*, (L.A.C.T. ed.), Vol. IV, pp. 155–157.
31. Quoted in More and Cross, *Anglicanism*, pp. 475–484.
32. loc. cit.
33. Quoted in More and Cross, *Anglicanism*, p. 471.
34. *The Final Report* (1982), p. 15.
35. *The Final Report* (1982), pp. 22, 24.
36. ib., p. 21.
37. *The Life and Writings of Jeremy Taylor* (1952) by C. J. Stranks, pp. 300–301.
38. *Works*, Vol. XV, pp. 209–213.

III Holy Sacrament and Holy Living

'The first life of Christ ever to be written in English' and 'it is a beautiful book. To Taylor it came as a splendid discovery. It taught him the magnificence of his strength and where that strength most truly lay.'[1] So wrote C. J. Stranks of Jeremy Taylor's *The Great Exemplar (1649)* or, to give its full title, *The History of the Life and Death of the Holy Jesus*. When it appeared, the author was accused by the Roman Catholic controversialist John Sergeant of plagiarizing from the *Vita Jesu Christi Redemptoris Nostri* by Ludolphus of Saxony, but this can hardly be sustained as the resemblances are very few and the format is different.

In spite of its great length, it is indeed a beautiful book. But no one seems to have remarked that it is really two books, fused and indissolubly merged by the creativity of a devout and attractive mind. One book recounts the life of Christ, centring on stages and incidents from 'The Bearing of Jesus in the Womb of the Blessed Virgin', through the Gospel story, to the crucifixion, resurrection and ascension of the Lord. Interwoven with the narrative are the devotional 'considerations' on each event and 'discourses' covering a wide range of aspects of religion according as the Life of Christ informs the daily life of the Christian. These constitute the second book and each depends on the other. *The Great Exemplar* is a rich example of the many-sidedness of Taylor, covering as it does so much of what is involved in Christian faith and practice. Yet, the work is unified by its central theme, that of the imitation of Christ: 'Every action of the life of Jesus, as it is imitable by us, is of so excellent merit, that, by making up the treasure of grace, it becomes full of assistances to us, and obtains of God grace to enable us to its imitation, by way of influence and impetration'.[2] This is what fuses together the devotional narrative, the considerations on it, the prayers and discourses. The latter deal with meditation, mortification, faith, repentance, charity, forgiveness, fasting, salvation (to mention some), and the sacraments.

What we have is, in fact, a remarkable book written by a moral/ascetic theologian whose understanding of the faith is deeply sacramentalist and whose whole thinking is suffused with the warmth of a devotion to the Sacred Humanity, reminiscent of *The Fire of the Altar* (1683) of his younger contemporary Anthony Horneck.[3] But because Taylor is so much a moral theologian, the devotional warmth and beauty are never divorced from the practicality of religion and from consonance with reason. Indeed, the dedication (to Christopher Hatton again) insists that 'I have chosen to serve the purposes of religion by doing assistance to that part of theology, which is *wholly practical*; that which makes us wiser, therefore, because it makes us better'.[4] Similarly, the Preface is designed to refute the allegation that Christianity is against reason and unreasonable. Again, in the *Exhortation to the Imitation of the Life of Christ* (9) he links this concept as instanced in 1 Peter 2: 21 and Romans 13: 14 with an appeal to its innate reasonableness; 'We find so much reason to address ourselves to a heavenly imitation of so blessed a pattern, that the reasonableness of the thing will be a great argument to chide every degree and minute of neglect'. The overall purpose, however, remains; 'My great purpose, is to advance the necessity, and to declare the manner and parts, of a good life'.[5] This is an integral part and purpose of his *Life of Christ* 'because I have observed, that there are some principles entertained into the persuasions of men, which are the seeds of evil life, such as are—the doctrine of late repentance, the mistakes of the definition of sins of infirmity, the evil understanding the consequents and nature of original sin, the sufficiency of contrition in order to pardon, the efficacy of the rites of Christianity without the necessity of moral adherencies, the nature of faith, of many other; I was diligent to remark such doctrines, and to pare off the mistakes so far, that they hinder not piety . . .'[6] There speaks the moral theologian and the passage reads like a pre-view or a digest of *Unum Necessarium* and *Ductor Dubitantium*, and we understand the grounds of his opposition to contemporary doctrines of original sin as being injurious to that piety and practical religion. Yet it is the flashes of a sensitive devotion to the Sacred Humanity which

light up and warm the book; 'He that gives alms to the poor,
takes Jesus by the hand; he that patiently endures injuries and
affronts, helps him to bear his cross; he that comforts his
brother in affliction, gives an amiable kiss of peace to Jesus; he
that bathes his own and his neighbour's sins in tears of penance
and compassion, washes his Master's feet: we lead Jesus
into the recesses of our heart by holy meditations and we
enter into his heart, when we express him in our actions'.[7]
The last sentence might be a description of the goal of
moral/ascetic theology. There is a meditation on 'his
holy hands', 'his holy breast . . . and . . . sacred heart',[8] and
meditation itself is described as going 'step by step with Jesus'.
But always devotion is linked with obedience,[9] and devotion
may not part company with reason, for meditation 'is a
composition of both ways; for it stirs up our affections by
reason and the way of understanding, that the wise soul may
be satisfied in the reasonableness of the thing, and the affec-
tionate may be entertained with the sweetnesses of the holy
Passion'.[10] The use of meditation, says Taylor, is 'to draw
from it rules of life' but after that comes what he calls 'mental
prayer and intercourse with God' and then one is 'swallowed
up with the comprehensions of love and contemplation.'[11]
This is the religion not of a pietist or a mere moralist, but of a
moral/ascetic theologian with a sense of deep spirituality when
he writes of 'the unitive way of religion' as 'a thing not to be
discoursed of, but felt'.[12] Inevitably, one recalls the text of
Rust's sermon at Taylor's funeral, 'It doth not yet appear what
we shall be' (1 John 3:2) and his observation that 'it is not
enough to believe aright, but we must practise accordingly',
which he illustrated by Taylor's 'solemn hours of prayer' and
the fact that, enjoying a large income when a bishop, he died
poor, for charity was his steward. Somehow, the writings and
the man are all of one piece and it comes through in *The Great
Exemplar* with considerable force, for the book is a rich
example of the many-faceted and profound wholeness of
outlook of its author.

Integral to his religion, and clearly so in the book, is Taylor's
sacramentalism. It is a constantly recurring element, as in
Section IX on the baptism of Jesus where Taylor emphasises
the ecclesial content of the sacrament since Jesus 'inserted
himself, by that ceremony, into the society and participation

of the holy people, of which communion himself was the Head and Prince'.[13] Sacraments are not forms automatically producing effects 'for there is nothing ritual, but it is also joined with something moral'. This is the essential sacramental principle 'and this truth is of so great persuasion in the Greek church, that the mystery of consecration in the venerable eucharist is amongst them attributed not to any mystical words and secret operation of syllables, but to the efficacy of the prayers of the church, in the just imitation of the whole action and the rite of institution'.[14] He devoted the whole of the lengthy Discourse VI to baptism, pointing out that Jesus had taken two Jewish rites and in each case 'transferred the rite to greater mysteries' making of each 'a perpetual sacrament . . . and a sacrament evangelical'.[15] In a very full analysis of the effects of baptism, Taylor expounds a strong doctrine of baptismal regeneration, for baptism is 'the laver of regeneration' and 'a new birth, by which we enter into the new world, the new creation'.[16] Christ told Nicodemus that this is 'the only door to enter . . . and by this regeneration we are put into a new capacity of living a spiritual life'.[17] The moral theologian ties in faith and repentance ('the whole doctrine of the Gospel') with the sacraments and their meaning and their place in the Christian life. Sins committed 'after baptism and confirmation, in which we receive the Holy Ghost' have to be accounted for but the necessity of repentance and a holy life must never drive people to despair. By the sacrifice of the Cross 'we are but once absolutely . . . and presentially forgiven' and our reconciliation is in virtue of the sacrifice of Christ 'and this sacrifice applied in baptism is one, as baptism is one and as the sacrifice is one'. Yet, men fall from grace but the mercy of God reaches to them and it is the duty of Christian ministers to 'restore a person overtaken in a fault'. Realistically, says Taylor, 'it is impossible we should be actually and perpetually free from sin . . . and without these reserves of Divine grace and after-emanations from the mercy-seat, no man could be saved'. Thus, the sacrifice would be unavailing save for 'newly-baptized persons, whose albs of baptism served them also for a winding-sheet'. Baptism, as well as being in order to the remission of what is past, reaches forward in its influence for the remainder of our lives; 'it hath admitted us into a lasting state of pardon, to *be renewed and actually applied by the sacrament of the Lord's Supper*.[18]

The Great Exemplar, as it sets out the power and compelling beauty of Christ's earthly life, insists that because He is the risen Lord, He is Life to all those baptized into Him who, with repentance and faith, come to the eucharist for more abundant life; 'By Christ we live and move . . . He took our life, that we might partake of his; he gave his life for us, that he might give life to us'—This, says Taylor, is the meaning of the eucharist.[19] The book is profoundly sacramental in its understanding of the Christian life and the means of grace available for living it. Marriage, too, was hallowed by Christ 'to a sacramental signification, and made to become mysterious'. In a splendid phrase Taylor says He 'new sublimed it by making it a sacramental representment of the union of Christ and his spouse, the Church'.[20] There is a sterness in his assertion that 'whoever dissolves the sacredness of the mystery (of marriage) . . . he dissolves his relation to Christ'. Similarly, he is severe on the subject of death-bed repentance. It was a subject much canvassed in the seventeenth century and one can detect in the Anglican moral theologians of the day a vein of rigorism in respect of it, though South was an exception.[21] Strictness in Taylor however is always tempered by his warm humanity. In *The Great Exemplar* he makes it clear that the impossible should not be expected from anyone. True, the Gospel-covenant was established on faith and repentance and 'consigned in baptism'. True, it is 'verifiable only in the integrity of a following holy life'. But that life is 'according to the measures of a man; not perfect, but sincere; not faultless, but heartily endeavoured'.[22]

II

It has, I hope, become clearer why I said that Taylor never sees the eucharist out of context, the context of the Christian's life in Christ. 'Christ who is our life' might be inscribed over his entire work. So it is especially in *The Great Exemplar*. The centrality of the eucharist for the Christian life is set out in such a way that at once the great themes of mystery and sacrament, of Life and Presence, of representment and of the heavenly altar, begin to appear in Taylor's eucharistic theology: 'As the sun among the stars . . . so is this action among all the instances of religion; it is the most perfect and consummate, it is an *union of mysteries*, and a consolidation of duties . . . this blessed sacrament is a consigning to us of all felicities, because after a *mysterious and ineffable manner, we receive him who is light and life*, the fountain of grace . . . so Christ hath remained in the world by the communication of this sacrament'.[23] The last phrase is strong sacramentalism indeed, even for Taylor. The passage at once links his major concepts of mystery and the transmission of Christ's life, and with this goes inevitably the concept of a presence neither figurative nor corporal—carnal, as he phrases it—but sacramental; '. . . because it is "life": the bread of the sacrament is the life of our soul, and the body of our Lord is now conveyed to us, by being the bread of the sacrament'. He develops this further in a passage containing the first hint of the concept of the altar in heaven which he will shortly develop as he explicates the meaning of the eucharistic sacrifice: 'In the sacrament, that body which is reigning in heaven, is exposed upon the table of blessing; and his body, which was broken for us, is now broken again and yet remains impassible'. He remains one, says Taylor, even 'while he is wholly ministered in ten thousand portions'. I do not think that this is Luther's doctrine of ubiquity because Taylor is insisting all the time that the whole point is that the manner of the sacramental presence is mystery: 'I suppose it to be a mistake to think whatsoever is real must be natural; and it is no less to think spiritual to be only figurative: that is too much, and this is too little . . . And if we profess we understand not the manner of this mystery, we say no more but that it is a mystery'. Mystery and sacrament are inseparable and since 'St. Paul calls it "bread" even after consecration (I Cor. 10: 16) . . . by Divine faith, we are taught to express our belief in *this mystery* in these words: The bread, when it is consecrated and made *sacramental*, is the body of our Lord; and the fraction and distribution of it is the communication of that body, which died for us upon the cross.'[24]

It is a point at which to stand back and consider Taylor's understanding of the eucharistic presence at this stage in his development. One may well wonder whether the term 'Laudian' for this type of viewpoint is not something of a misnomer seeing that the Windsor Statement (6) and (8) as already mentioned is using exactly the same ways of expressing the Presence of Christ. It is all there, in phrasing worth repeating since it is so similar to Taylor's: 'his true presence, effectually signified by the bread and wine which, in this mystery, become his body and blood'; 'the mystery of the eucharistic presence'; 'the sacramental body and blood of the Saviour'. The transmission of Christ's life and the resultant 'lifegiving encounter' are central. The elements are not mere signs and Christ's body and blood become really present and are really given.[25] In point of fact, Cranmer too in his *'Defence of the True and Catholic Doctrine of the Sacrament'* and in the *Answer* speaks of 'a sacramental conversion of bread and wine and of a spiritual eating and drinking of the body and blood' and asserts the true presence in the same way; 'Christ's flesh and blood be in the Sacrament truly present, but spiritually and sacramentally, not carnally and corporally'.[26] The ARCIC *Elucidation* (6) puts it thus, 'What is here affirmed is a sacramental Presence in which God uses realities of this world to convey the realities of the new creation: bread for this life becomes the bread of eternal life'.

If we can discern a kinship between the modern eucharistic agreement and Taylor's exposition, it is equally true that we can trace an earlier ancestry for his doctrine and find numerous parallels, as he himself did, in the writings of many Fathers. Nor is it beside the point to recall that it was not until the *Catechism* of the Council of Trent appeared in 1566 that the Roman Catholic Church *officially* declared that only the doctrine of transubstantiation was the true explanation of the mode of the eucharistic presence. The early patristic period displayed a variety of ways of expressing the real presence of Christ in which, as G. W. H. Lampe has demonstrated, realism and symbolism both played a part in how the different writers saw and understood the mystery of the eucharistic action.[27] Among the examples he quotes are many which parallel the Laudian approach—a presence which is real and also dynamic, life-giving, but not in any sense physical. The inward gift and the outward sign are real entities, and remain distinct. By the fourth century, says Lampe, 'there is an increasing tendency to speak of a "change" of the elements, by consecration, into the body and blood of Christ. This often co-existed

with a continued use of the language of symbolism.' A further
point is made by H. E. W. Turner about this critical period: 'By
the fourth century two main streams of interpretation began to
emerge—metabolism which asserts some change in the elements, not uniformly expressed or precisely identified, and
dualism which emphasizes a full co-presence of bread and
wine and body and blood'.[28] These streams flowed on through
the medieval period, the Reformation, and later times, and we
can detect the persistent presence of one of them in the writings
of Taylor and his fellow-Anglicans in the seventeenth century.
Bound up with, or even arising from, the metabolist strain,
there was, I would suggest, a development of the kind of
thinking which reifies the presence so that the unspoken
question is 'What is present?' rather than 'Who is present?'
Taylor escapes this because his understanding of the real
presence is personalist and dynamic, Christ giving himself to
us, his Life in ours—'we receive him who is light and life'. With
him, this is a permanent element in his eucharistic teaching.
The Johannine life-theme goes back very far in Christian
thought and liturgy. The Maronite anaphora called *Sharar*
begins with the words based on the fourth Gospel 'I am the
bread of life which came down from heaven so that mortals
may have life in me' and the Priest prays 'Make us live, O Lord,
through your true life . . . and grant us that we may obtain life
by your life-giving death'.[29] Centuries afterwards, Jeremy
Taylor is taking the same words and building on them for the
same purpose and to express the same meaning: 'He is the
bread which came down from heaven; the bread which was
born at Bethlehem; the house of bread was given to us to be the
food of our souls for ever. The meaning of which *mysterious
and sacramental* expressions, when they are reduced to easy
and intelligible significations, is plainly this: By Christ we live
and move and have our spiritual being in the life of grace . . .
He took our life that we might partake of his; he gave his life
for us, that he might give life to us.'[30]

It is worthy of note that this extract is from *The Worthy
Communicant* (1660), one of Taylor's later writings on the
subject and the persistence in his thought of this way of
expressing the eucharistic presence in terms of a sacramental
and life-imparting mystery is also noteworthy. While it may
suit our immediate purpose to call this view 'Laudian' we

do so in the knowledge that this type of eucharistic thinking both precedes and post-dates seventeenth-century Anglicanism.

The continuation of the same passage shows Taylor linking the life-transmitting theme with the Incarnation and the Paschal Mystery, and so can serve to lead us into a consideration of how, in *The Great Exemplar*, he understood the eucharist to be a sacrifice. He writes; 'The sum is this. Christ's body, his flesh and his blood, are therefore called our meat and our drink, because by his incarnation and manifestation in the flesh he became life to us: so that it is mysterious, indeed, in the expression, but very proper and intelligible in the event, to say that we eat his flesh and drink his blood, since by these it is that we have and preserve life.'

As we have seen, Richard Hooker makes precisely the same point that the eucharist provides 'continuance of life' for those who in baptism 'have attained the first beginning of a new life'.[31] Taylor completed the thought by expressing the direct link between the Cross and the eucharist, and suggesting that the *anamnesis* contains 'a visible word'. It seems to me that he is here saying more than that there is in the eucharistic action an aspect of a visual aid, a suggestion reinforced by Taylor's piling up of descriptive and explicative expressions. It seems more likely that he is striving to express a common patristic conviction about the role of the Word and of the Spirit's action in consecrating the bread and wine. At all events, Taylor is using antiquity here in his handling of the Johannine theme citing Clement of Alexandria and Tertullian in support.[32] He does not quote from St. Augustine but what he has to say parallels 'The word comes to the element and it becomes a sacrament, itself a kind of visible word' (*Tractatus* 80(3) on St. John's Gospel). We can pursue the line he takes in a later chapter. At this point, it sufficiently illuminates his perception of what is happening at Holy Communion to quote his summary; 'By his incarnation and manifestation in the flesh, he became life to us . . . but because what Christ began in his incarnation, he finished in his body on the cross, and all the whole progression of mysteries in his body, was still an operatory of life and spiritual being to us—the sacrament of the Lord's Supper being a commemoration and exhibition of his death, which was the consummation of our redemption by his body and blood, does contain in it *a visible word, the word in symbol and in visibility, and special manifestation.* Consonant to which doctrine, the fathers, by an elegant expression, called the blessed sacrament, 'the extension of the incarnation'.[33]

III

The Great Exemplar contains Jeremy Taylor's earliest exposition of how and in what sense the eucharist is a sacrifice. He was thirty-six at the time of its publication and the book, like *Holy Living (1650)* and *Holy Dying (1651)*, was part of the output of the years at Golden Grove when Taylor, like so many of his fellow-priests, lived in a sort of ecclesiastical limbo during the Protectorate. Frustrating and heart-breaking the times were for him 'when I had fixed my thoughts upon sad apprehensions that God was removing our candlestick, for why should he not, when men themselves put the light out'. Yet, he set himself to serve by his pen, putting 'a portion of the holy fire into a repository, which might help to re-enkindle the incense, when it shall please God religion shall return, and all his servants sing, "In convertendo captivitatem Sion", with a voice of eucharist'.[34] His situation did allow Taylor the time and the opportunity for thinking and writing, though what Rust called his 'indefatigable industry' was such that it is not easy to imagine circumstances in which he would have allowed his pen to lie idle.

Time and again throughout the book the eucharistic theme is part of the way in which the practice of Christian life is presented. For example, in Discourse XIII, fasting before Holy Communion—'a custom of the Christian Church and derived to us from great antiquity'—is commended. Its purpose is reverence 'that we might express honour to the mystery'.[35] Or, there is the comment on the relation of the eucharist to a ministry that is apostolic, in Section XV. The commandment to the apostles to celebrate the eucharist is a perpetual function for their successors. 'This was the first delegation of a perpetual ministry, which Jesus made to his apostles, in which they were to be succeeded in all generations of the church.' Once again, Taylor insists that what took place then was the turning of 'the ceremony into a mystery, (when) he gave his body and blood in sacrament and religious configuration; so instituting the venerable sacrament.'[36]

Thus, when he comes to Discourse XIX, devoted entirely to the eucharist, he has all along in a sense been leading up to the centrality of Holy Communion for the life of those whom he refers to as 'the holy people'. He has dealt with who rather than what is present: 'In the sacrament, that body which is reigning in heaven, is exposed upon the table of blessing; and his body, which was broken for us, is now broken again, and yet remains impassible'.[37] Now, he must answer, who or what is being sacrificed, since the great tradition has always asserted a sacrifice in the eucharist. With clarity he expounds the nexus between the Cross and the eucharist. In a passage of great density Taylor brings together as component elements the concepts of the re-presentation and pleading of the one perfect sacrifice in the eucharistic action, of the *anamnesis*, mystery and sacrament, and of the heavenly altar. The Offerer is being offered, 'as sacrificed', in conjunction with his perpetual self-offering to the Father, in heaven: 'There he sits, a high priest continually, and offers still the same one perfect sacrifice; that is, still represents it as having been once finished and consummate, in order to perpetual and never-failing events. And this, also, his ministers do on earth; they offer up the same sacrifice to God, the sacrifice of the cross, by prayers, and a commemorating rite and represented, according to his holy institution.'[38]

This is the core of the matter for Taylor and we need to look more closely at the components of his exposition of the eucharistic sacrifice, but let him first set it out more fully: 'For, as it is a commemoration and represented of Christ's death, so it is a commemorative sacrifice: as we receive the symbols and the mystery, so it is a sacrament. In both capacities, the benefit is next to infinite. First: for whatsoever Christ did at the institution, the same he commanded the church to do, in remembrance and repeated rites; and himself also does the same thing in heaven for us, making perpetual intercession for his church, the body of his redeemed ones, by representing to the Father his death and sacrifice.'[39] For Taylor, there is in the eucharistic action a parallelism which transcends time and space. The Church on earth re-presents to the Father His Son 'as sacrificed' and unites 'the offering' with that one perfect sacrifice which the Offerer Himself re-presents and pleads in His heavenly intercession. One is irresistibly reminded of *Windsor (5)* in which, having made the perpetual memorial of the Passion and entreated its benefits, the Church enters 'into the movement of his self-offering'.

Taylor elaborates this transcendent parallelism and spells out how the once-for-all sacrifice is commemorated and re-presented in the eucharistic action which thus itself becomes a sacrificial instrument: 'As Christ is a priest in heaven for ever, and yet does not sacrifice himself afresh, nor yet without a sacrifice could he be a priest; but, by a daily ministration and intercession, represents his sacrifice to God, and *offers himself as sacrificed: so he does upon earth, by the ministry of his servants*; he is offered to God, that is, he is, by prayers and the sacrament, represented or "offered up to God, as sacrificed"; which, in effect, is a celebration of his death, and the applying it to the present and future necessities of the church, as we are capable, by a ministry like to his in heaven'.

Because this parallelism is at the heart of the mystery, the sacramental celebration itself becomes a sacrifice instrumentally: 'It follows, then, that the celebration of this sacrifice be, in its proportion, an instrument of applying the proper sacrifice to all the purposes for which it first designed. It is ministerially, and by application, an instrument propitiatory; it is eucharistical, it is an homage and an act of adoration; and it is impetratory, and obtains for us and for the whole church, all the benefits of the sacrifice, which is now celebrated and applied; that is, as this rite is the remembrance and ministerial celebration of Christ's sacrifice, so it is destined to do honour to God . . . to beg pardon, blessings, and supply of all our needs.'[40]

Here, 'the heavenly altar' is inseparably linked with the earthly *anamnesis*, the making effective in the present of a past event, the once-for-all event of salvation, through the action of the Spirit for 'whatsoever the Spirit can convey to the body of the church, we may expect from this sacrament'.[41] The Spirit works through the eucharist which, says Taylor, is the offering of the whole people of God, by transmitting to them the Life of Christ: 'If we consider this, not as the act and ministry of ecclesiastical persons, but as the duty of the whole church communicating; that is, as it is a sacrament, so it is like the springs of Eden, from whence issue many rivers. . . . For whatsoever was offered in the sacrifice, is given in the sacrament; and whatsoever the testament bequeathes, the holy mysteries dispense . . . and every holy soul having feasted at his table, may say, as St. Paul, "I live, yet not I, but Christ liveth in me". So that "to live is Christ"; "Christ is our life", and he dwells in the body and spirit of every one that eats Christ's flesh and drinks his blood.'[42]

For such a sacrament, the true preparation is 'a disposition to life'; it is 'a new state of life' and 'a changed course'.[43] Justin Martyr is quoted with approval, that only the baptized, holding the true faith, and living 'according to the discipline of the holy Jesus', have the right to communicate.[44] Holy sacraments and holy living are inextricably merged in the economy of grace. And how often should I communicate? Seldom, for reverence, or often, for charity? This makes no more sense, says Taylor, than asking whether it is better to pray often or seldom, and 'if the necessities of the church were well considered, we should find that a daily sacrifice of prayer, and a daily prayer of sacrifice, were no more but what her condition requires'.[45] Taylor traces the decline in frequency of celebration from the early church to his own day, and pleads for the practice of communicating frequently, and this is echoed in the prayer which concludes the Discourse.[46]

Basic to Taylor's understanding of the unbloody sacrifice in the eucharist is his conviction that 'the holy table' is 'a copy of the celestial altar'. How he develops this still further we can note when examining his later exposition in *The Worthy Communicant*.[47] For the moment, it is appropriate that we look at his teaching in the light of the Great Tradition: Where does Taylor's doctrine of sacrifice root itself? How does it compare with later understanding of the theme? Can we discern a *mélange* of antiquity and modernity in his thought, justifying Porter's claim that, as far as medieval or protestant schools of thought are concerned, 'Taylor simply does not fall into their categories'?[48] This is a fair assessment so long as we bear in mind that his understanding of the sacrifice, and indeed of the presence, belongs in an earlier line of descent which reaches on, at least in part, to the present time. Taylor's eucharistic theology is not ready-made, 'without father or mother or genealogy.'

IV

If the sacrifice of Calvary is the once-for-all salvation-event, in what sense then can we call the eucharist a sacrifice? We have seen the shape of Taylor's answer at this stage: The eucharist is a commemoration and sacramental re-presentation of the unique sacrifice. It is offered by the Church in union with the heavenly offering by which Christ, eternally active and life-bestowing through His Cross, offers Himself 'as sacrificed'. It is also a sacrifice of praise and thanksgiving and an instrument by means of which, appropriated by faith, all the benefits of the Paschal Mystery are bestowed by the crucified, risen and glorified Saviour, through the Spirit. The manner of Christ's presence is a mystery only to be expressed in the language both of sacramental realism and of effectual sign. The eucharist, being the sacrament of Life, is a means for the continuance of the holy people in that new quality of life which ceaselessly flows from 'the high priest . . . who . . . offers still the same one perfect sacrifice'.

This sort of thinking is deeply rooted in the Great Tradition and has persisted in essence through the centuries in spite of aberrations and different understandings and misunderstandings of the meaning of sacrifice and of presence. It could not be otherwise in view of the New Testament institution narratives. In the Gospel accounts, Jesus places the bread and wine in the context of His approaching sacrifice—'This is my body; This is my blood'.[49] In the earliest account, that of St. Paul, the nexus between the one sacrifice and the eucharist is amplified so that one can distinguish three components, all of which continue in the history of eucharistic doctrine. There is sacramental realism and there is the unitive function of the eucharist which is a sacrificial meal.[50] It is when men began to meditate on and to think through the devotional and theological implications of this primal link between the Cross and the Table of Blessing that they felt impelled to ask what is meant by speaking of the eucharistic rite as a sacrifice. The process began early and Christians at the time of the *Didache* in the second century were seeing the eucharist as the 'pure sacrifice' foretold in Malachi 1: 11 since it was being offered everywhere. The theme persists in the early patristic writings and later, but the questions remained—what was the *nature* of this eucharistic sacrifice? Who, or what, was being offered and who was doing the offering? What relationship did it bear to the once-for-all sacrifice? This is not the place, even if one had the competence, to attempt to trace back in detail the various lines of development in respect of the idea of sacrifice, of the justice of God, and of propitiation. From the patristic writings however down to the scholastics and beyond, certain concepts, variously expounded, would seem to be fairly constant elements in answering the questions suggested above. These are the concept of commemoration which tended to shade into the concept of re-presentation. Close to them, but apparently not always identical, is the concept of memorial, of *anamnesis*, through which the past event is made effective in the here-and-now. There are also the kindred ideas of an unbloody sacrifice and of a mystical and sacramental sacrifice. Not unconnected with the latter is the concept of the heavenly altar, going back, for example, to Irenaeus. One is aware of the dangers and of the omissions in attempting such a sketch of a vast canvas. They are only too obvious. The purpose in attempting it is simply to indicate the emergence and persistence of certain ideas about the eucharistic sacrifice which are still with us. They can be recognized for example as persisting in the twelfth-century *Sentences* (IV, xii) of Peter Lombard: 'What is offered and consecrated by the priest is called a sacrifice and an immolation because it is a memorial and a representation of the true sacrifice and holy immolation made upon the altar of the cross. Christ died once upon the cross, and there he was immolated in his own self; and yet every day he is immolated sacramentally, because in the sacrament there is a recalling of what was done once.' They can be met with in the *Replication* of John Bramhall who consecrated Jeremy Taylor to the episcopate in 1661: 'The Holy Eucharist is a commemoration, a representation, an application of the all-sufficient propitiatory Sacrifice of the Cross. . . . We acknowledge an Eucharistical Sacrifice of praise and thanksgiving; a commemorative Sacrifice or a memorial of the Sacrifice of the Cross; a representative Sacrifice, or a representation of the Passion of

Christ before the eyes of His Heavenly Father; an impetrative Sacrifice, or an impetration of the fruit and benefit of His Passion by way of real prayer; and, lastly, an applicative Sacrifice, or an application of His merits unto our souls.'[51] Allowance should be made in such a bird's-eye view of the past for changes in the understanding of 'sacrifice'. A note in the *Final Report* (p. 13) of ARCIC reads; 'The early Church in expressing the meaning of Christ's death and resurrection often used the language of sacrifice. For the Hebrew *sacrifice* was a traditional means of communication with God.' Whatever the range of understanding of sacrifice in the earlier period (and even then it seems to have been a fairly fluid concept), we can say that Taylor and his colleagues were free from the narrow, propitiatory realism which infected some later eucharistic theologies.

When, in the year 1897, the English Archbishops replied to Pope Leo XIII's Bull, *Apostolicae Curae*, their document, *Saepius Officio*, was intended to be a declaration of Anglican belief. In the course of the Reply they had this to say on the meaning of sacrifice in the eucharist: 'Further we truly teach the doctrine of Eucharistic sacrifice and do not believe it to be a "nude commemoration of the Sacrifice of the Cross" . . . But we think it sufficient in the Liturgy which we use in celebrating the holy Eucharist—while lifting up our hearts to the Lord, and when now consecrating the gifts already offered that they *may become to us* the Body and Blood of our Lord Jesus Christ—to signify the sacrifice which is offered at that point of the service in such terms as these. We continue *a perpetual memory* of the precious death of Christ, who is our Advocate with the Father and the propitiation for our sins, according to His precept, until His coming again. For first we offer the *sacrifice of praise* and thanksgiving; then next we *plead and represent* before the Father the sacrifice of the cross, and by it we confidently *entreat* remission of sins and all other benefits of the Lord's Passion for all the whole Church; and lastly we offer the sacrifice of ourselves to the Creator of all things which we have already signified by the oblations of His creatures. This whole action, *in which the people has necessarily to take its part* with the Priest, we are accustomed to call the Eucharistic sacrifice.'[52] The persistence of the themes and the similarity with Taylor's exposition is noteworthy. We recall that

Taylor also insisted that 'the people are sacrificers too in their manner'. The Lima Report expresses the hope that 'in the light of the biblical conception of memorial, all churches might want to review the old controversies about sacrifice'. The Report stresses the concept of *anamnesis* as containing both 'representation and anticipation' and the Commentary speaks of 'the unique sacrifice of the cross, made actual in the eucharist and presented before the Father in the intercession of Christ', the heavenly altar theme. This is referred to again: 'In the memorial of the eucharist . . . the Church offers its intercession in communion with Christ, our great High Priest' and 'our prayer relies upon and is united with the continual intercession of the risen Lord'.[53] The *Windsor Statement* (5) and *Elucidation* (5) concentrate on expressing the nexus between the eucharist and the unique, unrepeatable sacrifice in terms of a memorial through which, by the Spirit's action, 'the once-for-all event of salvation becomes effective in the present'. The heavenly altar and the heavenly intercession do not appear although it is worth remarking that both documents emphasise that it is 'the glorified Lord' whom the faithful meet in the eucharistic celebration.

As to this latter theme, those who are familiar with the second edition (1714) of C. Wheatly's *A Rational Illustration of the Book of Common Prayer* may recall the frontispiece. It depicts a group of communicants kneeling on the chancel floor before the altar rails. At the altar the celebrant is consecrating the elements. Above him, in a cloud of glory spangled with the winged heads of cherubim stands the Saviour, hands raised before the heavenly altar. He is surrounded by a nimbus or halo in which one can detect the inscription 'Heb. IX, 11, 23. VII, 25'. It is a concept much favoured by Anglicans in the seventeenth century, and a major element in Jeremy Taylor's theology of the eucharist. Of course, it did not begin there as Rowan Williams has indicated in his short but illuminating piece on the eucharistic sacrifice.[54] The comment by J. L. Houlden covers the theme: 'The roots of it are so distinguished and comprehensive that it was bound to become prominent. They range from the Epistle to the Hebrews, through patristic texts and the Roman canon to the Protestant emphasis on the all-sufficiency of Calvary. It was a satisfying doctrine for those (like the seventeenth-century high Anglicans) who wished to give more *positive content to the traditional, above all, patristic, sacrificial teaching in relation to the eucharist*, while, at least to their own satisfaction, not abandoning their Protestant heritage.'[55] It would, however, be a mistake to imagine that the concept has disappeared in the twentieth century. As we have noted, a form of it is present in the Lima Report and we meet it in hymns regularly sung at the eucharist in Anglican churches. William Bright's hymn is possibly the best known:

> 'And now, O Father, mindful of the love
> That bought us, once for all, on Calvary's Tree,
> And having with us him that pleads above,
> We here present, we here spread forth to Thee,
> That only Offering perfect in thine eyes,
> The one true, pure, immortal Sacrifice.'

The same theme is found in another of Bright's well-known hymns, 'Once, only once, and once for all', as it is reflected in one by Archbishop William Maclagan:

> 'He pleads before the Mercy-seat;
> He pleads with God; he pleads for thee;
> He gives thee Bread from heaven to eat,
> His Flesh and Blood in mystery.'

Not surprisingly, in view of Taylor's influence on John Wesley, we meet it clearly set out in one of Charles Wesley's hymns:

> 'Yet may we celebrate below,
> And daily thus Thine Offering show:
> Exposed before Thy Father's eyes,
> In this tremendous Mystery—
> Present Thee bleeding on the Tree,
> An everlasting Sacrifice.'

Charles Gore, in *The Body of Christ* (1901), treating of the sacrificial aspect of the eucharist, discerned a linkage between the Sacrifice on the Cross, at the altar and in heaven. Dealing with the same theme of sacrifice, the Report *Doctrine in the Church of England* (1938) refers both to the concept of the eucharist in terms of a representation before the Father of the actual sacrifice of the Cross and to the doctrine of the Heavenly Altar at which we join in the perpetual offering by Christ himself and share the life of Christ crucified, risen and glorified. The persistence of the Heavenly Altar theme in Anglican eucharistic theology is due more to Taylor than to anyone else. We meet with it in the prayer for the dedication of the altar in the Irish consecration form of 1666 (possibly Taylor's work) and later still in Henry Dodwell's *Discourse Concerning one Altar and one Priesthood* (1683). It is to be found in the works of the Irish Non-Juror, Charles Leslie, but it was chiefly Taylor who took up the ancient theme, developed it and gave prominence to it in all his eucharistic writings.

For Jeremy Taylor, right up to the end of his life, the heavenly altar and the heavenly intercession are at the centre of his eucharistic theology and deep-set in his devotion. A prayer he wrote for use before receiving the sacrament contains the phrase 'I hear thy voice . . . thy blessed self making intercession for me at the eternal altar in heaven'.

As we endeavour to place Taylor's eucharistic theology (at this point of his development) within the context of Christian thinking about the eucharist before his own times, we can, I think accept that while Taylor cannot be categorised 'in terms of the major medieval or Protestant schools of thought', there are frequent resonances in his writings of earlier understandings of sacrifice and presence. Yet, with all this there remains in his work an individual quality which would develop further as he continued to think and write about the eucharist. Whether or not we consider this cluster of concepts as succeeding or failing in clarifying what kind of sacrifice there is in the eucharist, it is clear that they are part of a direct line of continuing affirmations of faith and that Taylor's thinking, as we can judge it to be in 1649, appears to be firmly located within that line of descent.

Notes

1. C. J. Stranks, loc. cit., pp. 96, 102.
2. *The Great Exemplar: An Exhortation to the Imitation of the Life of Christ*, (Hever ed. Vol. II, p. lxv).

3. Horneck's book of eucharistic devotions achieved a very wide circulation.

4. *Dedication*, (Heber ed.), Vol. II, p. xii.

5. *Preface*, ib., p. lviii.

6. *Preface* (44), ib., p. lvii. For an examination of Caroline teaching on repentance, contrition and distinction of sins, see my '*The Structure of Caroline Moral Theology (1949)*'.

7. *The Great Exemplar*, Exhortation to the Imitation (15), ib. p. lxix.

8. *The Great Exemplar*, Part I, Ad Section III, (7)–(9), ib., pp. 26–27.

9. loc. cit., Discourse III (9), ib. p. 110.

10. loc. cit., Discourse III (11), ib., p. 112.

11. ib.

12. ib., (20) and (21), ib., p. 118.

13. Section IX (2), ib. p. 185.

14. Ad Section IX (3), ib. pp. 190–191.

15. Ad Section IX (11), ib., p. 239.

16. loc. cit. (16), ib., p. 242.

17. Section XI (2), ib., p. 335.

18. Discourse IX, (10)–(17), ib., pp. 398–407.

19. *The Worthy Communicant*, C. I, Section II, ib. Vol. XV, p. 412.

20. *The Great Exemplar*, Part II, Ad Section X (8) ib., Vol. II, p. 315.

21. See H. R. McAdoo, *The Structure of Caroline Moral Theology* (1949), pp. 131–137.

22. Discourse IX (12), ib. Vol. II, p. 400.

23. Part III, Section XV, Discourse XIX (1), ib. Vol. III, p. 289.

24. This and the three preceding extracts are from Discourse IX (2)–(4), ib. Vol. III, pp. 290–294.

25. *The Elucidation (1979)*, commenting on 'become the body and blood' of *Windsor (10)*, notes that *becoming* 'does not imply that Christ becomes present in the eucharist in the same manner that he was present in his earthly life. It does not imply that this *becoming* follows the physical laws of this world' (*Final Report*, p. 21).

26. Quoted in Essay 4 by C. W. Dugmore in *Eucharistic Theology Then & Now* (1968), pp. 68–9.

27. See Essay 3 (G. W. H. Lampe) in *Eucharistic Theology Then & Now* (1968).

28. See Essay 7 (H. E. W. Turner) in *Thinking about the Eucharist* (1972).

29. *Addai and Mari—The Anaphora of the Apostles* (ed. Bryan D. Spinks), Grove Books (1980), p. 19.

30. *The Worthy Communicant*, Ch. I, Section II (1), ib. Vol. XV, p. 412.

31. *Ecclesiastical Polity*, V, lxvii, 1.

32. *The Worthy Communicant*, Ch. I, Section II (2)–(13), ib. Vol. XV, pp. 413–414.

33. loc. cit. (4), pp. 419–420.

34. From the dedication of the book to Christopher Hatton.

35. Discourse XIII (1), ib. Vol. III, p. 95.

36. Section XV (17), ib. Vol. III, p. 250.

37. Discourse XIX (4), ib. Vol. III, p. 294.

38. *Discourse* XIX (4), ib. Vol. III, p. 296.
39. ib.
40. ib.
41. *Discourse* XIX (9), ib. Vol. III, p. 300.
42. *Discourse* XIX (8), ib. Vol. III, p. 298.
43. *Discourse* XIX (14), ib. Vol. III, p. 308.
44. *Discourse* XIX (12), ib. Vol. III, p. 303.
45. *Discourse* XIX (18), ib. Vol. III, p. 312.
46. ib. Vol. III, p. 318.
47. See in particular, Chap. I, Section IV, 4 (2), ib. Vol. XV, pp. 437–8.
48. *Jeremy Taylor: Liturgist* (1979) by Harry Boone Porter, pp. 67–8.
49. Mark 14: 22–25; Matthew 26: 26–29.
50. cp. 1 Cor. 10: 16–17 and 1 Cor. 11: 17–34.
51. Ch. II, section vii and Ch. IX, section vi. (*Works*, L.A.C.T. ed. Vol. II, pp. 88, 276).
52. *Saepius Officio* XI, (1977 ed., pp. 13–14).
53. 'The Eucharist as Anamnesis or Memorial of Christ', B, (5)–(13) and Commentary (8), in *Baptism, Eucharist and Ministry* (1982), pp. 11–12.
54. *Eucharistic Sacrifice: The Roots of a Metaphor* (1982), see in particular pp. 13–17.
55. *Thinking about the Eucharist* (1972), p. 94.

IV Holy Living and Holy Sacrament

No book of Taylor's has been more generally known and used and none has survived better in the interest of ordinary people than *The Rules and Exercises of Holy Living* (1650). I have a 'New Impression' printed as late as 1938, containing also the companion work, *The Rules and Exercises of Holy Dying* (1651). Both books were an early influence on the young John Wesley at Oxford and John Keble wrote to J. T. Coleridge that 'that book is enough to convert any infidel'.[1] Jeremy Taylor thus touched the beginnings both of Methodism and of the Oxford Movement. H. Trevor Hughes, through a careful comparison of Wesley's *Diary* and *Holy Living*, has demonstrated 'a very marked dependence' on Taylor. He has even shown that Wesley's famous experience of 1738 in the room at Aldersgate was begun in 1725 when, on reading *Holy Living and Holy Dying*, 'I was exceedingly affected . . . Instantly I resolved to dedicate all my life to God, all my thoughts, and words and actions'. The stricter life and rules which Wesley then planned for himself 'sprang from his acquaintance with the writings of Jeremy Taylor'.[2] Dean Farrar ranked the book with *The Imitation of Christ* and with *Pilgrim's Progress*. *Holy Living and Holy Dying* are indeed beautiful books and it would be hard to better the phrases of C. J. Stranks: 'Taylor's sentences lie like a handful of jewels, each one complete in its own beauty' and 'In the first chapter of *Holy Dying* Taylor reaches the height of his literary glory. He did few things as well and nothing better in his after days.'[3] Behind the latter book lies personal tragedy and loss. Taylor's 'dear wife' and his admired patroness both died in 1651. In the dedication, he made it clear that Lady Carbery had suggested the writing of *Holy Dying* but she did not live to read it. Inevitably, there is 'more personal feeling in it than any other of Taylor's books'.[4] Heber believes that 'the extensive popularity of the *Great Exemplar* produced the *Holy Living*, and the *Holy Dying*'. He is certainly right in grouping all three together in their shared objective, 'the promotion of practical holiness'.[5] Undoubtedly, the one followed hard upon the other in theme as well as in time.

The books belonged together in the Golden Grove period of Taylor's life in Wales during the Civil War. The house was the seat of Richard Vaughan, Earl of Carbery, to whom Taylor acted as chaplain, living close by and keeping a school at Newton Hall with his partners William Nicholson and William Wyatt. These were the years when the country underwent the doubly traumatic experience of civil war and of the abolition of the monarchy—Charles I was executed in the year that the *Great Exemplar* was published. Taylor himself had not escaped being touched by these events which also cast him on the charity of others. Against such a troubled background, Golden Grove was the haven from which, in the midst of upheaval in the State and the overthrow of the Church, he launched out as a writer, at least seven major works belonging to his time in Wales. The aim of *Holy Living* is similar to that of *An Introduction to the Devout Life* (1609) of St. Francis de Sales. There is a rather similar range of subject-matter, in general terms, but there the resemblance ceases. The French work has a more pedestrian flavour and the structure of Taylor's work is quite different, as is the style. Their objective, however, remains the same and both deal with prayer and meditation, humility and obedience, chastity, instructions for the married and for widows. *Holy Living* is, however, far richer in range and deeper in its treatment. One has only to compare the sections on 'hearing and reading the Word of God' to see the difference of quality.[6] The one book not recommended here in the *Devout Life* is the Bible! If Taylor knew the earlier work, as quite possibly he did, *Holy Living* remains indisputably his own book.

So, what sort of books are *Holy Living* and *Holy Dying*, and to what extent do they advance our understanding of the eucharistic theology of Jeremy Taylor? Once again, we find his teaching on the eucharist locked into the context of his teaching on the Christian life. The three 'general instruments of holy living' are care of our time, purity of intention and the practice of the presence of God. The first chapter consists of a practical analysis in depth of these in which Taylor's keenness of human observation and his sensitivity are very evident. The remaining three chapters are built around Christian sobriety, Christian justice and Christian religion. This is the central structure of *Holy Living*: 'Christian religion . . . according to the apostle's arithmetic hath but these three parts of it; 1. Sobriety, 2. Justice, 3. Religion. "For the grace of God bringing salvation hath appeared to all men, teaching us that, denying ungodliness and worldly lusts, we should live, 1. Soberly, 2. Righteously, and, 3. Godly, in this present world . . ." The first contains all our deportment in our personal and private capacities, the fair treating of our bodies and our spirits. The second enlarges our duty in all relations to our neighbour. The third contains the offices of direct religion, and intercourse with God.'[7]

Holy Living is moral/ascetic theology adapted to and designed for the home, the market-place, for work and leisure and the ordinary relationships and situations of life—its proper and natural habitat, since at all these levels a man's 'worldly employment . . . is a serving of God'.[8] Attractively and with practicality Taylor paints the picture of holy living. The internal and external aspects of religion are related to everyday reality. There is counsel on chastity and sexual behaviour, on the right use of food and drink, on modesty, humility and contentedness, on the working out of justice in its various aspects, on the problems of anger, envy and covetousness. Faith, hope and love are made central and help is given on prayer ('wandering thoughts' and 'tediousness of spirit'), on meditation, on fasting and almsgiving and on 'the acts and parts of repentance'. All leads up to the concluding section, on preparation and 'how to receive the holy Sacrament'.[9]

What does this part of *Holy Living* reveal concerning Taylor's eucharistic beliefs and teaching? Is there substance in the comment of Stranks that 'his practice was more in line with the Laudians than his theology'?[10] Does the section confirm the suspicion of C. W. Dugmore that 'it may be that we have here the beginnings of the Central Churchmanship which he adopted in the fifties and sixties'?[11] Dugmore contends that Taylor's later work shows the influence of his friend William Nicholson, and this is something to be pursued when examining Taylor's *Real Presence and Spiritual* (1654) and the *Dissuasive* (1664) and the *Worthy Communicant* (1660). All the time, I would suggest, there is a certain elusiveness, a resistance to categorisation, in Taylor. It is an element in his theological constitution which makes for caution in assessment. We recall too his attitude in questions of faith and reason and of original sin, for in matters theological Taylor remains very much his own man as well as a man conscious of his roots.

II

Holy sacraments are for holy living and so Taylor's advice to the communicant is that those who have communicated are 'in conjunction with Christ, whom you then have received' and because of this are 'more fit to pray' for others 'in the celebration of that holy sacrifice, which then is sacramentally presented to God'. For one's self, having given thanks 'for the passion of our dearest Lord' one must pray for 'a holy perseverance in well-doing'.[12] The heart of the matter is Christ's Life in ours, and ours in Him through grace and through the imitation of Christ:

'After the solemnity is done, let Christ dwell in your hearts by faith, and love, and obedience, and conformity to his life and death: as you have taken Christ into you, so put Christ on you . . . Remember, that now Christ is all one with you; and therefore, when you are to do an action, consider how Christ did, or could do, the like, and do you imitate his example . . . and contract his friendships; for then you do every day communicate; especially when Christ thus dwells in you, and you in Christ, growing up towards a perfect man in Christ Jesus.'[13]

What has Taylor to say in this Section X of *Holy Living* on the themes which he has already opened up in the *Great Exemplar*, mystery, sacrifice and presence? As he expounds the meaning of the Eucharist in the context of discipleship and devotion, one is struck afresh by the depth of Taylor's own reverence and devotion entwined as it is with a practicality of Christian behaviour the end of which is glory, for Christ makes us partakers of the divine nature.[14] There is a total and thrilling simplicity in such a phrase as 'in this feast, all Christ . . . is conveyed'.[15]

This is the living context of the eucharist within which, once again, he sets out the eucharistic sacrifice in terms of re-presenting, of sacramental memorial and of mysterious presence:

'When I said, that the sacrifice of the cross, which Christ offered for all the sins and all the needs of the world, is *represented to God by the minister in the sacrament, and offered up in prayer and sacramental memory*, after the manner that Christ himself intercedes for us in heaven (so far as his glorious priesthood is imitable by his ministers on earth), I must of necessity also mean, that all the benefits of that sacrifice are then conveyed to all that communicate worthily.'[16] The same passage repeats further on the emphasis on 'his intercession in heaven' with which Taylor sees the Church's eucharistic offering as inextricably entwined. The heavenly altar and the sacramental presentation of 'this one sufficient sacrifice' which was perfect, and could be but one, and that once[17] are at the heart of his teaching. He does not hesitate to spell it out again, as he did in the *Great Exemplar*, and with even stronger emphasis:

'As Christ is pleased to represent to his Father that great sacrifice as a means of atonement and expiation for all mankind and with special purposes and intendment for all the elect, all that serve him in holiness: so he hath appointed, that the same ministry shall be done upon earth too, in our manner, and according to our proportion; and therefore hath constituted and separated an order of men, who, by "shewing forth the Lord's death" by *sacramental representation*, may pray unto God after the same manner that our Lord and high priest does; that is, *offer to God and represent in this solemn prayer and sacrament, Christ as already offered*: so sending up a gracious instrument, whereby our prayer may for his sake and in the same manner of intercession, be offered up to God in our behalf, and for all them, for whom we pray, to all those purposes, for which Christ died.'[18] Once more, we are back to who offers and who is being offered. Once more, Taylor is saying that the celebrant offers Christ, re-presents Christ, as already sacrificed once for all. He does so in union with, and through the grace of, the ascended Christ who continues to re-present in intercession to his Father that one perfect sacrifice. Again Taylor underlines the instrumentality of the eucharistic offering. Obviously, it is not surprising to see him reproducing the sort of exposition set out in the *Great Exemplar*, since only a year separates the two books. The importance of the 'heavenly altar' theme for the understanding of his eucharistic theology declares itself repeatedly. It is part of the individual stamp on his writings, though it goes back very far in origin and was being used by fourth-century theologians to explain the eucharistic sacrifice. For example, students of Taylor will recall how frequently he quotes from St. Ambrose. In his book *Table and Tradition*, Alasdair Heron makes the intriguing suggestion that the 'heavenly altar' theme may 'offer a way round the impasse in which Roman Catholic and Protestant thinking have often found themselves—the one linking the Eucharist very closely with Christ's own sacrifice, the other tending to distinguish sharply between them. The continuing intercession of Christ for us can be seen as offering a bridge between the cross and the Eucharist.' Heron quotes St. Ambrose as an example of the 'heavenly altar' theme, common in the Fathers. He links it with another key-theme, that of Christ being 'the primary actor in the Eucharist . . . and the action is that of his unique and inexhaustible sacrifice which has already been made'.[19] Here he instances St. Chrysostom, another favourite of Taylor's, and one can discern clearly some of the patristic roots which strike deeply into the theology and the devotion of the Golden Grove books. *Who is offered?* Because the parameters of his thinking on the eucharistic sacrifice are the heavenly altar and 'Christ as sacrificed', on the one hand, and on the other, a sacramental re-presentation and anamnesis, and because he rejects transubstantiation, Taylor betrays no nervousness about saying that we offer Christ: 'that is, offer to God and represent in this solemn prayer and sacrament, Christ as already offered'. Because of this parallelism, because Christ is both priest and sacrifice, and because, for Taylor, the whole life-bestowing eucharistic action is mystery—in the sense of unexplained reality—there is no room left for literalist interpretations of 'offering Christ'.

In Anglicanism, as already noted, the theme of the 'heavenly altar' was seen as illuminating the mystery of the eucharist, not by philosophical explanation, but by adding a transcendent dimension to what was taking place in the eucharistic action. William Forbes died fifteen years before the *Great Exemplar* was published and his *Considerationes Modestae et Pacificae* was not published until 1658, twenty-four years after his death. His use of the theme thus predates Taylor's probably by a couple of decades. Having written of 'the presence of Christ the Lord in the Sacrament, Who is present in a wonderful but real manner', Forbes goes back to patristic sources: 'The holy Fathers say very often that the Body of Christ itself is offered and sacrificed in the Eucharist, as is clear from almost number-less places; but not in such a way that all the properties of a sacrifice are properly and actually preserved, but by way of commemoration and representation of that which was per-formed once for all in that One Only Sacrifice of the Cross whereby Christ our High Priest consummated all other sac-rifices, and by way of pious prayer whereby the Ministers of the Church most humbly beseech God the Father on account of the abiding Victim of that One Sacrifice, Who is seated in Heaven on the right hand of the Father and is present on the Holy Table in an ineffable manner, to grant that the virtue and grace of his perpetual Victim may be efficacious and healthful to His Church . . .'[20]

As he writes further of the heavenly intercession, Taylor speaks of the part of the people in the eucharistic sacrifice and he links the Church's offering of Christ with the self-offering of the worshippers—here too there is an echo of John Chry-sostom: 'As the ministers of the sacrament do, in a sacramental manner, present to God the sacrifice of the cross, by being imitators of Christ's intercession; so the people are sacrificers too in their manner: for besides that, by saying *Amen*, they join in the act of him that ministers, and make it also to be their own; so when they eat and drink the consecrated and blessed elements worthily, they receive Christ within them, and there-fore may also offer him to God, while, in their sacrifice of obedience and thanksgiving, they present themselves to God with Christ, whom they have spiritually received . . .'.[21] The final prayer in *Holy Living* is a post-communion prayer which begins 'O blessed and eternal high-priest, let the sacrifice of the cross, which thou didst once offer for the sins of the whole world, and thou dost now and always represent in heaven to thy Father by thy never-ceasing intercession, and which this day hath *been exhibited on thy holy table sacramentally*, obtain mercy and peace . . . to thy holy church which thou hast founded upon a rock, the rock of a holy faith'.[22] This might be a description of the illustration in Wheatly's book. Devotionally as well as theologically the concept is central to Taylor's exposition of what, for him, is and cannot be other than 'the sum of the greatest mystery of our religion; it is the copy of the passion, and the ministration of the great mystery of our redemption ... this celebration is our manner of applying or using it'.[23]

Taylor never shys away from the term 'mystery' and never treats the concept as a refuge. Rather, he embraces it and constantly refers to it. The whole eucharistic action representing the one sacrifice is 'mystery': the manner of the presence is 'mystery': the elements are 'these holy mysteries': the manner of receiving Christ in the eucharist is 'mystery': 'There our bodies are nourished with the signs, and our souls with the mystery'.[24] The relation (the term is that of Aquinas) of Christ to the elements in the eucharist is a mysterious one in any presentation of it save, of course, a purely symbolist interpretation. The intermingling of realist and figurative terminology discernible in some early writers can be detected also at times in Taylor. The reason is not, as Stranks suggested, that he is prone to self-contradiction in his view of the eucharistic presence.[25] Rather is it that, for him, the mystery of the eucharist requires both modes of expressing what happens at Holy Communion. For in the last resort words cannot encompass the mystery of how Christ's life is conveyed to the communicant for 'there our bodies are nourished with the signs, and our souls with the mystery'. Nor can we begin to grasp Taylor's admittedly complex thought on the eucharist—so akin in certain respects to some modern presentations—if we forget his constant assertion that both the presence and the re-presenting of the Sacrifice are *sacramental*.

In a passage, later to be expanded in the *Worthy Communicant*, and derived from Chrysostom's *Treatise on the Priesthood*, Taylor gathers up many of the insights of his thinking hitherto in a beautiful and theologically profound devotional passage on the eucharistic mystery:

'When the holy man stands at the table of blessing and ministers the rite of consecration, then do as the angels do, who behold, and love, and wonder that the Son of God should become food to the souls of his servants; that he, who cannot suffer any change or lessening, should be broken into pieces, and enter into the body to support and nourish the spirit, and yet at the same time remain in heaven, while he descends to thee on earth . . . that . . . by his death he should bring thee to life, and by becoming a man he should make thee partaker of the Divine nature. These are such glories, that although they are made so obvious, that each eye may behold them, yet they are also so deep, that no thought can fathom them: but so it hath pleased him to make these mysteries to be sensible, because the excellency and depth of the mercy is not intelligible . . . but yet it is so great, that we cannot understand it'.[26] The passage breathes the spirit of,

> 'Pange, lingua, gloriosi
> Corporis mysterium',

perhaps especially,

> 'Praestet fides supplementum
> Sensuum defectui'.

As in Aquinas's hymn, this section of *Holy Living* is rich with the sense of the mystery of salvation and of the mystery of the Saviour's self-giving presence in the eucharist. No wonder Taylor can assert and claim 'so Christ hath remained in the world, by the communication of this sacrament'.

What does the Christian receive at the altar? Not mere signs, not simply spatial objects and not bread and wine physically changed. Rather, says Taylor, the crucified, risen and glorified Lord takes the consecrated elements into union with himself and through them conveys to the faithful communicant his Life, which is His Body and His Blood. So what has Taylor to say specifically about the effect of consecration and about the eucharistic elements? In the year before he published *Holy Living* he had declared, in the *Great Exemplar*, that 'the bread, when it is consecrated and made sacramental, is the body of our Lord: and the fraction and distribution of it is the communication of that body which died for us on the cross'. The words 'made sacramental', together with the term 'mystery' offer us the key to Taylor's understanding of Christ's presence in the eucharist. There *is* a change in the elements, a sacramental change, and one recalls Cranmer's 'sacramental

conversion'. Thorndike had developed more fully this understanding of the elements and of consecration. He asserts that
all the fathers 'acknowledge the elements to be changed,
translated, and turned into the substance of Christ's body and
blood; *though as in a sacrament, that is, mystically*; yet,
therefore, by virtue of the consecration, not of his faith that
receives'.[27] In the *Real Presence and Spiritual* (1654) we shall
find Taylor making precisely the same claim for the patristic
use of such terms as 'conversion, mutation, transition, migration, transfiguration'. Here, in *Holy Living*, he is, of course,
working at another level, that of the devotional life of the
faithful communicant. He counsels, 'In the act of receiving,
exercise acts of faith with much confidence and resignation,
believing it not to be common bread and wine, but holy in their
use, holy in their signification, holy in their change, and holy in
their effect: and believe, if thou art a worthy communicant,
that thou dost as verily receive Christ's body and blood to all
effects and purposes of the Spirit, as thou dost receive the
blessed elements into thy mouth . . .'[28]

It is at this point that Dugmore thinks to detect signs of a
modification in Taylor's teaching, due to the influence of his
colleague, William Nicholson: 'There is more emphasis upon
the sacred use to which the elements are appointed, and it may
be that we have here the beginning of the Central Churchmanship which he adopted in the fifties and sixties. Nevertheless, he still exhorts his readers to "believe that Christ in the
holy sacrament gives thee His body and His blood. He that
believes not this is not a Christian"'.[29] Dugmore's last comment is puzzling indeed but possibly means that Taylor at this
stage still holds the 'Laudian' view of the presence as mystery.
Certainly, the rest of this section shows no abatement in the
use of the concept. The elements are 'these holy mysteries',
the 'weakness' of which 'adds wonder to the excellency of the
sacrament'.[30] The communicant is advised, 'Dispute not concerning the secret of the mystery, and the nicety of the manner
of Christ's presence: it is sufficient to thee, that Christ shall be
present to thy soul, as an instrument of grace, as a pledge of the
resurrection, as the earnest of glory and immortality . . . he
that believes so much, needs not to inquire further, nor to
entangle his faith by disbelieving his sense'.[31] Earlier, I suggested that terms like 'Laudian' and 'Central' are at the best

merely convenient indicators, a point with which Dugmore agrees. The fact is that Taylor's view of the eucharist is rich and comprehensive, embracing many emphases all of which he considers to belong to some aspect of the mystery of the eucharist. Certainly in the passage from *Holy Living* to which Dugmore refers there is an emphasis on the sacred use to which the elements are appointed. They have ceased to be 'common bread and wine, but holy in their use'. But has Dugmore given any weight to the phrase 'holy in their change'? This surely points back to the effect of consecration, referred to in the *Great Exemplar*, the sacramental change: 'the bread when it is consecrated and made sacramental is the body of our Lord'. It echoes the sense of Lancelot Andrewes when he writes 'we allow that the elements are changed'. The manner of that change is sacramental; 'At the coming of the almighty power of the Word, the nature is changed so that what before was the mere element now becomes a Divine Sacrament, the substance, nevertheless remaining what it was before'. At this stage of the development of his thought, I would submit that Taylor's view of the eucharistic presence is controlled by the concepts of 'sacrament' and 'mystery'. All the time, his thought seems to resist even provisional cataloguing. Stranks is correct that 'It may be doubted whether in his own mind Taylor ever committed himself to any one school of thought about the eucharist'.[32] He is surely wrong in suggesting receptionism or virtualism as a possible category for Jeremy Taylor. The section closes with counsel on prayer for all men, after communicating, and on thanksgiving for the passion, 'in the celebration of that holy sacrifice, which then is sacramentally represented to God'.[33] Thus, the sacramental presence and the sacramental representing of the sacrifice of the Cross are at the heart of the mystery which, because 'now Christ is all one with you', has as its goal for each person 'growing up towards a perfect man in Christ Jesus'.[34]

Characteristically, and with a luminous simplicity, the last page of *Holy Living* has an ejaculation for use 'any time that day, after the solemnity is ended',—'O Jesus, be a Jesus unto me'.

III

The Rules and Exercises of Holy Dying can hardly be read by modern people in the same way that their seventeenth-century forbears read it. Too much has happened in the interval to thought and experience, to religion and to medicine, to men's attitude to dying and to death. Yet there is in the book a quiet acceptance that death is natural and inevitable which has a perennial quality about it, new to his own times and acceptable to ours. Taylor's theme is simplicity itself, that the best preparation for holy dying is holy living: 'It is a great art to die well, and to be learnt by men in health'.[35] We are vulnerable —'Death meets us everywhere and is procured by every instrument and in all chances'—and our true protection is a life of charity 'with its twin-daughters, alms and forgiveness'.[36] The literary quality of the book is high and the beauty of the phrasing and imagery is sustained. Rust's tribute to Taylor that 'he was a rare humanist . . . and had thoroughly concocted all the ancient moralists, Greek and Roman, poets and authors' is confirmed by the number of classical references and allusions woven into the text. Here, perhaps more than anywhere else, he wrote prose as a poet. Nevertheless, it is as pastor and guide, as moral/ascetic theologian, that Taylor handles the subject. Indeed, his favourite term for the priest ministering to the dying patient is 'guide'. *Holy Dying* is moral and pastoral theology as it bears upon the situation, the fears, the sufferings and the hopes of those who are terminally ill and on the service of those who minister to them. There is the temptation of impatience and that of the fear of death. For the first, Taylor offers as a remedy the recreation of attitudes—be thankful for mercies, 'Remember that thou art a man, and a Christian', so you must accept your illness or 'you must renounce your religion'. Think of 'the holy Jesus upon the cross' and strive to conform your sufferings to His, which were so much greater. Cultivate a spirit of hope, for 'hope is designed in the arts of God and of the Spirit to support patience'.[37] He sets out the practice of the graces which the sick man can reach on—the practice of patience, the making of acts of faith, the practice of repentance, and he provides aids and prayers.[38] The fifth chapter is in effect a little treatise for the 'clergy-guides' on this special part of their ministry as confessors and as comforters.

Throughout the book Taylor's religious matter-of-factness is illuminated by his human sensitivity. He is anxious, for example, to banish the bogey-man of death but he does not sentimentalize about Sister Death. 'It is a thing that is no great matter in itself'; 'It is a thing that everyone suffers'; 'It is necessary, and therefore not intolerable'; 'Take away but the pomps of death, the disguises and solemn bugbears . . . and then to die is easy . . .'.[39] Fortitude and prudence are security against the fear of death and remembering always 'that above there is a country better than ours'. With a gentle understanding bred of personal and pastoral experience and with great delicacy of feeling, Taylor adds 'After all this, I do not say it is a sin to be afraid of death . . . our blessed Lord was pleased to legitimate fear to us by his agony and prayers in the garden'.[40] That liberality which runs through his writings keeps company with a pastoral concern for fundamental realities at this crucial stage for 'Now is the time, in which the faith appears most necessary, and most difficult'. The passage tells us something about Taylor the man and Taylor the 'guide': 'Let the sick man mingle the recital of his creed together with his devotions, and in that let him account his faith . . . for some over-forward zeals are so earnest to profess their little and uncertain articles, and glory so to die in a particular and divided communion, that, in the profession of their faith, they lose or discompose their charity. Let it be enough, that we secure our interest of heaven, though we do not go about to appropriate the mansions to our sect: for every good man hopes to be saved, as he is a Christian, and not as he is a Lutheran, or of another division'.[41]

Here, the context of the eucharist is that of confession, repentance and reconciliation. From his own experience, as he tells us, Taylor has seen the results of calling in the priest when it is too late—'and the curate shall say a few prayers by him, and talk to a dead man, and the man is not in a condition to be helped, but in a condition to need it hugely'. The work of the confessor is 'to execute the office of a restorer and judge' but Taylor's fellow-feeling and understanding are evident—'at first he needs a comfort, and anon something to make him willing to die'.[42] At the ministration of the eucharist, 'let the exhortation be made proper to the mystery, but fitted to the man'.[43] The eucharist is the final step in the restoration of the penitent as it is the comfort and strength of the sufferer, for at the heart of the action is the perfect pardon-bestowing, life-imparting Sacrifice now made sacramentally present in the sick-room: 'let all the circumstances and parts of the Divine love be represented, all the mysterious advantages of the blessed sacrament be declared; that it is the bread which came from heaven; that it is the representation of Christ's death to all the purposes and capacities of faith, and the real exhibition of Christ's body and blood to all the purposes of the Spirit; that it is the earnest of the resurrection, and the seed of a glorious immortality. . . . that this is the sacrament of that body, which was broken for our sins, of that blood, which purifies our souls, by which we are presented to God pure and holy in the beloved; that now we may ascertain our hopes, and make our faith confident'.[44]

As we pass in review the substance of Taylor's eucharistic theology as revealed in his writings hitherto with their continuing emphasis on mystery in respect both of the presence and the sacrifice, one cannot but be struck, by way of comparison, with what one may call the modern rediscovery, even the rehabilitation, of the concept of mystery in the eucharist. One thinks not only of the ARCIC and Lima statements referred to earlier but to such a contemporary document as the famous Dutch Catechism, commissioned by the Roman Catholic bishops of the Netherlands and issued with their Foreword. 'This is a mysterious presence', says the *New Catechism*, and it asserts 'This presence is linked with the bread. His words proclaim it: This is my body. And the bread itself shows it. He is as close and life-giving as food, in his presence. Hence bread is the symbol in which he is among us. Ordinary bread has become for us bread of eternal life: Christ.[45] —But then, what happens to this bread? It remains the same as regards outward appearance and taste. Otherwise the symbol in which he wills to be among us would disappear. What then is changed?' The passage then refers to substance and accident theories as a 'way of expressing the mystery' and continues: 'When we consider the matter in terms of present-day thought one should therefore say that the reality, the nature of material things is what they are—each in its own way—for man. Hence it is the essence or nature of bread to be earthly food for man. In the bread at Mass, however, this nature becomes something quite different: Jesus' body, as food for eternal life. Body in Hebrew means the person as a whole. Bread has become Jesus' person. —This is a mysterious presence'. The section concludes by rejecting both physical literalism and pure symbolism.[46]

Is not this what, centuries before and at this stage of his development, Taylor wishes to convey by 'the mystery of his presence', by saying that 'the bread, when it is consecrated, and made sacramental, is the body of our Lord', and by such phrases as 'the body of our Lord is now conveyed to us, by being the bread of the sacrament'? For him, the concept of sacramentality is declared to be 'mystery', for the true *mustērion* is Christ,[47] in whom the Father is revealed, man is reconciled to God and in whom, through the Spirit, the new life is imparted. This is the ground and authentication of all sacramentality.

Notes

1. C. J. Stranks, loc. cit., p. 115. Both books went into many editions in the seventeenth century alone.
2. H. Trevor Hughes, *The Piety of Jeremy Taylor* (1960), pp. 175–177.
3. C. J. Stranks, loc. cit., pp. 108, 113.
4. C. J. Stranks, loc. cit., p. 112.
5. *Works*, Vol. I, p. cxl.
6. *Holy Living*, Ch. IV, Section IV; *The Devout Life*, Part II, Ch. XVII.
7. *Holy Living*, Ch. II, Section I, ib. Vol. IV, p. 56.
8. loc. cit., Ch. I, Section I, ib., p. 14.
9. Ch. IV, Section X, ib. Vol. IV, pp. 265–274.
10. C. J. Stranks, loc. cit., p. 138.
11. *Eucharistic Doctrine in England from Hooker to Waterland* (1942), pp. 94–5.
12. loc. cit., Ch. IV, Section X (12), ib. Vol. IV, p. 272.
13. ib. (13), ib., p. 272.
14. ib. Ch. IV, Section X (8), ib. Vol. IV, p. 270.
15. ib. Ch. IV, Section X (4), ib. Vol. IV, p. 268.
16. ib. 'The effects and benefits of worthy communicating', ib. Vol. IV, p. 273.
17. ib. Ch. IV, Section X (2), ib. Vol. IV, p. 265.
18. ib. Ch. IV, Section X (4), ib. Vol. IV, p. 266.
19. *Table and Tradition* (1983), pp. 77–79.
20. Quoted in *Anglicanism*, ed. More & Cross, pp. 472–3.
21. ib. Ch. IV, Section X (5), ib. Vol. IV, p. 266.
22. ib. Prayers for Several Occasions, ib. Vol. IV, p. 312.

23. ib. Ch. IV, Section X (6), ib. Vol. IV, p. 267.

24. ib. 'The effects and benefits of worthy communicating', ib. Vol. IV, p. 273.

25. C. J. Stranks, loc. cit., p. 137.

26. ib. Ch. IV, Section X (8), ib. Vol. IV, pp. 269–270.

27. Herbert Thorndike, *Works* (L.A.C.T. ed.), Vol. IV, p. 73.

28. loc. cit., Ch. IV, Section X (10), ib. Vol. IV, p. 271.

29. C. W. Dugmore, loc. cit., pp. 94–95.

30. ib. Ch. IV, Section X (9), ib. Vol. IV, p. 270.

31. ib. Ch. IV, Section (10), ib. Vol. IV, p. 271.

32. C. J. Stranks, loc. cit., p. 137.

33. ib. Ch. IV, Section X (12), ib. Vol. IV, p. 272.

34. ib. Ch. IV, Section X (13), ib. Vol. IV, p. 272.

35. From the Dedication, ib. Vol. IV, p. cccix.

36. *Holy Dying*, Ch. II, Section III, ib. Vol. IV, pp. 381–4.

37. ib. Ch. III, Section V, ib. Vol. IV, pp. 404–408.

38. ib. Ch. IV, ib. Vol. IV, pp. 445–503.

39. ib. Ch. III, Section VII, ib. Vol. IV, pp. 423–425.

40. ib. Ch. III, Section VIII (6), ib. Vol. IV, p. 434.

41. ib. Ch. IV, Section III (2), ib. Vol. IV, pp. 461–2.

42. ib. Ch. V, Section II, (1)–(14), ib. Vol. IV, pp. 506–522.

43. ib. Ch. V, Section IV (11), ib. Vol. IV, p. 531.

44. ib. Ch. V, Section IV (11), ib. Vol. IV, p. 531.

45. Compare, ARCIC *Elucidation* (1979), (6): 'bread for this life becomes the bread of eternal life'.

46. *A New Catechism* (English translation, 1967), pp. 342–3.

47. cp. Eph. 3:4, Col. 1: 13–28.

V The Celebration and the Celebrant

Clerus Domini is a short title for a short treatise. Its secondary title is rather longer and explanatory: 'A Discourse of the Divine institution, necessity, sacredness, and separation, of the Office Ministerial, together with the nature and manner of its power and operation'. The book was published in 1651 and the second edition in 1655 described it as written by special command of Charles I. When Taylor published his first major work, *Episcopacy Asserted* in 1642, it had received the King's warm approval and the degree of D.D. was conferred on the author by royal command. The smaller book may be regarded as a sequel in which Taylor did for the second order of ministry what he had done for the first in *Of the Sacred Order and Offices of Episcopacy*. Evidently, from the title-page, it may be assumed that the King had requested this completion of the defence of the sacred ministry.

The book bases its appeal in the opening section on tradition and reason in that wise nations have always 'had their priests and presidents of religious rites'. Taylor points out that 'all great and public things' require people with proper and fitting skill and learning and it would be totally unreasonable if 'only religion should lie in common, apt to be bruised by the hard hand of mechanics'[1]—a splendid seventeenth-century phrase not applicable apparently to fishermen. 'The very natural design of religion' he insists 'forces us to a distinction of persons, in order to the ministration.' Yet he emphasises that the difference in the celebrant is that his calling, and 'assignment' are holy and he himself is 'taught to be holy', and not that he is a superior being, for the ministers of religion are 'yet our brethren in nature'.[2] The section cites numerous classical authors in support of the general principle.

In Christianity, however, the office of priesthood is more than a reasonable tradition analogous to the developments in other settings which he has been describing. It is also a divine commission established on Christ's promise 'to the apostles in the capacity of church-officers' to be with them to the end of the world: 'and therefore, for the verification of the promise . . . so long as the benefit was to be dispensed, so long they were to be succeeded to'.[3] Consideration of 'the power and graces' committed to the apostles which were not of a temporary nature, 'but lasting, successive, and perpetual' requires the conclusion that the ministry itself is perpetual.[4] Taylor instances four elements in this commission, the power of binding and loosing, preaching the gospel, the administration of baptism and the celebration of the eucharist. The first of these powers is not only confessional but disciplinary and he identifies it with the Pauline ministry of reconciliation. The instance in the epistle of St. James proves 'that this power fell into succession' since the presbyters did not receive 'the commission immediately from Christ'.[5] The second power was the commission to the apostles to preach the gospel. Because they 'were created doctors of all the world', the apostles instructed those 'whom they sent out upon the same errand'.[6] Taylor then deals with the results of this preaching 'when by miracle God dispensed great gifts to the laity and to women'. In his view these charismata were 'miraculous verifications' of the Father's promise to send the Spirit. He insists that 'these gifts were given extra-regularly' and conferred 'no other commission, to speak in public'. In his view 'women were not capable of a clerical employment' and, while he recognizes the institution of deaconesses in the primitive Church, he quotes early writers to the effect that 'whatsoever these deaconesses could be, they could not speak in public'. His point is that they were not a ministerial order, being 'reckoned in the laity, because they have no imposition of hands', according to the Council of Nicaea. The same applies to men 'who had gifts extraordinary of the Spirit. . . . they had no pretence to invade the chair'.[7] Taylor brings the application of this into the context of his own disordered times with a condemnation of preaching by persons who have neither authority nor commission.[8]

His strong sacramentalism, noted in earlier chapters, is very much to the fore in his handling of baptism, 'a sacred ministry, a sacrament and a mysterious rite, whose very sacramental and separate nature requires the solemnity of a distinct order of persons for its ministration'.[9] He puts the arguments for and against lay-baptism in emergencies and is clearly unhappy about the practice since it blurs the distinction between the layman and the deacon whose special function he holds it to be. As to the claim that strictness here would imperil an infant Taylor says that God who loves mercy is not that sort of God. It is to argue 'as if God loved this ceremony better than he loved the child'. There are resonances here of the thinking which in a couple of years' time would be fully developed in *Unum Necessarium* and *Deus Justificatus*.[10] He leaves it to the Church to decide but adds that the rubric in the first liturgy of Edward VI 'permitting midwives to baptize in cases of extreme danger . . . was left out in the second liturgies', indicating, he believes, that at least the Church of England left the matter undetermined. Unusually, he regards baptism as part of the exercise of the power of the keys in virtue of its essential linking with repentance, and therefore to be performed by an ordained person. Here again Taylor's theological individuality and the admixture of 'Laudian' and 'liberal' in his make-up are evident.

II

As he looks at the fourth element, in the ministerial commission, the celebration of the eucharist, Taylor is teaching the teachers as well as explaining the nature of their office. He is explaining what happens in the eucharist as well as describing the rôle and function of the celebrant. The note at once struck is that of the mystery of the eucharist—'the most solemn, sacred and divinest mystery in our religion; that in which the clergy in their appointed ministry do *diakonountes mesiteuein* "stand between God and the people", and do fulfil a special and incomprehensible ministry, which "the angels themselves do look into" with admiration'.[11] The eucharistic mystery at the earthly altar is merged with and actuated sacramentally (the words are Taylor's) by the great High Priest's offering of Himself, as sacrificed, in perpetual intercession at the heavenly altar. The priest re-presents and commemorates the same sacrifice as he celebrates the eucharist. The now-familiar themes are woven even more closely by Taylor into his understanding of priesthood: 'for certainly there is not a greater degree of power in the world, than to remit and retain sins, and to consecrate the sacramental symbols into the mysteriousness of Christ's body and blood . . . to handle the sacrifice of the world, and to present the same, which, in heaven is presented by the eternal Jesus'.[12] Taylor quotes from numerous Fathers on the priestly function and rôle and in particular from two of his favourites, John Chrysostom's *De Sacerdotio* and what he believed to be Ambrose's *De Dignitate Sacerdotali*, not nowadays reckoned as authentic.[13] Nor is he afraid, supported by patristic authors, to use phrases not especially acceptable or popular today—'the priestly power', 'the power of celebrating this dreadful mystery'. He distances himself very distinctly, however, from any suggestion that the celebrant's 'power' in the eucharist is something akin to the magical: 'for the power God hath given, is indeed mystical; but it is not like a power operating by way of natural or proper operation: it is not "vis" but "facultas" . . .'.[14] The priest receives a 'solemn *capacity*, to intervene between God and the people'. By his office he is 'an intercessor with God' because 'all the ministries of the Gospel are *in genere orationis*'. His intercession is on the pattern of, and linked with, the heavenly intercession. Taylor explains that 'That is not to lessen the power but to understand it: for the priest's ministry is certainly the instrument of conveying all the blessings of the people, which are annexed to the ordinary administration of the Spirit. But when all the office of Christ's priesthood in heaven is called "intercession" for us, and himself makes the sacrifice of the cross effectual to the salvation and graces of his church by prayer—since we are ministers of the same priesthood, can there be a greater glory than to have our ministry like to that of Jesus?'

He drives home his point that this power cannot be understood in any other terms because it is a power 'not operating by virtue of a certain number of syllables, but by a holy, solemn, determined, and religious prayer, in the several manners and instances of intercession: according to the analogy of all the religions in the world, whose most solemn mystery was then most solemn prayer: I mean it in the manner of sacrificing; which also is true in the most mysterious solemnity of Christianity in the holy sacrament of the Lord's supper, which is hallowed and lifted up from the common bread and wine by mystical prayers and solemn invocations of God. And therefore St. Dionysius calls the form of consecration "prayers of consecrations": and St. Cyril . . . says the same: "The eucharistical bread, after the invocations of the Holy Ghost, is not any longer common bread, but the body of Christ"'.[15]

What then is the meaning of this 'priestly power' or, to put it another way, how is the 'sacramental change' brought about? Is consecration effected by the words of institution or by the power of the Holy Spirit in response to prayers of the Church offered by the priest? Clearly, Taylor favours the latter view which he associates with the early liturgies and those of Eastern Orthodoxy. It is his contention that the Church of England so understands the prayer of consecration.[16] His treatment of the question is full and illuminates his own thinking on the eucharist. The words of institution are absolutely essential to the 'completion' of the rite, 'yet even those words also are part of a mystical prayer'. They are not just 'narrative' but 'invocation' also. They are 'retained as a part of the mystery . . . manifesting the signification of the rite, *the glory of the change*, the operation of the Spirit, the death of Christ, and the memory of the sacrifice'. Taylor makes much at this point of the invocation and coming of the Holy Spirit. But whether the Greek or the Latin understanding is correct, the ministry of the celebrant in consecration 'is still by way of prayer. Nay, further yet, the whole mystery itself is operative in the way of prayer'. He is underlining his view of the priestly power as definable *in genere orationis* and he continues 'All the whole office is an office of intercession, as it passes from the priest to God, and from the people to God. And then for that *great mysteriousness, which is the sacramental change*, which is that which passes from God unto the people by the priest, that also is obtained and effected by way of prayer'. Taylor's conclusion is that 'the Holy Spirit is the consecrator' who is not 'called down by the force of a certain number of syllables' but 'by the prayers of the church, presented by the priests'.[17] Thus we see emerging a picture of the celebration and the celebrant in which come together major elements in his eucharistic theology: the concepts of 'mystery' and of 'sacramental change'; the Spirit as consecrator, invoked in his operation by the prayers of the Church; the consecration effected not 'in any one instant, but *a divine alteration* consequent to the whole ministry—that is, the solemn prayer and invocation': the celebrant whose 'power' is not supernatural but the invoking of God's power by prayer and by intercession which mirrors or reflects the intercession of the great High Priest at the heavenly altar; the sacramental representation of the one Sacrifice perpetually pleaded by Him who is both high-priest and sacrifice, 'to use the words of St. Cyprian'.

This is a rich doctrine of the eucharist and of the ministry and Taylor summarises it and in the process makes clear the sense in which he believes the priesthood to have a sacrificial rôle:

'Now Christ did also establish a number of select persons to be ministers of this great sacrifice, finished upon the cross; that they also should exhibit and represent to God, in the manner which their Lord appointed them, this sacrifice, commemorating the action and suffering of the great priest; and by way of prayers and impetration, offering up that action in behalf of the people, *epi to anō thusiastērion anapempsas tas thusias*, as Gregory Nazianzen expresses it, "sending up sacrifices to be laid on the altar in heaven": that the Church might be truly united unto Christ their head, and, in the way of their ministry, may do what he does in Heaven.' Taylor is saying that the eucharistic parallelism of the heavenly altar continues on into the functions and rôle of the ministers of the eucharist, but with the essential qualifications: 'in the way of their ministry', 'as it becomes ministers, humbly, sacramentally'. This he develops further: 'For he exhibits the sacrifice, that is, himself, actually and presentially in heaven: the priest on earth commemorates the same, and, by his prayers, represents it to God in behalf of the whole catholic church; presentially too, by another and more mysterious way of presence; but both Christ in heaven, and his ministers on earth, *do actuate the sacrifice*, and apply it to its purposed design by praying to God in the virtue and merit of that sacrifice; Christ himself, in a high and glorious manner; the ministers of his priesthood (as it becomes ministers) humbly, *sacramentally*, and according to the energy of human advocation and intercession; this is the sum and great mysteriousness of Christianity, and is now to be proved'.[18]

Taylor has been at pains to explain very carefully what he means by the sacrificial rôle of the priesthood. One is accordingly impelled to ask how he understands the relationship between the High Priesthood of Christ and 'the ministerial priesthood in the Church'—a phrase he uses in *Clerus Domini* V (8). The outline of an answer is sketched in the closing sentences of the paragraph just quoted and now Taylor turns to Scripture to give more detail and content to the picture. According to *Hebrews*, Christ is a priest for ever with an unchangeable priesthood and 'he lives for ever to make intercession for us'. Taylor comments: 'This he does as priest, and therefore it must be by offering a sacrifice; "for every high-priest is ordained to offer gifts and sacrifices"; and therefore "it is necessary he also have something to offer", as long as he is a priest, that is, "for ever", till the consummation of all things. Since therefore he hath nothing new to offer, and something he must continually offer, it is evident, he offers himself as the medium of advocation, and the instance and argument of a prevailing intercession; and this he (i.e. the author) calls "a more excellent ministry"; and by it, "Jesus is a minister of the sanctuary, and of the true tabernacle;"—that is, he, as our high-priest, officiates in heaven, in the great office of a mediator, in the merit and power of his death and resurrection'.

Taylor is saying that the teaching of the epistle is that as there is but one Sacrifice, so there is but one High-Priest, and that therefore his priesthood is unique and intransmissible, *aparabaton echei tēn hierōsunēn* (Heb 7: 24). The ministerial priesthood is parallel but on another plane, that of '*sacramental presentation*'. The phrase is from *Holy Living* where he has already made the distinction: As Christ represents to the Father the one Sacrifice 'so he hath appointed that the same ministry shall be done upon earth too, *in our manner, and according to our proportion*'.[19] It is a totally different, but *related*, priesthood and the relation consists in the commemorative presentation of the unique sacrifice of the one High-Priest. This is similar to the position advanced in the ARCIC statement on *Ministry and Ordination* (13). Thus, continues Taylor, 'What Christ does always *in a proper and most glorious manner, the ministers of the gospel also do in theirs: commemorating the sacrifice upon the cross*, "giving thanks", and celebrating a perpetual eucharist for it'. He returns to his definition of the power of this ministerial priesthood which, as he notes elsewhere, 'is wholly from

God'.[20] It is intercessory and in this sense is sacrificial: 'By declaring the death of Christ, and praying to God in the virtue of it, for all the members of the church, and all persons capable; it is "in genere orationis", a sacrifice, and an instrument of propitiation, as all holy prayers are in their several proportions'.[21] In other words, it is a case of parallelism and not of identity of priesthood.

This is an important matter both in the doctrine of the eucharist and in that of the ministry, that nowhere in Taylor's work, so far as I am aware, is there any trace of the view that the ministerial priesthood and/or the royal priesthood of believers is a sharing in the priesthood of Christ. Quite the contrary, since for Taylor it is clear that there are two planes or frames of reference. Only once, in a passage already quoted, is there a loose phrase, 'since we are ministers of the same priesthood'. This is immediately corrected by the following words 'can there be a greater glory than to have our ministry *like to that of Jesus*'. The context makes it clear that it is a likeness of intercession. In Section VI (2), Taylor speaks of the 'excellent and supernatural abilities' of the ministerial priesthood as 'deriving from Christ upon his ministers', by *delegation* from Him who is 'the fountain of evangelical ministry'.

This assertion of sharing in the priesthood of Christ would seem to me to be questionable theology. It is to be met with in the *Report* of the Lambeth Conference of 1968: 'All Christians share in the priesthood of their Lord'.[22] The 1971 report on *The Ministerial Priesthood* made to the Synod of Bishops in Rome, while describing Christ as 'exercising a supreme and unique Priesthood by the offering of himself' speaks of 'this special participation in Christ's Priesthood' on the part of the hierarchical ministry.[23] The report of the International Theological Commission (of the Roman Catholic Church), dated October 10th, 1970, on *The Priestly Ministry* ends with six propositions, one of which reads 'In the New Testament there is no other priesthood but that of Christ ... all the faithful in the Church are called to share in it'.[24]

It would appear to me that Christians do not share in the priesthood of Christ which is unique and radically incommunicable—the word in Heb. 7:24 being *aparabatos*. What we share in is the effects of the great High Priest's unique and unrepeatable sacrifice. We share in what the Book of Common Prayer terms 'remission of our sins and all other benefits of his passion'. The fruits of the Paschal Mystery are seen in the new life of the new and apostolic household of faith. We share in the life of faith and love, through the sacrifice of Christ. What Romans 12: 1 calls 'the living sacrifice' of ourselves is wholly dependent on the sacrifice of the great High Priest and is the fruits and effect of his self-offering. Jean Tillard would seem to me to be correct in his assessment of the relevant New Testament passages: 'None treats explicitly of the Christian ministry. It even seems necessary to add that none establishes, in a clear and inescapable way, any relation between the Priesthood of Christ and that of the Church as a whole other than the following: because of the Priesthood of Christ, the faithful can offer sacrifices acceptable to God (Hebrews); because of the *Sacrifice* of Christ, the baptized are the People who bear the holy priesthood which is exercised in spiritual sacrifices (1 Peter). Nowhere is it said that the Priesthood of the Church (a royal Priesthood, a priesthood of holiness of life) constitutes a participation in the priesthood of Christ. Nowhere is there any question of a relationship between this Priesthood of the Church and that which is exercised in ritual worship'.[25] In a valuable and closely-argued booklet, his conclusion on the ministerial priesthood follows from his rejection of this concept of sharing in the priesthood of the sole *archiereus*, Christ Jesus: 'We have rather to do with a priesthood *sui generis*, wholly relative to the unique priestly act of Jesus, intended to assure the contact of the community with that act in the *hic et nunc*. This priesthood only yields up its meaning when read in the light of the *Memorial* (in the technical sense of the term) which is the sacramental mirror reflecting *hic et nunc* to the Church the event of the Passover of Christ. Thanks to this priesthood the community can sit at the table where the sacrificial death of the unique Priest is celebrated'.[26] This is largely the position set out in ARCIC's agreed statement, *Ministry and Ordination* (13): 'The priestly sacrifice of Jesus was unique, as is also his continuing High Priesthood. Despite the fact that in the New Testament ministers are never called priests (hiereis), Christians came to see the priestly role of Christ reflected in these ministers and used priestly terms in describing them. Because the eucharist is the memorial of the sacrifice of Christ, the action of the presiding minister in reciting again the words of Christ at the last supper and distributing to the assembly the holy gifts *is seen to stand in a sacramental relation to what Christ himself did in offering his own sacrifice'*.

As one looks back over what Taylor has been saying about the celebrant and the celebration, comparing this with the matter which we have been discussing, we are aware of the anticipatory quality of Taylor's teaching in this respect. It is another of those sudden flashes of what I ventured to call his modernity which keeps company with his reverence for and use of antiquity, so sustained in this particular treatise on ministry. For Taylor, too, the point at which the ministerial priesthood fully reveals its meaning is in the celebration of the eucharist commemorating the unique sacrifice. The 'heavenly altar' reveals the inner dynamism of the eucharistic action and at the same time makes clear the uniqueness of Christ's 'continuing High Priesthood'. Perhaps the similarity of viewpoint is not so surprising since both Taylor and the moderns have returned to sources, to Scripture and tradition, for their starting point. The three-fold appeal is an explicit criterion in *Clerus Domini* as it is throughout Taylor's work.[27] His treatment of the priesthood of all the faithful is brief and unsatisfying, clericalized and almost rabbinical. He argues that since St. Peter takes 'the royal priesthood' from the Mosaic law in Exodus 19: 6, then the situations are analogous. The old Israel was a kingdom in which priests were appointed by God, 'a kingdom, in which nothing is more honourable than the priesthood . . . and yet the people were not priests, in any sense, but of a violent metaphor'. Taylor then draws the parallel with the new Israel: 'and therefore the Christian ministry having greater privileges, and being honoured with attrectation of the body and blood of Christ, and offices serving to "a better covenant", may, with greater argument, be accounted excellent, honourable, and royal; and all the church be called "a royal priesthood"; the denomination being given to the whole, from the most excellent part; because they altogether make one body under Christ the head, the medium of the union being the priests, the collectors of the church, and instrument of adunation'.[28] Whatever one may feel about special pleading here, there is no doubt about Taylor's general position as to the rôle of the celebrant and the nature of the celebration:'This being the great mystery of Christianity, and the only remanent express of Christ's sacrifice on earth, it is most consonant to the analogy of the mystery, that this commemorative sacrifice be presented by persons as separate and distinct in their ministry, as the sacrifice itself is from, and above, the other parts of our religion'.[29] That says it all—a compendium of Taylor's doctrine of the eucharist and of the ministry. The word 'analogy' too is somehow suggestive of a parallelism of ministries which are distinct.

III

'Taylor's experiences as an active priest under an actively persecuting government gave birth in 1658 to a book of major interest . . .' So writes Harry Boone Porter of Taylor's *Collection of Offices*.[30] His detailed and scholarly study makes much use of the book which he regards as a unique achievement by Taylor: 'He alone among his Anglican contemporaries had the ability and the boldness on his own initiative to compile single-handed a whole new liturgy, and to publish it for public use'.[31] The book reveals yet another aspect of the many-faceted genius of Jeremy Taylor. Its publication also demonstrated his courage and it is generally accepted that his brief imprisonment in the Tower of London at this time was caused by the 'popish' frontispiece of the *Collection*. It is convenient to include it here because of its date of publication and because it is likely that these were the offices used by Taylor in Wales when the Book of Common Prayer was proscribed and suppressed. Part of the contents also fit with consideration of the celebrant and the celebration since the book contains 'An Office or Order for the Administration of the Holy Sacrament of the Lord's Supper according to the way of the Apostolical Churches, and the Doctrine of the Church of England'.[32] This office from the *Collection* presents in terms of liturgy what he has been expressing in his eucharistic theology. Porter has given us a thorough and illuminating discussion of the rite. He draws attention to Taylor's borrowings and translations from the Liturgy of St. James. This would have been one of the earliest rites with which the seventeenth century was conversant, and, in *Clerus Domini* Taylor writes of its importance. His use of it in his *Collection* would have been because of his devotion to the early tradition but also because his own sense of the profound mystery of the eucharist finds liturgical expression in the Liturgy of St. James. There is an epiclesis and an anamnesis (from St. James), a prayer from the Liturgy of St. John Chrysostom, a translation of the Cherubic Hymn, and, curiously, no creed. His use of acclamations foreshadows modern liturgical revisions and, I would add, a prayer for use by the communicants, 'Lord, I am not worthy that thou shouldest come under my roof' is echoed in the modern Roman rite 'Lord, I am not worthy to receive you'. Clearly, we have in Taylor's liturgical work yet a further example of his almost disconcerting capacity to be at times ahead of his own times. Porter observes that 'he anticipates the teaching of the present liturgical revival, and some of his ideas will be more acceptable to readers today than they were to his contemporaries'.[33] That is well said, and is confirmed, as we have seen, by other instances of this 'modernity' which in some respects made Taylor atypical as far as his own period is concerned.

Original and often beautiful though his work as a liturgist is, it is to its content in respect of his theology of the eucharist that we turn in examining the rite. No matter what the liturgical sources upon which he draws, it is noteworthy that the title of the office affirms that the order is 'according to . . . the doctrine of the Church of England'. Taylor's assertion that there is nothing idiosyncratic about his teaching but that it is firmly Anglican is a recurring feature of his work. Obviously he thought it necessary here in a new liturgy to make this clear to the worshippers who were now forbidden to use the Book of Common Prayer and who might fear that new forms of worship implied new doctrines.

The prayer of consecration begins with an epiclesis (from St. James) and a statement of the presence: 'Send thy Holy Ghost upon our hearts, and let him also descend upon these gifts, that by his good, his holy, his glorious presence, he may sanctify and enlighten our hearts, and he may bless and sanctify these gifts;

That this bread may become the holy body of Christ. Amen.

And this chalice may become the life-giving blood of Christ.

Amen. That it may become unto us all, that partake of it, this day, a blessed instrument of union with Christ . . .'.[34]

The modern Roman rite follows Taylor in transposing the epiclesis from its place at the end of the consecration prayer in St. James to precede the institution narrative. It is worthy of note that two of the Roman eucharistic prayers (I and II) use the words 'become for us' while III and IV, like Taylor, have simply 'become'. The Scottish office of 1637 had 'may be unto us' and the modern rite changed this to 'may become'. This was the phrase both in the Scottish rite of 1764 and in the American rite of Bishop Seabury. Bucer had objected to the prayer of invocation of the Holy Spirit that the elements 'may be unto us the Body and Blood of Christ', which was the form in the Book of Common Prayer of 1549.[35] We know that Taylor had a favourable view of the 1549 Prayer Book but he does not hesitate to use the simple and direct petition 'may become the holy body of Christ'. He has no qualms about the Scriptural realism and for very good reason since his theology hitherto is that of a real, a true, presence which is sacramental. We have had occasion already to note the ARCIC statement (*Windsor*, (6)–(8)): 'his true presence, effectually signified by the bread and wine which, in this mystery, become his body and blood'; 'the sacramental body and blood of the Saviour are present as an offering to the believer awaiting his welcome'; 'who gives himself sacramentally in the body and blood of his paschal sacrifice'. Once again, in his liturgy, Taylor stresses the dynamism of the presence by emphasising the instrumentality of the eucharist in creating for the believer 'union with Christ'.

As the one sacrifice, the heavenly altar and the unbloody sacrifice are at the heart of his theology so it is in his eucharistic office. In the opening prayers after the Lord's Prayer, and which are adaptations of the Great Entrance prayer and the offertory prayer from St. James, the celebrant prays by way of preparation: 'Thou hast given us . . . confidence and commandment to present ourselves before thee at thy holy table to represent a holy, venerable, and unbloody sacrifice for our sins, and for the errors and ignorances of all thy people'

and

'Grant that with a holy fear, and a pure conscience, we may finish this service, presenting a holy sacrifice holily unto thee, that thou mayest receive it in heaven, and smell a sweet odour in the union of the eternal sacrifice, which our blessed Lord perpetually offers'.

The celebrant's prayer of preparation petitions 'by the power of the Holy Ghost, make me worthy for this ministry, accepting this service for his sake, whose sacrifice I represent, and by whose commandment I minister'.[36] The prayer of oblation reads 'We ... do humbly present to Thee, O Lord, this present sacrifice of remembrance and thanksgiving' and the prayer for the Catholic Church, which follows the Communion, begins 'Receive, O eternal God, this sacrifice for and in behalf of all Christian people, whom thou hast redeemed with the blood of thy Son'.[37] As a result of our study so far of Taylor's eucharistic theology we must readily concur with Porter's evaluation of his liturgy for the administration of the holy sacrament of the Lord's Supper: 'The composition of this service gave Taylor the opportunity to frame a complete liturgical expression of his own eucharistic belief and devotion. As we have seen, his teaching and his private prayers on this topic were coherent and consistent and had appeared over the years, especially in the *Psalter*, *Great Exemplar*, *Holy Living* and *Worthy Communicant*. It is this same consistent position which is expressed in Taylor's liturgy, although this has not always been perceived by modern writers'.[38]

Notes

1. *Clerus Domini*, Section I (8), ib. Vol. 14, p. 421.
2. *Clerus Domini*, Section I (8)–(10), ib. Vol. 14, pp. 421–2.
3. *Clerus Domini*, Section II (2), ib. Vol. 14, p. 427.
4. *Clerus Domini*, Section II (3), ib. Vol. 14, p. 427–8.
5. *Clerus Domini*, Section II (4)–(5), ib. Vol. 14, pp. 428–9.
6. *Clerus Domini*, Section III (2), ib. Vol. 14, p. 432.
7. *Clerus Domini*, Section III (4)–(8), ib. Vol. 14, pp. 433–437.
8. *Clerus Domini*, Section III (9)–(15), ib. Vol. 14, pp. 437–442.
9. *Clerus Domini*, Section IV (3)–(12), ib. Vol. 14, pp. 444–450.
10. See Chapter I, pp.
11. *Clerus Domini*, Section V (1), ib. Vol. 14, p. 452.
12. *Clerus Domini*, Section V (10), ib. Vol. 14, p. 459.
13. *Clerus Domini*, Section V (11), ib. Vol. 14, p. 460, and Ch. V (6).
14. *Clerus Domini*, Section VII (3), ib. Vol. 14, p. 467.

15. *Clerus Domini*, Section VII (4)–(5), ib. Vol. 14, pp. 467–469.

16. *Clerus Domini*, Section VII (10), ib. Vol. 14, p. 473. 'The Church of England does most religiously observe it according to the custom and sense of the primitive liturgies; who always did believe the consecration not to be a natural effect and change, finished in any one instant, but *a divine alteration* consequent to the whole ministry—that is, the solemn prayer and invocation.'

17. *Clerus Domini*, quotations from Section VII (4)–(10), ib. Vol. 14, pp. 468–473.

18. *Clerus Domini*, Section V (2), ib. Vol. 14, pp. 452–3.

19. *Holy Living*, Ch. IV, Section X (4).

20. *Clerus Domini*, Section VI (7).

21. *Clerus Domini*, Section V (3), ib. Vol. 14, pp. 453–4.

22. *Report*, p. 100.

23. pp. 9, 13.

24. Editions du Cerf (Paris, 1971).

25. Jean Tillard, *What Priesthood has the Ministry* (1973), p. 14.

26. loc. cit., p. 27.

27. *Clerus Domini*, Section VII (13), ib. Vol. 14, p. 475.

28. *Clerus Domini*, Section V (9), ib. Vol. 14, pp. 457–8.

29. *Clerus Domini*, Section V (5), ib. Vol. 14, p. 454.

30. *Jeremy Taylor: Liturgist* (1979), p. 16.

31. loc. cit., p. 18.

32. Heber, Vol. 15, p. 290.

33. *Jeremy Taylor: Liturgist* (1979), p. 1.

34. Heber, Vol. 15, pp. 299–300.

35. cp. Procter & Frere's '*A New History of the Book of Common Prayer*' (1932 ed.), pp. 74, 510–517.

36. Heber, Vol. 15, pp. 291–2.

37. ib. Vol. 15, pp. 301, 303.

38. loc. cit., p. 81.

VI Really Present

'The tree of life is now become an apple of contention' wrote Jeremy Taylor, as he sadly reflected on how the debates and discussions on the manner of Christ's presence in the eucharist have made of the sacrament a source of division instead of being 'a union of Christian societies to God'.[1] Indeed, the polemics involved were distasteful to him, for Taylor was a reluctant controversialist whose chief concern was, as we have seen, with the reality of the eucharist and with its place and effect in the life of the Christian. So, in *The Real Presence and Spiritual in the Blessed Sacrament* and in the epistle dedicatory to the Bishop of Rochester, he insists that he is 'accidentally engaged in the question of transubstantiation' and that it is 'against my resolution and proper disposition'. Ten years later, in the preface to the *Dissuasive* (1664), he would describe controversial skill as 'the worst part of learning' and would regret that the Irish bishops had chosen him for the task—'the lot fell upon Matthias; and that was my call'. He had no taste for polemics but 'I had nothing left me but obedience; though I confess that I found regret in the nature of the employment'.[2] His dedication of the *Real Presence* to the Bishop of Rochester is a tribute from one victim of persecution to another, for 'the diminution of your outward circumstances cannot render you a person unfit to patronise this book'. The immediate reason for writing the book is thought to have been the proselytising activities in Wales of John Sergeant, a Roman Catholic controversialist.

The Real Presence and Spiritual in the Blessed Sacrament is an outstanding example of the classical Anglican three-fold appeal to Scripture, to the teaching of the Primitive Church, and to reason. This provides the broad structure of the book which, heavy going though it may be at times, has both breadth and depth in its treatment and is of importance in evaluating the eucharistic theology of Jeremy Taylor. Its full title is *The Real Presence and Spiritual of Christ in the Blessed Sacrament proved against the Doctrine of Transubstantiation.* This suggests that, for the purpose of further clarifying Taylor's views, we have two areas requiring investigation: what he is here saying about the real presence and what he thinks the other side in the debate is saying. In both there are problems to be considered.

Straight away, Taylor re-affirms what is for him the central concept in respect of the eucharistic presence, that of mystery: 'so we may in this mystery to them that curiously ask, what, or how it is? "Mysterium est"; "It is a sacrament, and a mystery"; by sensible instruments it consigns spiritual graces; by the creatures it brings us to God; by the body it ministers to the spirit.'[3] It is the strength of the affirmation of the real, spiritual presence of Christ that 'this account does still leave the article in his deepest mystery'.[4] For him, the assertion of the mystery of the eucharist is no side-stepping of the issue but a vital element in a position deliberately taken. The working of the Spirit is essentially mysterious and, in Taylor's view, only this way of describing the presence of Christ in the eucharist protects this truth of experience: 'the word "spiritual" is so general a term, and operations so various and many, by which the Spirit of God brings his purposes to pass, and does his work upon the soul, that we are, in this specific term, very far from limiting the article to a minute and special manner. Our word of "spiritual presence" is particular in nothing, but that it excludes the *corporal and natural manner*; we say it is not this, but it is to be understood figuratively, that is, *not naturally*, but to the purposes and in the manner of the Spirit and spiritual things; which how they operate or are affected, we know no more than we know how a cherub sings or thinks'—a typical flash of unexpected imagery.[5] Moreover, says Taylor, this description of the presence fits the theology and experience of the first thousand years when there was liberty in interpreting the mystery. With approval he quotes Cuthbert Tunstall's observation that before the Lateran council 'it was free for everyone to opine as they please, and it were better it were so now'. Taylor is here in the direct Anglican line from Andrewes onwards which refuses to define what is by its very nature indefinable in the last resort. So it was, he maintains, that in the primitive Church also 'many of the fathers laid their hands

upon their mouths, and revered the mystery'.[6] The case of us
latter-day Christians is that if we had not 'looked too far into
the sanctuary . . . we had kneeled before the same altars, and
adored the same mystery, and communicated in the same rites,
to this day'.

The source of our present divisions was the defining of the
how of the eucharistic presence and the enforcement of the
definition as *de fide*, a definition which he proposes to show
to be unacceptable 'by Scripture, by reason, by sense, and by
tradition'.[7] This is the structure of his work and, as he sees it,
the catalyst producing the controversy has been and is the
definition of transubstantiation: 'For, in the thing itself, there
is no difference amongst wise and sober persons; nor ever was,
till the manner became an article, and declared or supposed to
be of the substance of the thing'.[8] Such is the state of the
question as Taylor understands it and before commencing his
investigation he makes what he deems to be an Anglican
confession of faith: 'The doctrine of the Church of England
and generally of the Protestants, in this article, is—that after
the minister of the holy mysteries hath rightly prayed, and
blessed or consecrated the bread and wine, *the symbols become changed into the body and blood of Christ, after a
sacramental, that is, in a spiritual real manner*: so that all that
worthily communicate, do by faith receive Christ really, effectually, to all the purposes of his passion . . . the result of which
doctrine is this: *It is bread, and it is Christ's body. It is bread in
substance, Christ in the sacrament*; and Christ is really given to
all that are truly disposed, as the symbols are; *each as they can;
Christ as Christ can be given; the bread and wine as they
can*. . . . It is here, as in the other sacrament . . . there and here
too, *the first substance is changed by grace, but remains the
same in nature.*'

That this is the doctrine of the Church of England, is
apparent in the church-catechism; affirming 'the inward part
or thing signified by the consecrated bread and wine to be "the
body and blood of Christ, which are verily and indeed taken
and received of the faithful in the Lord's Supper" . . . and the
same is repeated severally in the exhortation, and in the prayer
of the address before the consecration, in the canon of our
communion; "verily and indeed" is "reipsa", that is, "really
enough"; that is our sense of the real presence'.[9] All this is a

reiteration of what Taylor has already set out in the *Great Exemplar* on the mystery of the sacramental presence which is both real and spiritual.[10] There is more than a chance or coincidental resemblance between part of the passage just quoted and the extract from the Dutch Catechism given at the close of Chapter IV. There is a similarity of thought on the relation of Christ to the elements, even a similarity in expressing that relation. It is a further instance of this oddly anticipatory quality which I have loosely termed Taylor's modernity.

Now he turns to a clarification of terms and it is in the process of this analysis that there is a further revealing of the richness and the complexity of his own thought. The matter of terms and their meaning is all-important, as twentieth-century ecumenical conversationalists have discovered afresh in their rigorous search for agreed formulas. Taylor was well aware of what was involved and gives two reasons why 'I have been the more careful to explain the question, and the use of these words according to our meaning in the question'. His first reason will be familiar to all participants in modern dialogues on the eucharist: 'Until we are agreed upon the signification of the words, they are equivocal; and by being used on both sides to several purposes, sometimes are pretended as instruments of union, but indeed effect it not'. The outcome, says Taylor, is often the reverse because 'each suspects the word in a wrong sense'. The second reason bears more directly on the purpose of his book but is still directed to the terms under discussion, being concerned with how and in what sense these terms are used by the writers of the patristic period. The contemporary relevance of this is underlined by the attention given by modern writers to the variety of eucharistic thought and terminology in the Fathers. Taylor's point which he will sustain in detail later in the book is that 'because the words do perfectly declare our sense, and are owned publicly in our doctrine and manner of speaking, it will be in vain to object against us those sayings of the fathers, which use the same expressions'. The nub here from the angle of proving his view as against transubstantiation is that when the Fathers use those words, 'really, substantially, corporally, verily, and indeed, and Christ's body and blood' it has to be demonstrated that they 'speak for transubstantiation . . . for we use the same words'. What has to be shown is that 'these words can be proved in them (i.e. the Fathers) to signify more than our sense of them does import'.[11] It is Taylor's contention that the appeal to antiquity shows the consistency of the doctrine of the real, spiritual presence as Anglicans expound it with the doctrine of the primitive Church and this he asserts in the lengthy Section XII where he sets himself to 'inquire after the doctrine of the church, in this great question'.

The terms 'real' and 'spiritual' first engage his attention. With these are closely involved the words 'corporal' and 'natural'. Behind all four terms lies the long history of the evolution from an undifferentiated sacramental realism to the concept of the elements being changed in substance. Deep within this evolutionary process was the problem of the relationship of the consecrated elements to the original, the 'physical', body of Christ in heaven. This problem in turn lay behind Berengar's rejection of 'conversionism' in the eleventh century, a rejection which obliged him to recant and to affirm that the Body of Christ in the sacrament is the true body of Christ which was born of the Virgin. It is not certain that Berengar denied all change but in any event it was the same problem which later led Luther to formulate his doctrine of ubiquity. The effects of this continuing debate together with the philosophical refinements of Aquinas and the moderate distinction made by the Council of Trent produced an unclear situation, theologically speaking, in the sixteenth and seventeenth centuries. This is reflected in what Taylor says about his own views and about the views to which he is opposed. A further complication was created by the popular realism of some elements in contemporary Roman Catholicism. To do Taylor justice he has little to say (and that only in the epistle dedicatory) about tales of eucharistic 'miracles' and apparitions, contenting himself with a reference to the 'horrible words' in the *Stella Clericorum* where the priest is called 'the creator of his Creator'. In the book itself he deals fairly and often astringently with authentic positions and with genuine arguments by leading figures and theologians of repute. How far both sides of the debate really entered into one another's positions is matter for investigation. Nor can one appreciate the argument of both sides without becoming aware of the effects of the current thinking about location and corporeality. It shows itself as much in the Book of Common Prayer—'the *natural* Body and Blood of our Saviour Christ is in Heaven, and not here; it being against the truth of Christ's natural Body to be at one time in more places than one'—as in the Trent decree, 'Nor is there any contradiction between these things, that the Saviour himself sits always at the right hand of the Father in heaven according to his *natural* mode of existence, and that he should nonetheless also be present *sacramentally in his own substance* in other places by that mode of existence which, although we can scarcely express it in words, we can conclude it is possible with God'.[12] That Taylor is alive to these matters and their implications becomes evident as his book develops. One thing remains constant and clear however—the value and importance of his continued assertion of the concept of sacramentality and the sacramental presence as he endeavours to set out the manner of Christ's presence in the eucharist.

If you believe that the gifts of the Spirit are 'real graces', says Taylor, then you will realise that 'the spiritual is also a real presence'. Indeed, were it possible for Christ's body to be 'in the sacrament naturally or corporeally, it could be but in order to this spiritual, celestial, and effective presence'. The proof of this, agreed by the Roman theologians, is that the unworthy communicant, receiving the elements 'in the natural and corporal manner fall short of that for which it is given, that is, of the blessings and benefits'.[13] In support he quotes Bellarmine and the Egyptian liturgy. The error here is *the word 'real' is taken for 'natural'*; and does not signify 'transcendenter'.[14]

The next term to be considered is the word 'substantial' and Taylor makes favourable mention of the article of the Council of Trent. The eirenic quality which sees the possibility, however remote, of agreement peeps out here as it does even more markedly in *The Worthy Communicant*. What is striking about Taylor's liberality, judged by the standards of his times, is that in his circumstances he could have such feelings, let alone put them in print, for he is writing as a sequestered priest of a Church suppressed by Puritans and triumphed over by 'the emissaries of the church of Rome . . . (who) ask, Where is your church now?'[15] He writes, 'The word "substantialiter" is also used by Protestants in this question: which I suppose may be the same with that which is in the article of Trent; . . . "in substance, but after a sacramental manner": which words if they might be understood in the sense, in which the Protestants use them, that is, really, truly, without fiction or the help of fancy, but "in rei veritate" . . . *it might become an instrument of a united confession*; and this is the manner of speaking which St. Bernard used . . . "In the sacrament is given us the true substance of Christ's body or flesh, not carnally, but spiritually". The importance of such phrases as "sacramentally", "in a sacramental manner" or "as in a sacrament" for the understanding of Taylor's doctrine of the real presence is a recurrent. Taken thus, the term "substantially" presents no problem, "but they mean it otherwise, as I shall demonstrate by and by".'

It is remarkable, continues Taylor, that Bellarmine, quoting the same passage from St. Bernard, appears to be in agreement; 'for he says, "that Christ's body is there truly, substantially, really; but not corporally; nay, you may say spiritually:" and now a man would think we had him sure; but his nature is labile and slippery, you are never the nearer for this; for first he says, "It is not safe to use the word 'spiritually', nor yet safe to say, he is not there 'corporally', lest it be understood, not of the manner of his presence, but to the exclusion of the nature". Taylor is obviously conscious that this sort of argument may look like shadow-boxing so he insists that "this caution and exactness in the use of the word 'spiritual' are, therefore, carefully to be observed, lest the contention of both parties should seem trifling, and to be for nothing". Since both sides maintain, says Taylor, that Christ is present in the sacrament really but spiritually, "Where now is the difference? Here, by 'spiritually' they mean 'present after the manner of a spirit'; by 'spiritually' we mean 'present to our spirits only' . . . but their way . . . implies a contradiction; a body not after the manner of a body, a body like a spirit".'[16]

The interdependence of the various terms, to say nothing of the subtleties in their use, is daunting even to Taylor and he adds 'that which seems of hardest explication is the word "corporaliter"'. Even so, he presses on to seek a consensus of meaning though not with notable success: 'the expression may become warrantable, and consonant to our doctrine; and means no more than "really" and "without fiction", or "beyond a figure": like that of St. Paul "In Christ dwelleth the fulness of the Godhead bodily".' The Fathers used the word *sōma*, body, to mean what is real and has a proper being 'So that we, receiving Christ in the sacrament "corporally" or "bodily", understand, that we do it really, by the ministry of our bodies receiving him into our souls. And thus we affirm Christ's body to be present in the sacrament; not only in type or figure, but in blessing and real effect.' He suggests that the word is also acceptable 'when by it is only understood a corporal sign'.[17]

Finally in his examination of terms, Taylor looks at what from early times underlies the expressions of sacramental realism and the various theories of change in or transmutation of the elements, namely, the nature of Christ's Body present in the sacrament. *Was it the body born of Mary or not?* It is the question variously dealt with by Ratramn, Radbert and Berengar, subsequently re-appearing in the sixteenth century, and answered from one side by the doctrine of transubstantiation, the concept of a change of substance. Taylor's solution is both simple and subtle: 'It is much insisted upon, that it be inquired whether, when we say we believe Christ's body to be "really" in the sacrament, we mean "that body, that flesh, that was born of the Virgin Mary", that was crucified, dead, and buried?' He instances some of the Fathers, such as Jerome and Clement of Alexandria who reply in the negative but 'the meaning is easy; they intend that it is not eaten in a natural sense'. Thus their term a spiritual body is an affirmation of the manner not a distinguishing of one kind of body from another. The reality, says Taylor, is that the physical and the risen and glorified body of Christ is one, but differently apprehended. To the question he replies 'I know none else that he had, or hath: there is but one body of Christ natural and glorified; but he that says, that body is glorified, which was crucified, says it is the same body, but *not after the same manner: and so it is in the sacrament*; we eat and drink the body and blood of Christ, that was broken and poured forth; for there is no other body, no other blood of Christ; but though it is the same which we eat and drink, *yet it is in another manner*.'[18] Taylor sees his answer as entirely consistent with the Resurrection narratives and with the affirmation of a sacramental presence that is real and spiritual. He is very much aware of the persistent echoes of a debate which both here and in the *Dissuasive* he surveys in patristic, scholastic and later writings.

Having sorted out terms as a necessary preparatory exercise how does he view the state of the question and how will he tackle it? How well has he understood his opponents' position and how well has he clarified his own? The question now is 'not whether the symbols be changed into Christ's body and blood, or no? For it is granted on all sides: but whether this conversion be sacramental and figurative? Or whether it be natural and bodily? Nor is it, whether Christ be really taken, but whether he be taken in a spiritual, or in a natural manner? We say, the conversion is figurative, mysterious, and sacramental; they say it is proper, natural, and corporal. . . . This thing I will try by Scripture, by reason, by sense, and by tradition.'[19] This is what he thinks he must test and this will be the method of his book.

II

As in his other works, Taylor unequivocally asserts a change in the eucharistic elements and the change is 'mysterious and sacramental', a position from which he never deviates. It is when he comes to assess what the other side in the debate is saying that problems arise. For example, in the extract just cited he asserts that the Roman Catholic position is that the change or conversion is 'proper, natural and corporal', while 'we say, the conversion is figurative, mysterious, and sacramental'. Aquinas never said this nor did the Council of Trent from which Taylor has quoted approvingly. Everything seems to hinge on the words 'substantially' and 'natural'. Clearly, in the light of his own warning about the danger of terms being ambiguous until meanings are agreed, Taylor is suspicious of the content given to the word 'substance' particularly when taken in any association with the 'natural' body of Christ. It is clear from the text that the agile footwork of Bellarmine has helped in the confusion surrounding 'substantialiter' and 'sacramentaliter' and which is compounded by current thinking on corporeality and locality in respect of the natural body of Christ. Has Taylor grasped the difference which Aquinas (leaving others aside) makes between *materia*, the physicality of a thing, and *substantia*, what differentiates a thing from all other things and gives it its identity? Or is he on a different line of approach as he examines what he calls the natural and philosophical impossibilities of the doctrine of transubstantiation, quoting the words of Aquinas that 'there are more difficulties in this conversion of the sacrament, than in the whole creation'.[20] We shall find, I think, that while Taylor agrees that a substance is 'that which can subsist in itself without a subject of inherence', he affirms that a body is that 'which hath a finite quantity, and is determined to one place'. From this his argument then follows that for the body of Christ to be 'upon so many altars . . . is to make a body to be a spirit'.[21] His handling of this in respect of the word 'sacramentaliter', that 'Christ's body is sacramentally in more places than one, which is very true' is interesting and fits in with what I would regard as the strongly personalist view of the eucharistic presence in Taylor's thought: 'This is not a natural, real being in a place, *but a relation to a person'.*[22]

The second question, as we try to unravel this section of *The Real Presence and Spiritual*, is what weight Taylor gives to the affirmation of Trent that there is no contradiction between the heavenly session of Christ 'according to his natural mode of existence' and his presence 'sacramentally in his own substance in other places'.

Though the argument is close and convoluted, Taylor's over-all contention is clear, namely, a rejection of the substance and accidents explication which, even if one grants the validity of its own philosophical terms of reference, requires not one but two perpetually-repeated miracles in order to be true. Secondly, his affirmation that faith cannot be against reason is integral to his treatment. This, of course, was a favourite theme with the Cambridge Platonists such as his friend and correspondent, Henry More. Taylor's line of approach here is that it is no part of divine omnipotency to 'reconcile contradictions' and that nothing 'could be, and not be, at the same time'. Or, to put it another way, 'nothing is impossible but that which naturally repugns the understanding'. He then applies this to the miraculous conversion of substance: 'our adversaries do not deny, but that in the doctrine of transubstantiation, there are a great many impossibilities, which are such naturally and ordinarily; but by Divine power, they can be done; *but that they are done, they have no warrant*, but the plain literal sense of the words of "Hoc est corpus meum". Now this is so far from proving, that God does work *perpetual miracles to verify the sense of it*, that the working of miracles ought to prove that to be the sense of it . . . for concerning the words themselves there is no question, and therefore now no more need of miracles to confirm them; *concerning the meaning of them in the question*'. Such a 'daily extraordinary' is against reason and is not necessary to establish the reality of Christ's presence and he quotes Scotus, and not for the first time, that 'the truth of the eucharist may be saved without transubstantiation'.[23] Ockham is several times mentioned as is Gabriel Biel to the effect that neither in the Scripture nor in the Fathers is the doctrine of transubstantiation expressed.[24] In another place, Taylor groups them all with Durand and, very interestingly, observes 'and those men were for consubstantiation; that Christ's natural body was together with natural bread, which although I do not approve . . . it was their doctrine, that after the consecration bread still remains'.[25] Leaving aside for the moment the phrase 'natural body', the conclusion is an integral part of Taylor's doctrine of the eucharistic mystery. Elsewhere he refers to this again and more accurately, 'if Luther's and the ancient schoolmen's ways be true that Christ's body be present together with the bread —in that sense Christ's words might be true, though no transubstantiation; and this is the sense which is followed by the Greek church'. He adds Pico della Mirandola's phrase which he renders 'that it may be bread and Christ's body too'.[26] Twice he refers to the terms of Berengarius's recantation noting on one occasion that they were approved by Bellarmine with some very 'scholastic' glosses.[27]

It is remarkable how Taylor's assessment of the historical development of eucharistic doctrine tallies with modern evaluations such as, for example, that of Brilioth, made three centuries later. Distinguishing between what he calls the crude form of transubstantiation appearing in the Berengarius controversy and the sophisticated teaching of Thomas Aquinas which denied any physical transmutation of the elements, Brilioth notes the impanation theory as an attempt 'to find a middle way between symbolism and realism: the bread is not transubstantiated, its substance remains, but the *personal* presence of Christ is added to it as a heavenly substance'. There are resonances here for what we have seen hitherto of Taylor's own views although it might be fairer to describe these (as quoted earlier in this chapter) in terms of a dualist concept in which both bread and the body of Christ are simultaneously present as a result of the sacramental change in the symbols . . . the substance being changed by grace but remaining the same in nature. Brilioth characterises impanation as an attempt 'to preserve something like a spiritual interpretation; it was to be revived by Scotus and Ockham, and passed on by them to Luther', figures to whom Taylor pays particular attention. In the same way, the points made by Brilioth concerning transubstantiation are precisely those dealt with by Taylor, often at wearisome length, in the course of *The Real Presence*: 'Yet the definition (of 1215) left wide scope for variety of interpretation. For a long time it had been held that the body of Christ was present not only in every host but in every particle of every host. And when the later scholastics, Bonaventura, Thomas, or Scotus, seek to state this thought with precision, and to relate it to the doctrine of transubstantiation, by some hair-splitting analysis of the quantitative, dimensional, or substantial presence of the body of Christ, what is this but an unconscious effort to blunt the edge of a formula which had been forced on theology by the materialism of popular piety? What sort of corporeity belongs to a body which lacks size and dimensions, and is "substantially" present at every conceivable mathematical point in another body?'[28] These are exactly the threads which Taylor tries to unravel, commenting that in the doctrine of transubstantiation 'fantastical and mathematical bread . . . is represented on the table'.[29] He has correctly read the history of eucharistic doctrine so how then to account for his apparent ignoring of what Aquinas and the Tridentine decree were saying? The Carolines and their predecessors understood perfectly well what was at issue in the doctrine of transubstantiation and they rejected the doctrine on theological and philosophical grounds. Taylor states the general case fairly: 'There are three strange affirmatives of which the fathers never dreamed. 1. That the natural being of bread is wholly ceased . . . 2. That the accidents of bread and wine remain without a subject, their proper subject being annihilated, and they not subjected in the holy body. 3. That the body of Christ is brought into the place of the bread, which is not changed into it, but is succeeded by it. These are the constituent propositions of transubstantiation, without the proof of which, all the affirmations of conversion signify nothing to their purpose, or against ours'.[30]

It is when he comes to the real presence and what he believes the other side of the debate to be saying about it that the problem crystallises—'the word "real" is taken for "natural"'.[31] Throughout this part of his book Taylor continues to affirm that the Roman Catholic church teaches that there is a 'corporal presence', a 'carnal presence', of 'the natural body' of Christ in the consecrated elements. The only conclusion would appear to be that he is reading the theological situation in the light of what happened to the doctrine of transubstantiation since Aquinas's time. This colours his exposition and one has to remember that Roman Catholic polemic in the earlier part of the seventeenth century lent itself at times to a debased interpretation of the doctrine at the same time that Andrewes and Bellarmine were in debate on a higher level of understanding.[32] The fact is that by the early part of the sixteenth century the phrases 'natural body' and 'material body' of Christ were being used in a way that in effect negatived Aquinas's denial of a physical transmutation or of a local presence, Christ being present only *per modum substantiae*. The confusion was added to by the fact that Ridley himself used the phrase 'natural body'. The effects of this continued through Taylor's life-time and were debated as late as at the Savoy Conference of 1661, resulting in the rubric in the 1662 Prayer Book being altered to 'any Corporal Presence of Christ's natural Flesh and Blood' instead of the phrase 'real and essential presence'. Different explanations for the change have been advanced but Bishop Burnet (of Queen Anne's Bounty fame) claimed that 'the author of that change' was Bishop John Gauden who believed that the body of Christ 'was both in heaven and in the elements' and that the intention of the change in the rubric was to convey 'that a corporal presence signified such a presence as a body naturally has, which the assertors of Transubstantiation itself do not, and cannot pretend is in this case; where they say the body is not present corporally but spiritually, or as a spirit is present.'[33] Gauden, the probable author of *Eikon Basilike*, was a slightly older contemporary of Taylor and he either understood transubstantiation in its pure form better than Taylor did or he was less alive to the continuing effects of the trend which, in effect, was a resurrection of the eleventh century debate. That the trend was real and persistent from the mid-sixteenth century onwards has been amply documented by Darwell Stone and he summarises the reasons for it: 'It is to be noticed that in the formal statements of belief and in the articles of indictment the phrases "natural body" and "material body" of Christ occur in descriptions of the body which is present in the Euchar-ist . . . the phrases . . . were probably used, like the phrase "natural body" in some of the formularies of foreign Refor-mers, to emphasise that the body in the Eucharist is the same body as that which was born of the Virgin and suffered on the cross; the expression that the body of Christ is "broken" to emphasise that the consecrated Sacrament is the body. As in the Berengarian controversy, the influence of panic produced by denials of what was held dear may have had much to do with the choice of language which would not be congenial to the more careful advocates of Transubstantiation. That the phraseology "natural body" and "material body" begins after the widespread denials of Transubstantiation and of the Real Presence in the reign of Edward VI, and that the phrase declaring the body of Christ to be "broken" should have been revived at this particular time *after being laid aside for cen-turies*, tends to indicate that such an influence was at work. But this is not the whole explanation of the use of such language. That the body of Christ was said to be "broken" denotes much forgetfulness of the philosophic teaching by the aid of which the doctrine of Transubstantiation was developed in the thir-teenth century; and the application of the words "natural" and "material" to the body of our Lord in its present state shows that the change in the condition of His body at the resurrec-tion, which had been much emphasised in the middle ages, was but little remembered'.[34] This last point was one which, as we recall, Taylor took up when discussing the relation of Christ's body to the eucharistic action and elements.

Stone's assembly of evidence is impressive and helps one to understand, at least in part, the strength of the trend and why its continuance led Taylor (and others) to take the line they did, although we may consider nowadays that he was mis-directing his fire: '*Becoming* does not here imply material change. . . . It does not imply that Christ becomes present in the eucharist in the same manner that he was present in his earthly life. It does not imply that this *becoming* follows the physical laws of this world. What is here affirmed is a sacramental presence.'[35] ARCIC I is nearer to St. Thomas Aquinas than are Bishop Bonner's interrogatories or the Statute of the Six Articles, and also nearer to Taylor's own understanding of the eucharistic presence.

That the revived use of this terminology was not a vagary of some theologians is clear from instances of its use in official and semi-official doctrinal statements in the second half of the sixteenth century. (To get the time-scale in perspective, Cranmer and Ridley suffered death a half-century or so before Taylor was born). The Statute of the Six Articles, passed by parliament and with the royal assent, uses the phrase 'natural body'. It occurs also in the questions addressed by the bishops to John Frith, whose book had been answered by Sir Thomas More.[36] Later, in 1554, among the propositions ordered by Convocation to be submitted to Cranmer, Ridley and Latimer was the affirmation that 'the natural body of Christ which was conceived of the Virgin Mary is actually present under the species of bread and wine; also His natural blood'.[37] Similarly, the phrasing 'the true and natural body and blood ... the self-same in substance, though not in outward form and appearance, which was born of the Virgin Mary and suffered on the cross' occurs in all the interrogatories of Bishop Bonner.[38] Stone gives examples of the same teaching from the writings of Tunstall and Watson. What was happening was that the scholastic stress on the difference between how Christ was present in heaven and present in the eucharist, a difference to be emphasised also by the Council of Trent, was being forgotten. Stephen Gardiner, a more careful theologian, expounded the concept of the presence in a way which Taylor could have accepted: 'When we acknowledge by faith Christ's body present, although we say it is present truly, really, substantially, yet we say our senses be not privy to that presence, or the manner of it, but by instruction of faith; and therefore we say Christ's body to be not locally present nor by manner of quantity, but invisible, and in no sensible manner, but marvellously in a Sacrament and mystery truly, and in such a spiritual manner as we cannot define and determine'. He notes that 'the word "corporally" may have an ambiguity' and

that the truth of the presence exceeds 'our capacity to comprehend the manner "how"'. He denies that 'Catholic teaching'
understands the matter 'grossly, carnally', but then he adds the
qualification 'a spiritual manner of presence, and yet there is
present by God's power the very true *natural* body and blood
of Christ, whole God and Man, without leaving His place in
heaven'.[39] This was not precisely what Aquinas (or Trent)
taught and the confusion was further compounded on the
other side by the use of the phrase 'the identical and natural
body of Christ' in the Belgic Confession of 1561 which
ultimately became the received statement of the Dutch and
Belgian Reformers, being adopted at Dort in 1619.[40] Furthermore, Ridley himself, at his final examination before the
commissioners, had allowed a qualified use of the phrase: 'if
you take really for *vere*, for spiritually by grace and efficacy,
then it is true that the natural body and blood of Christ is in the
Sacrament *vere et realiter*, indeed and really; but if you take
these terms so grossly that you would include thereby a *natural
body having motion* to be contained under the forms of bread
and wine *vere et realiter*, then really is not the body and blood
of Christ in the Sacrament . . .'.[41] This would be nearer to the
position of Taylor but the word 'natural' would be a problem
for him, and indeed for Trent. Aquinas had denied that the
body was 'movably in this sacrament . . . because Christ is not
in this sacrament as in a place'. (III, Q. 76, art. 6). Nevertheless
Ridley uses the concept of a 'natural body' as he sets out a
doctrine of the change in the elements along the lines which
would later be taken by such as Andrewes, Forbes and Taylor
himself: 'Both you and I agree herein, that in the Sacrament is
the very true and natural body and blood of Christ, even that
which was born of the Virgin Mary, which ascended into
heaven, which sitteth on the right hand of God the Father . . .
only we differ *in modo*, in the way and manner of being. . . . I
confess Christ's natural body to be in the Sacrament indeed by
spirit and grace . . . and you make a grosser kind of being,
enclosing a natural, a lively, a moving body under the shape or
form of bread and wine. . . . In the Sacrament is a *certain
change* in that that bread, which was before common bread, is
now made a lively presentation of Christ's body, and not only
a figure, but effectually representeth His body . . . such a
sacramental mutation I grant to be in the bread and wine,

which truly is no small change, but such a change as no mortal man can make, but only the omnipotency of Christ's word . . . the bread ceaseth not to be bread'.[42]

During the boyhood of Jeremy Taylor's barber-father, Nathaniel, the martyrdoms on both sides would have been fresh in men's memory and that about which they contended did not disappear either. In 1653, the year before Taylor's *Real Presence* was published, we find John Bramhall making a perceptive analysis of what he sees as the original confusion: 'The first doubt about the Presence of Christ's Body in the Sacrament seems to have been moved not long before the year 900 in the days of Bertram and Paschasius; but the controversy was not well formed, nor this new article of Transubstantiation sufficiently concocted in the days of Berengarius, after 1050, *as appeareth by the gross mistaking and misstating of the question on both sides.* First Berengarius, if we may trust his adversaries, knew no mean between a naked figure or empty sign of Christ's Presence and a corporeal or local Presence, and afterwards fell into another extreme of *impanation.* On the other side, the Pope and the Council made no difference between Consubstantiation and Transubstantiation, they understood nothing of the spiritual or indivisible being of the Flesh and Blood of Christ in the Sacrament'. Discussing the difficulties in the development of the doctrine of transubstantiation, Bramhall put his finger on the point: 'Then grew up the question, what is the proper adequate Body which is contained under the species or accidents; whether a material Body, or a substantial Body, or a living Body, or an organical Body, or a human Body.'[43]

The theological after-effects of this ambiguity in the meaning of terms, reinforced by aspects of popular Roman Catholic piety, were felt well on into the late seventeenth century. C. W. Dugmore furnishes instances from the controversial literature on both sides in which 'corporal presence' and 'natural body' are at issue.[44] Nor, as he points out, was it just pamphleteers but men of theological standing who were involved in the debate. As late as 1736, John Constable, an English Jesuit, published a reply to John Johnson's *Plain Account* (1735). Dugmore's comment is something to be borne in mind by anyone attempting to create a clear picture of the theological situation of the period: 'This treatise . . . is a good example of that inability of the Papists to distinguish between the reality of the substance of Christ's body sacramentally present in the Eucharist (High Anglicanism), on the one hand, and the presence of the substance itself (Papism) on the other, which was only equalled by the inability of the Anglicans to distinguish between the presence in the sacrament of Christ's substantial body spiritually (Tridentine belief) and the presence of it carnally (popular superstition).[45] While the conclusion of the last sentence needs to be qualified by recalling that much of the confusion was *theological* rather than *popular* in its origin, the comment stands as a warning. It is against this background and in the light of his own explicit conviction that by substance '*they mean it otherwise*' that we have to read Taylor's criticism of transubstantiation as the true way of understanding and expressing the real presence of Christ in the blessed sacrament.

III

With the *Summa Theologica*, and in particular, Part III, QQ LXXV–LXXVII, we are far removed from any theory of 'carnal' or physical mutation in the eucharistic elements. Provided always that we are prepared to grant that the terms of this philosophy correspond to reality, Aquinas's theory is a remarkable restatement of the doctrine and an intellectual *tour de force*. There is a considerable and acknowledged debt to Aquinas on the part of the Anglican moral theologians, Taylor among them, in the field of law and human acts. In eucharistic theology however transubstantiation and the philosophy underlying it are rejected, as in Article XXVIII; 'The change of the substance of Bread and Wine' is here rejected on the grounds that it cannot be proved from Scripture; contradicts Scripture which speaks of the element after consecration as bread; overthrows the nature of a sacrament in that the reality of the outward sign is destroyed; gives rise to superstition and materialist concepts of the sacrament. Basically, this is Taylor's approach though, to his credit, he makes no use of tales of bleeding hosts in his argument . . . 'but these things are too bad'.[46] Bearing in mind the later developments in the use of the words 'natural body', we have to try to discern when he is writing specifically about Aquinas how Taylor comes to grips (if he does) with the subtlety of St. Thomas's exposition.

In the *Summa*, the presence of Christ's true body and blood in the sacrament are detectable 'by faith alone' (Q. 75, art. 1). Christ's body is not present 'as a body in a place ... but sacramentally' (ib.). Aquinas refuses the opinion that the elements and the body and blood of Christ are simultaneously present (Q. 75, art. 2). The substance of the elements is not 'annihilated but changed into the body of Christ' (Q. 75, art. 3). The conversion is supernatural (Q. 75, art. 4). 'The entire Christ is in this sacrament' by this conversion and 'from natural concomitance' (Q. 76, art. 1). The conversion has nothing to do with dimensions (for there is no physical change) but is a conversion of 'substance into substance'. Christ's body is therefore in the sacrament 'by way of substance and not by way of quantity'. (Q. 76, art. 1) The consequence is that 'Christ's body is not in this sacrament as in a place, but after the manner of substance' (Q. 75, art. 5). Christ's original body is in heaven (Q. 75, art. 2 and Q. 76, art. 6) and so Christ is not in the sacrament 'movably'. To say that Christ is under this sacrament is to 'express a kind of relationship to this sacrament' (Q. 76, art. 6). All the time, Aquinas is talking of a transformed substance and not of a localised presence: 'Christ's body is here after a fashion proper to this sacrament' (Q. 75, art. 1). The conversion of the substance 'is not like natural changes, but is entirely supernatural' (Q. 75, art. 4). The purpose of the eucharist is seen by Aquinas in terms of Christ bestowing life, just as Hooker and Taylor visualised it: 'The effect of this sacrament ought to be considered, first of all and principally, from what is contained in this sacrament, which is Christ; who ... also, by coming sacramentally to man, causes the life of grace' (Q. 79, art. 1).

It is noteworthy that this carefully articulated and refined exposition of the eucharistic presence rejects any concept of a physical mutation in the elements and avoids the ambiguities consequent on using such phrases as 'the natural body' to describe Christ present in the sacrament. Nevertheless—and Aquinas himself declares it— the transforming of substance requires, first, a miracle by which the substance of bread and wine are changed into the substance of Christ's body and blood, and, second, a miracle by which the accidents of bread and wine remain when 'the substance of the bread and wine . . . is changed into the body of Christ' (Q. 75, art. 3). Furthermore, in order to ensure that 'the entire Christ' himself is present in the sacrament the concept of concomitance has to be introduced, a third 'daily extraordinary' as Taylor puts it. Laud called the concept 'a fiction of Thomas of Aquin' and Taylor's partner, Nicholson, wrote of 'the chimera of Thomas' brain, concomitancy'.[47]

Whatever the impact and force of Taylor's argument in the theological situation of his own times, its effect for us is in part vitiated by his insistence that transubstantiation implies the presence in the eucharist of Christ's 'natural body'. That there were reasons for Taylor's suspicion of double-speak is undeniable in the light of the growth of this terminology from the middle of the preceding century onwards. What is less justifiable is his apparent inability to take Aquinas or Trent at face-value or to separate totally their careful statements from the theologically cruder expressions which the latter half of the sixteenth century had revived and imported into the debate. Thus, and typically, he insists that *corpus* must be 'taken in a spiritual sense; *sacramental and mysterious*; not a natural and presential'. This, he says, 'will not please the Romanists, unless "est", "is", signify properly without trope or metonymy, and "corpus" be "corpus naturale". Inevitably, the heavenly session is introduced, Aquinas and Trent seemingly being ignored, and Taylor then sets out what he conceives to be the truth of the eucharistic presence; 'that Christ's natural body is now in heaven definitively, and nowhere else; and that he is in the sacrament as he can be in a sacrament, in the hearts of faithful receivers, as he hath promised to be there; that is, in the sacrament *mystically*, *operatively*, as in a moral and divine instrument, in the hearts of believers by faith and blessing; this is the truth and the faith of which we are to give a reason and account to them that disagree'.[48]

Taylor's line is that if the doctrine of transubstantiation can be shown to affirm contradictions then it is impossible for it to be true. He presses his assertion that the doctrine is 'against the nature and essence of a body', accusing Bellarmine of prevaricating when he claims that since we do not fully understand 'the essence of things' a body might well be in many places at once.[49] The heart of what elsewhere Taylor calls 'the eternal

intricacies and inextricable riddles'[50] is to be found in the
conjunction of the two concepts of a body and of substance
with the presence of Christ's natural body in heaven. The
argument becomes very involved and I would suggest that the
point here is not so much whether Taylor fully appreciated the
Thomist notion of substance as that he is questioning whether
the concept has any real meaning when applied to 'body'. Can
the one concept carry the other in any way that is meaningful
for the understanding of Christ's presence in the eucharist?
'Here is the first contradiction', he writes 'the body of Christ is
in the sacrament. The same body is in heaven. In heaven it
cannot be broken naturally; in the sacrament, they say, it is
broken naturally and properly; therefore the same body is and
is not, it can and cannot be broken.' To this they answer that
'this is broken under the species of bread; not in itself. . . . For
if being broken under the species, it be meant that the species
be broken alone, and not the body of Christ—then they take
away in one hand, when they reach forth with the other'.
Taylor then asks 'how can species, that is, accidents, be broken
but when a substance is broken? for an accident properly . . .
hath of itself no solid and consistent, nor indeed any fluid
parts'.[51] Taylor is asking how this thought-form can be reconciled with perceived reality—'I demand, when we speak of a
body, what we mean by it?' Here, his difficulty with the
meaning and application of this terminology in respect of the
eucharistic presence surfaces. He defines substance as 'that
which can subsist in itself, without a subject of inherence'. An
accident is that the very essence of which is 'to be in another'.
By 'body' we mean that 'which hath a finite quantity, and is
determined to one place'. The consequence of this, says
Taylor, is 'to make the body of Christ to be in a thousand
places at once, and yet to be but one body—to be in heaven
and to be upon so many altars . . . is to make a body to be a
spirit, and to make finite to be infinite'.[52] This, in his view, is
not to affirm the real spiritual presence of Christ because there
is a difference between 'present after the manner of a spirit'
and 'present to our spirits'. This is the contradiction 'a body
not after the manner of a body, a body like a spirit, a body
without a body'. One recalls Bramhall's analysis of what kind
of body is under the species and Brilioth's question 'What sort
of corporeity?' When Bellarmine asserts that Christ's body is

present truly, substantially and really, but not corporally, Taylor believes that what this is saying is that 'a body should be substantially present, that is, with the nature of a body, naturally, and yet be not as a body but as a spirit'. The conclusion must be that the Body that 'was upon the cross' is truly present there 'but not after the manner of all or any body, but after the manner of being as an angel is in a place—that is their spiritually'.[53] Dugmore's comment on mutually unintelligible positions comes to mind. At this stage one gets the feeling of a series of near misses in the argument due to the confusion of thought surrounding the terms 'body' and 'substance' and to the consequent impossibility of melding the substance and accidents theory (which Taylor understood very well) with the concept of the natural body of Christ being present in the eucharist (which Taylor apparently believes to be the contemporary Roman Catholic position). It is like two billiard balls repeatedly coming into contact and then going off tangentially. This refusal to give full value to what Aquinas and Trent said about Christ's body being 'naturally' in heaven but 'substantially' in the eucharist persists throughout the *Real Presence*. Taylor even goes so far as to say that the doctrine of transubstantiation 'contradicts an article of faith', that of Christ's heavenly session.[54] Practically the whole of Section VII is given to showing that the natural body of Christ is not under the accidents of bread. Section IX refers to some rather grim medieval arguments concerning digestion—'not so fitted for edification', comments Taylor. The words 'mysterium fidei' applied to the chalice in the Roman canon predate the doctrine of transubstantiation and 'prevent the literal and natural understanding of the other words'.[55] One can only conclude that the effects of the sixteenth-century switch of emphasis and use of questionable phrases persisted longer and went deeper than may have been supposed. In defence of Taylor it must be admitted that he appears to have been faced with a good deal of imprecision. Commenting on the papal encyclical of 1965, *Mysterium Fidei*, which affirms that the bread and wine 'contain a new "reality" which we are right to call *ontological*', Alasdair Heron asks why transubstantiation is claimed as a suitable and accurate name for this. He concludes that 'there remains here a continuing unclarity in the official Roman Catholic position'. In his view it is not apparently every detail of Aquinas's doctrine which is being affirmed in this encyclical, and that precision is still lacking.[56]

How then does Taylor deal with Aquinas specifically? We shall find that his seeming inability to accept at face value the position set out in the *Summa* is not due solely to the lingering effects of the theological trend just mentioned. Rather does it seem to spring more from his conviction that the concept of 'substance' as applied to 'body' in expressing Christ's presence in the eucharist is in fact meaningless; 'to say that a body is there, not according to the nature of a body, but of a "substance" *is not sense*; for besides that, by this answer, it is a body without the nature of a body, it says that it is also there determined by a manner, and yet that manner is so far from determining it, that it makes it yet more undetermined and general than it was. For "substance" is the highest genus in that category: and "corpus" or "body" is under it, and made more special by a superadded difference'. The meaning of this according to Taylor is that a body becomes not a species but a genus, 'that is, more universal by being made more particular. For impossible it is for wise men *to make sense* of this business'. He is here specifically discussing the key-phrase of Aquinas that 'the body of Christ is not in the sacrament, in the manner of a body, but of a substance, and so is whole in the whole'. According to Aquinas himself, says Taylor, such substances are neither divisible nor multiplicable, so how then can Christ's body 'be multiplied, by the breaking of the wafer or bread, upon the account of the likeness of it to a substance that cannot be broken, or if it could, yet were not multiplicable?' One recalls his reference to 'mathematical bread' and, again, one has the curious sensation of neither side of the debate making real contact at this particular juncture. Following on from his original contention that all this amounts to making a body to be a spirit, he asserts that '*substantia* hath in it no relation to a place, till it be specificated to a body or a spirit'.[57]

Taylor then turns to the denial in the *Summa* of a local presence: 'Aquinas hath yet another device to make all whole —saying, that one body cannot be in divers places "localiter", but "sacramentaliter", not "locally", but "sacramentally" —But first I wish the words *were sense* and that I could tell the meaning of being in a place locally, and not locally. . . . But if by "sacramentally" in many places, is meant "figuratively", as before I explicated it, then I grant Aquinas's affirmative; Christ's body is in many places sacramentally, that is, it is represented upon all the holy tables or altars in the Christian church. But if by "sacramentally" he means "naturally and properly", then he contradicts himself; for that is it he must mean by "localiter", if he means anything at all'.

The feeling keeps recurring that the argument is going in a circle and the feeling is not dispelled by a contradictory quotation from Bellarmine to the effect that if a body cannot be in two places at once 'locally', then neither can it 'sacramentally'.[58] Yet one cannot say categorically that Taylor has totally failed to understand the *Summa*: Writing on the sentence 'Hoc est corpus meum' he notes 'Thomas Aquinas and his scholars affirm, that "this" demonstrates neither bread, nor the body, nor nothing, nor the accidents, but a substance indefinitely, which is under the accidents of bread'.[59] Rather is it the case that he finds this whole system defective and its categories incapable of conveying the truth of the eucharistic mystery in a way that is consonant with reason, with the patristic writings and with Scripture. The concept of 'substance' simply will not bear the weight of meaning and interpretation placed upon it, in Taylor's view. Like Durand (whom he quotes) he finds the word 'transformation' better than 'transubstantiation' for the simple reason that the latter is fundamentally *'unintelligible'*.[60] 'The sum is this; as substances cannot subsist without the manner of substances; no more can accidents, without the manner of accidents; quantities, after the manner of quantities; qualities, as qualities; for to separate that from either, by which we distinguish them from each other, is to separate that from them, by which we understand them to be themselves. And four may well cease to be four, and be reduced to unity . . .'[61]

Behind Taylor's criticism of the concept of substance lies the necessity he feels to hold together the reality both of bread and body ('It is bread and Christ's body too'). Hence, his search for a term such as 'transformation' which will cover this and one is reminded of William Temple in *Christus Veritas* (1924) who, discarding the concept of substance and replacing it with that of value, chose the term 'convaluation' to express the two realities in the eucharistic element.

IV

When Jeremy Taylor published the *Dissuasive* in 1664 his life had but three more years to run. Three years previously he had been consecrated Bishop of Down and Connor by Archbishop Bramhall who, at a Service in St. Patrick's Cathedral, Dublin, on 27 January 1661, had consecrated two archbishops and ten bishops, thus virtually reconstituting the gravely depleted Irish episcopate. Unusually, though perhaps not unexpectedly, Taylor preached the sermon in the course of which he plainly set out to the enormous congregation the doctrine of the apostolic succession.[62] His death at the age of fifty four prompts reflection on the vast extent of his literary output, the range of his learning and his capacity for writing with beauty and with force. It was an astonishing achievement accomplished over a period of less than three decades during a life-time which up to the end was fraught with difficulties, dangers, problems and controversy. It is ironic that his last book should have been extracted from him, a reluctant controversialist, but satisfying to remark the note of liberality which persisted in Part I. Discussing transubstantiation, Taylor writes: 'Now, from these premises we are not desirous to infer any odious consequences in reproof of the Roman Church, but we think it our duty to give our people caution and admonition; that they be not abused by the rhetorical words and high expressions, alleged out of the fathers, calling the sacrament, "The body or the flesh of Christ". *For we all believe it so and rejoice in it.* But the question is—After what manner it is so—whether after the manner of the flesh, or after the manner of spiritual grace and sacramental consequence? We, with the holy Scriptures and the primitive fathers, affirm the latter'.[63]

The book suffers at times from a tendency to treat the practice of the Roman Catholic Church in some places as if it were mandated by official authority. It was the supreme irony that in spite of the passage quoted above from Part I and his avowed disinclination and distaste for controversy, an attack on the book by his old opponent John Sergeant provoked the only piece of 'personal abuse he ever wrote, though it only runs to a page and a half'.[64] This was at the beginning of Part II of the *Dissuasive* which contains a reply to Sergeant's criticisms and which was Taylor's final piece of writing. His health had been failing and he died at Lisburn on 13th August 1667, having caught a fever from a patient whom he was visiting.

Considering the nature and purpose of the book, to serve the 'watchfulness over their flocks' of his fellow-bishops, it is hardly to be expected that he will bring much fresh material to the consideration of the nature of the real presence and of the doctrine of transubstantiation, 'a mere stranger to antiquity'. Taylor summarises the history of the development of the doctrine, noting, as he did in the larger book, that men like Scotus, Ockham, Biel and Fisher grant that nowhere in Scripture is it expressed. Numerous patristic writers are called on to show that in using terms such as 'figure', 'image', 'antitype', although 'they speak perfectly against transubstantiation, yet they do not deny the real and spiritual presence of Christ's body and blood; which we all believe as certainly, as that it is not transubstantiated or present in a *natural and carnal* manner'.[65] Thus, Taylor's reading of the theological situation had not changed during the ten years since the publication of the *Real Presence*: 'For Christ's body being in heaven, glorious, spiritual, and impassible, cannot be broken'. The positive implications of what took place at the Last Supper when Christ spoke the words of institution in his own person 'do force us to understand the sacrament in a sense not natural, but spiritual, that is, *truly sacramental*. And all this is besides the plain demonstrations of sense, which tells us, it is bread and it is wine naturally as much after as before consecration'.[66] Nor had his view changed in the last year of his life when Part II of the *Dissuasive*, replying to his Roman Catholic critics appeared (1667); 'that the bread is no more bread in the natural sense, and that it is naturally nothing, but the natural body of Christ; that the substance of one is passed into the substance of the other, this is not affirmed by the fathers'.[67] At this point Taylor introduces one piece of fresh material in the form of a discussion of Peter Lombard's *Sentences IV* concerning which one of his opponents had assailed him. He refuses to withdraw his remark that Lombard 'could not tell, whether there was a substantial change or no'. Exactly the same point had been made earlier by Andrewes in his *Responsio* (*Works* L.A.C.T. ed., VIII, 265): 'Not long before the Lateran Council the Master of the Sentences himself says "I am not able to define".' Lombard had suggested four ways[68] in which the change might be explained and Taylor's point is that 'if they who (in Peter Lombard's time) believed Christ's real presence were good Catholics, although they believed no transubstantiation or consubstantiation, that is, did not descend into consideration of the manner, why may they not be so now? . . . Why is the way to heaven now made the narrower than in Lombard's time? For the Church of England believes according to one of these opinions; and therefore is as good a catholic church as Rome was then, which had not determined the manner'.[69] He discusses the four theories of the change involving consubstantiation, transformation, annihilation, or 'the substance of bread being made the flesh of Christ but ceasing not to be what it was'. The point, however, maintains Taylor, is not which theory of the change Lombard favoured. The point is that at the time of the Master of the Sentences those who differed in their judgment had freedom to do so in respect of 'whether there was a substantial change or no'.[70]

Such is the nature of Taylor's understanding of what the other side in the debate was saying. That there are problems here and that both parties displayed strengths and weaknesses is evident. In view of the purpose of both books, this is the necessarily negative aspect of his eucharistic theology. The question of greater moment is the shape taken by his positive affirmations of faith. What does Taylor himself believe concerning the real presence of Christ in the blessed sacrament?

Out of all this learned wrangling emerges a sentence which may lead us forward to an evaluation of what in these two books, his last, Taylor himself thought: 'For we say as they said, Christ's body is truly there, and there is *a conversion of the elements into Christ's body*; for what before the consecration in all senses was bread, is, after consecration, in some sense, Christ's body'.[71]

Notes

1. *The Real Presence and Spiritual of Christ in the Blessed Sacrament, proved against the Doctrine of Transubstantiation* (1654), Section I (1), ib. Vol. IX, p. 421.

2. *A Dissuasive from Popery* (1664), Preface, ib. Vol. X, p. cxv.
3. *Real Presence*, Section I (1), ib. Vol. IX, p. 421.
4. Section I (2), ib. Vol. IX, p. 423.
5. ib.
6. ib.
7. Section I (13), ib. Vol. IX, p. 432.
8. Section I (3), ib. Vol. IX, p. 424.
9. Section I, (4) and (5), ib. Vol. IX, pp. 424–5.
10. *The Great Exemplar*, Discourse IX (2)–(4), ib. Vol. III, pp. 290–294. See Ch. III, pages
11. Section I (10), ib. Vol. IX, p. 430.
12. See the Black Rubric at the end of the Communion Office in the B.C.P. and the Council of Trent decree (Cap. I. *De reali praesentia*), Enchiridion Symbolorum, ed. Denzinger-Schönmetzer, 1636 (1965 ed. p. 385).
13. Section I (6), ib. Vol. IX, p. 425.
14. Section I (8), ib. Vol. IX, p. 427.
15. Epistle Dedicatory to the *Real Presence*, ib. Vol. IX, p. ccccxiv.
16. Section I (8), ib. Vol. IX, pp. 427–9.
17. Section I (9), ib. Vol. IX, pp. 429–430.
18. Section I (18), ib. Vol. IX, p. 431.
19. Section I (13), ib. Vol. IX, p. 432.
20. Section XI (8), ib. Vol. X, p. 26.
21. Section XI (13), ib. Vol. X, pp. 28–9.
22. Section XI (17), ib. Vol. X, p. 33.
23. Section XI (7), ib. Vol. X, pp. 23–26.
24. Section II (2)–(4), ib. Vol. IX, pp. 433–4.
25. Section V (10), ib. Vol. IX, p. 479.
26. Section XI (1), ib. Vol. X, pp. 16–17. The phrase is 'Paneitas possit suppositare corpus Domini'.
27. Section III (5), ib. Vol. IX, pp. 442–3.
28. Yngve Brilioth, *Eucharistic Faith and Practice Evangelical and Catholic* (1939 ed.), pp. 86–87.
29. Section XI (7), ib. Vol. X, p. 25.
30. Section XII (6), ib. Vol. X, p. 63.
31. Section I (8), ib. Vol. IX, p.
32. For instances, see C. W. Dugmore *Eucharistic Doctrine in England*, pp. 26–29.
33. Quoted in *A History of the Doctrine of the Holy Eucharist* (1909), Vol. II, pp. 319–320, by Darwell Stone.
34. *A History of the Doctrine of the Holy Eucharist* (1909), Vol. II, p. 168.
35. *Final Report* of ARCIC I, p. 21.
36. Stone, loc. cit., Vol. II, p. 118.
37. ib., p. 162.
38. ib., pp. 164–167.
39. ib., pp. 153–4.
40 ib., p. 57.
41. ib., pp. 192–3.

42. ib., pp. 192–3.
43. John Bramhall, *An Answer to M. de la Milletière*, *Works* (L.A.C.T. ed.) Vol. I, pp. 7–23.
44. C. W. Dugmore, *Eucharistic Doctrine in England* (1942), pp 123–131.
45. ib., pp. 162–3.
46. *Dissuasive*, ib. Vol. X, pp. 162–3.
47. Laud, *Works* (L.A.C.T. ed.), Vol. II, p. 338; William Nicholson *An Exposition of the Catechism of the Church of England* (1685), Parker ed. 1842, p. 180.
48. *Real Presence*, Section VI (1), ib. Vol. IX, p. 481.
49. ib. Section XI (10–11), ib. Vol. X, pp. 26–27.
50. Section IV (1), ib. Vol. IX, p. 457.
51. Section XI (12), ib. Vol. X, pp. 27–8.
52.
53. ib. Section I (8), ib. Vol. IX, pp. 427–9.
54. Section VI (14), ib. Vol. IX, p. 491.
55. Section VII (10), ib. Vol. IX, p. 499.
56. *Table and Tradition* 1983), pp. 166–7.
57. Section XI (20), ib. Vol. X, pp. 34–5.
58. Section XI (21), ib. Vol. X, pp. 35–6.
59. Section V (3), ib. Vol. IX, p. 468.
60. Section XI (37), ib. Vol. X, p. 55.
61. Section XI (34), ib. Vol. X, p. 51.
62. For an account of the occasion, see *History of the Church of Ireland* (1933), ed. Walter Alison Phillips, Vol. III, pp. 120–121.
63. *Dissuasive*, Part I, Ch. I, Section V, ib. Vol. X, p. 161.
64. Stranks, loc. cit., p. 268.
65. Part I, Ch. I, Section V, ib. Vol. X, pp. 155–159.
66. ib., p. 163.
67. Part II, Book II, Section III, ib. Vol. XI, p. 100.
68. ib. Vol. XI, pp. 96–100.
69. ib., p. 98.
70. ib., p. 97.
71. ib., p. 99.

VII   Present in Reality

'Sublimed to become the body of Christ' is how Jeremy Taylor describes the bread in the eucharist which, he says, following Justin Martyr, is no longer common bread but 'it is made sacramental and eucharistical'. That which before the consecration was known to be natural bread is now 'bread and something more'.[1] His friend William Nicholson said much the same: 'They remain in substance what they were; but in relation to Him are more'.[2] The thought echoes on into the twentieth century, and, perhaps surprisingly, we find it in Armitage Robinson: 'They are what they were, but they are more than they were before'. His phrase concerning the bread and wine being identified for a spiritual purpose with the Body and Blood of Christ would suggest a type of virtualism: 'They are the means by which Christ gives us participation in the virtue signified by His Body and His Blood'. Taylor occasionally speaks of something rather like this as when in the *Real Presence* he declares that 'This bread is the communication of Christ's body, that is, the exhibition and donation of it, not Christ's body formally, but *virtually and effectively*; it makes us communicate with Christ's body in all the effects and benefits'.[3] At this point he goes on to emphasise that what was common bread is now made sacramental and that there is a change. Interestingly, Armitage Robinson says the same thing ('The bread and wine do not remain *mere* bread and wine') and that the Articles which refute the change of substance 'do not deny all change'. The elements 'are raised to a higher power. They have become our spiritual food, so that we may eat the flesh of the Son of Man and drink his blood, as we read in the sixth chapter of St. John's Gospel. This is indeed a mysterious change'.[4] Virtualism is easy to caricature but not so easy to characterise. There must be an element stressing the received '*virtus*' in every serious doctrine of the eucharist and particularly if the theologian happens to be a moral/ascetic theologian as Taylor is. The whole concept of Life transmitted is involved and 'All other benefits of His Passion' has to do with the real effects of communicating. But if it is of the essence of virtualism that the communicant receives the virtue of Christ's body and blood, which are themselves absent, when he receives the bread and wine which continue to exist unchanged after the consecration, then it does not seem possible to slot Taylor into either a virtualist or a receptionist category as Stranks does, following Darwell Stone.[5] Taylor's frequent assertion of a change in the elements makes both unacceptable. 'The symbols become changed into the body and blood of Christ after a sacramental, that is, in a spiritual and real manner';[6] 'The change is . . . sacramental and spiritual; exhibiting what it signifies'.[7] 'In this mystery . . . the bread when it is consecrated and made sacramental, is the body of our Lord'; 'that body which is reigning in heaven, is exposed upon the table of blessing; and his body which was broken for us, is now broken again and yet remains impassible'.[8] The last two extracts are from the *Great Exemplar* and the others from the *Real Presence*, five years later. Stranks was on safer ground when he observed that 'Taylor is a hard man to classify'. It never does to forget that the controlling factor in Taylor's eucharistic theology is a constant blending of the concepts of mystery and sacramentality. His eucharistic theology is deep and subtle and at times almost elusive as he strives to unite in one richness of interpretation the many aspects of the eucharistic action and its implications for Christian living. The comparison with Armitage Robinson is instructive and not only in respect of the continuance of concepts but in respect of a difference of depth. Taylor may say something similar about the elements but his notion of the real spiritual presence is richer and more profound. Armitage Robinson even associates the eucharistic celebration with 'the Eternal Sacrifice which the Ascended Lord presents at the heavenly altar', but there the similarity ends. For him, the sacrifice being offered in the eucharist is ourselves and our oblations, 'an earthly sacrifice', while for Taylor this sacrifice of ourselves is subsumed under a tapestried concept of the eucharistic sacrifice in which the Church's *anamnesis* and the heavenly altar are indissolubly linked, the offering with the self-offering, Christ Himself being both priest and feast.

Similarly, the receptionist view that the presence is conditional upon the faith of the receiver and is to be sought only in the heart of the worthy communicant, cannot be attributed to Taylor. His frequent assertion that the symbols are changed after they have been consecrated rules this out completely —'the symbols are changed into Christ's body and blood'; 'it is bread and Christ's body too'; . . . 'that great mysteriousness which is the sacramental change'. The celebrant is the representative of the worshipping people of God and the mysterious and sacramental change is effected 'after the minister hath rightly prayed and blessed or consecrated the bread and wine'.[10] Taylor elsewhere notes that 'the Greek church universally taught, that the consecration was made by the prayers of the ministering man' but it is always the Church's offering, the priest being the officiant.[11] The change is not effected by the conjunction of certain syllables 'in any one instant, but is a *divine alteration* consequent to the whole ministry—that is, the solemn prayer and invocation'.[12] He takes the view, widely held today, that the change results from the entire eucharistic action: 'If these words, which are called the words of consecration, be exegetical, and enunciative of the change, that is made by prayers and other mystical words; it cannot possibly be inferred from these words, that there is any other change made than what refers to the whole mystery and action'. The consequence is, says Taylor, that the words 'take', 'eat', and 'this do' 'are as necessary to the sacrament as "Hoc est corpus"; and declare that it is Christ's body only in the use and administration; and therefore not *natural* but *spiritual*'. Commenting on the order of these sayings in the synoptic gospels, Oulton remarks 'A noteworthy point in this order is that the words "This is my body", "This is my blood", were spoken in connection with the "taking" and the "eating" or "drinking" of the elements; that is to say, they are not *isolated* sayings, but sayings within the context of a relationship of an intimate kind, and sayings related to persons. This fact is not easily expressed in liturgical action, but is more successfully expressed in some liturgies than in others'.[13] Taylor has of course much to say about faith's place and function in the eucharistic economy. It receives and apprehends the gift but it does not create the gift in any sense. It does create the worthy communicant.

In effect, Taylor's writings on Holy Communion repeatedly

remind us of one of those three points earlier adjudged to be fundamental, namely, Who rather than what is present and received? It is the whole Christ in His grace and power who is present and received, not entities however sacred, the 'substance' of his body and blood under the *species* of bread and wine. In order to exclude materialist concepts of the presence, it has to be insisted that not 'entities' but a Person is present in and through the sacramental elements. Aquinas achieves this by affirming a doctrine of concomitance and Taylor by asserting a real spiritual presence. In this he was following a line already established in Anglican eucharistic theology. The Hampton Court Conference of 1604 had produced, among other things, questions and answers on the sacraments to be included in the Church Catechism. These are generally attributed to John Overall, subsequently Bishop of Norwich, who died six years after the birth of Jeremy Taylor. Overall in his *Praelectiones* linked both concepts: 'In the Sacrament of the Eucharist or the Lord's Supper the body and blood of Christ, and therefore the *whole Christ*, are indeed *really present*, and are really received by us, and are really united to the sacramental signs, as signs which *not only signify but also convey*, so that in the right use of the Sacrament, and to those who receive worthily, when the bread is given and received, the body of Christ is given and received; and when the wine is given and received, the blood of Christ is given and received; and therefore *the whole Christ* is communicated in the Communion of the Sacrament. Yet this is not in a *carnal*, gross, earthly way by Transubstantiation or Consubstantiation, or any like fictions of human reason, but in a way *mystical, heavenly, and spiritual*, as is rightly laid down in our Articles'. This, and not virtualism or receptionism, is the tradition to which, more than any other, Taylor's theology belongs. Yet he is not a standard specimen of that tradition but brings to it at various points an originality both of understanding and exposition. The eucharist is 'the sum of the greatest mystery of our religion' says Taylor, both in *Holy Living* and *Clerus Domini*.[14] He seems to think that no doctrinal explication is capable of fully encapsulating its meaning and one of the advantages of the affirmation of the real and spiritual presence is that it leaves 'the article still in his deepest mystery'. Another advantage is that richness of meaning in the eucharist comes from many sources and 'our word of "spiritual presence" is particular in nothing, but that it excludes the corporal and natural manner'.[15] Taylor himself seems—if one may so put it—to skim the cream from both virtualism and receptionism and yet to combine such insights with the assertion of a presence which is real and given, the dynamic presence of Christ Himself bestowing a gift and imparting life. Unlike the view noted by Turner as current in Reformed circles concerning Christ being 'really but spiritually present' which, though reaching towards a personalist approach, has a vagueness about it particularly in respect of the relation between the presence and the elements, Taylor *has* a theology of the elements.[16] This is grounded firmly both in the conviction that the eucharist is primarily and unconditionally a mystery and in the concept of sacramental change—'the change is not natural and proper, but figurative, sacramental, and spiritual; exhibiting what it signifies';[17] 'the conversion is figurative, mysterious, and sacramental';[18] 'the body of our Lord is now conveyed to us by being the bread of the sacrament'.[19] No virtualist or receptionist could say that 'the bread, when it is consecrated and made sacramental, is the body of our Lord'[20] or 'it is bread and Christ's body too'; that is, it is 'bread naturally' and 'Christ's body spiritually'.[21] The elements are 'holy mysteries' and must be reverently 'honoured' and received as the first food of the day.[22] While standing within the position established by Lancelot Andrewes that the presence is real but the mode of it not to be defined as *de fide*, Taylor has something to say about the relation of the bread and wine to Christ's person. What he has to say reveals two aspects. The first, as we have been noting, appears to be a kind of dualist interpretation by which both the bread and wine and the body and blood of Christ are equally and at the same time present, a view having its origins very far back in eucharistic thinking. The second aspect is a distinctly personalist emphasis.

It is Christ Himself who is the gift in the eucharist: 'Christ is as really given to all that are truly disposed, as the symbols are; each as they can; *Christ as Christ can be given*; the bread and wine as they can'.[23] 'The sacrament is life'[24] and 'the holy mysteries' so dispense Christ's life that the faithful communicant can say 'to live is Christ' and 'Christ is our life' since he dwells in everyone 'that eats Christ's flesh and drinks his blood'.[25] The blessed sacrament 'is an union of mysteries' because 'after a mysterious and ineffable manner, we receive Christ, who is light and life, the fountain of grace'.[26] At the eucharist, the people, who with the priest 'are sacrificers too after their manner, . . . when they eat and drink the consecrated and blessed elements worthily, they receive Christ within them'.[27] Taylor's writings are full of such expressions: 'Wonder that the Son of God should become food to the souls of his servants'.[28] Communicants receive 'the flesh and blood of the incarnate Jesus'[29] and taking 'the holy elements . . . you have taken Christ into you after a manner which you do not understand'.[30] They are not the rhetoric of devotion but the expression of his doctrine of the real and spiritual presence of Christ. If we link this doctrine, as Taylor does with his insistence on the heavenly altar theme, we understand that it is the whole Christ, God and man, crucified, risen and ascended, who through the Spirit gives Himself to the faithful communicant: after the 'sacramental and mysterious conversion . . . we affirm that Christ is really taken by faith, by the Spirit, to all real effects of his passion'.[31] He develops this by returning to the parallelism between Christ representing in heaven his death 'in the way of intercession' and the Church's ministerial representation: 'so it is in the sacrament after our manner, "This is my body given for you", that is, "This is the sacrament of my death, in which my body is given for you".' The words 'by which the thing is sacramental' says Taylor 'signify something beyond those words'. They carry the reality of Christ's redeeming work on our behalf: 'It is but an imperfect conception of the mystery to say, it is the sacrament of Christ's body only, or his blood; but it is . . . a sacrament of the death of his body; and to us a participation or an exhibition of it, as it became beneficial to our sacrifice'.[32] *The reality of the Sacrifice is inextricably bound up with the reality of the Presence, as we can see from Taylor's prayers and his Collection of Offices.* His whole approach to the concepts of 'presence' and 'sacrifice' takes the same line as does the explanatory note to the ARCIC resolution passed by the Lambeth Conference of 1988 which comments that 'Both are areas of "mystery" which ultimately defy definition'. Taylor would have felt that his successors were speaking his language. What he is talking about is the heavenly presence of Christ, crucified and

ascended, mediated by the Spirit through the symbols which
He has taken into union with Himself.

The symbols are changed in a manner that is real and
spiritual and the relation of Christ to the sacramental elements
is, as he has stressed elsewhere, 'a relation to a Person'.[33] This
is as far as Taylor can go, or rather, as far as he thinks
Scripture, the experience of the Church, and reason will allow
him to go, in defining how Christ's presence can be related to
the outward elements in the eucharistic action. Some necessary
glosses he will make, however, on the terms 'real' and 'spiritual'. There are two ways of mistaking the meaning, he writes
in the *Great Exemplar*: 'Some so observe the literal sense of the
words that they understand them also in a natural: some so
alter them, by metaphors and preternatural significations, that
they will not understand them at all in a proper'. If any proof
were needed of Taylor's belief in the real, spiritual presence of
Christ, the reality of the person of Christ in his sacramental
body and blood encountered in faith by the communicant, the
passage which follows furnishes it. Literalism and pictorialism
are both inadequate because we are confronted with what is
essentially 'mystery'. Our senses tell us it is bread but Christ
also said 'This is my body'. If faith can create 'an assent as
strong as its object is infallible, or can be as certain of its
conclusion, as sense is as certain in its apprehensions, *we must,
at no hand, doubt but that it is Christ's body*'. So long as we no
more doubt our faith than we do our senses 'then our faith is
not reprovable'. Taylor grants that 'it is hard to do so much
violence to our sense, as not to think it bread' but equally 'it is
more unsafe to do so much violence to our faith, as not to
believe it to be Christ's body'. There is a distant echo of his
discussion of faith and reason when he says that 'to believe
both what we hear and what we see' can in no way disavow the
interest of religion or the 'sacredness of the mystery'. He
reaffirms the position which he consistently holds that it is
'bread, and yet verily Christ's body'. Certainly, this implies the
action of 'God's omnipotence' and those who believe the
change of substance and cannot 'reconcile its being bread with
the verity of being Christ's body' are reminded that the
doctrine of transubstantiation has far more difficulties, contradicts reason and 'the testimony of sense', and requires more
miracles. To affirm that the element is bread and Christ's body

too means that 'we shall no more be at war with reason, nor so much with sense, and not at all with faith', a candid assessment. He then turns to those 'of contradictory persuasion, who, to avoid the natural sense, affirm it only to be figurative'. Their purpose, says Taylor, is 'only to make this sacrament to be Christ's body in the sense of faith, and not of philosophy'. Presumably, these would be those now thought of as pure virtualists and pure receptionists. He reminds them of the meaning of 'real' and 'spiritual' and that the one is not a synonym for 'natural' or the other for 'figurative' and once again the key concept is mystery: 'its being really present does not hinder but that *all that reality may be spiritual*; and if it be Christ's body, so it be not affirmed such in a natural sense or manner, it is still only the object of faith and spirit; and if it be affirmed only to be spiritual, there is then no danger to faith in admitting the words of Christ's institution, "This is my body". I suppose it to be a mistake, to think whatsoever is real must be natural; and it is no less to think spiritual to be only figurative: *that is too much, and this is too little*. Philosophy and faith may well be reconciled; and whatsoever objection can invade this union may be cured by modesty. And if we profess we understand not the manner of this mystery, *we say no more but that it is a mystery*'.

The institution of the eucharist shows the power, the wisdom and the 'unspeakable charity of Christ in making the symbols to be the instruments of conveying himself to the spirit of the receiver . . . and makes the spirit to be united to his body, *by a participation of the Divine nature*. In the sacrament, that body which is reigning in heaven, is exposed upon the table of blessing; and his body, which was broken for us, is now broken again, and yet remains impassible. Every consecrated portion of bread and wine *does exhibit Christ entirely* to the faithful receiver; and yet Christ remains one, while he is wholly ministered in ten thousand portions'.[34] In simple terms, it is the whole Christ who is present dynamically and in reality and who is apprehended through faith.

In *The Real Presence*, as we have already remarked, Taylor repeats the same interpretation of 'real' and 'spiritual', affirming it to be the Church's official position in the Catechism and the Prayer Book: 'verily and indeed' is 'reipsa', that is, 'really enough'; that is 'our sense of the real presence'. He adds 'now that the spiritual is also a real presence, and that they are hugely consistent, is easily credible to them, that believe that the gifts of the Holy Ghost are real graces, and a spirit a proper substance'.[35]

It is against the background of these affirmations that the eucharistic action is mystery and that the element is 'bread and Christ's body too' that we have to understand Taylor's concept of the real spiritual presence. Nor can we have failed to note that its full implications are not evident until we take account of the obvious, that Holy Communion cannot ultimately be comprehended apart from Holy Spirit: 'Whatsoever the Spirit can convey to the body of the Church, we may expect from this sacrament; for as the Spirit is the instrument of life and action, so the blood of Christ is the conveyance of his Spirit'. We glimpse here a thought which Taylor will further develop in *The Worthy Communicant*, but here he affirms that if we gather together all the Scriptural references to 'the effects of Christ communicated in the blessed sacrament' they cannot adequately describe 'this spiritual secret, and excellent effects of the Spirit'.[36] In the *Real Presence* when he declares that 'by "spiritually" we mean "present to our spirits only"'' Taylor is not suggesting that our spiritual attitude creates the presence. He is contrasting this with what he believes Bellarmine to be saying—'present after the manner of a spirit'—and insisting that Christ's presence is discernible not to sense but to 'faith or spiritual susception'. He is present 'as the Spirit of God is present in the hearts of all the faithful'. This is the manner of our receiving but it is Christ really present who is received: 'we eat and drink the body and blood of Christ, that was broken and poured forth; for there is no other body, no other blood, of Christ: but though it is the same which we eat and drink, yet it is in another manner'.[37] Taylor's views can sometimes appear difficult to pin down if we lose sight of his constants, namely, mystery and sacramentality. The central elements in his teaching can be grasped through a succession of phrases gathered from a single paragraph:

(1) 'Christ's natural body is now in heaven definitively, and nowhere else'.
(2) ' "corpus" is taken in a spiritual sense; sacramental and mysterious'.

(3) Christ 'is in the sacrament as he can be in a sacrament'.
(4) Christ 'is in the hearts of faithful receivers, as he hath promised to be there'.
(5) Accordingly, Christ is 'in the sacrament mystically, operatively, as in a moral and divine instrument, in the hearts of receivers by faith and blessing'.[38]
(6) The 'change' or 'conversion' in the elements is 'figurative, mysterious and sacramental'; it is 'sacramental and spiritual; exhibiting what it signifies'.[39]
(7) It 'is bread and verily Christ's body'.

Link these with the rich and profound concept of the eucharistic sacrifice which runs through all his writings on the eucharist and one has an outline of Taylor's understanding of the sacrament. It is an understanding at once both simple and complex. We have been attempting to construct from this *ébauche* a fuller and more detailed picture. In the process the deep roots of his eucharistic theology as well as his individuality of understanding and exposition are gradually revealed. Yet there is more still as we shall see from his handling of the Johannine material, the Alexandrian emphasis on the flesh as Christ's word and the blood as His Spirit, and on the relation of sacramental to non-sacramental in the economy of grace.

II

At this stage, however, as previously indicated, there is said to be a problem or at any rate a question in respect of the eucharistic theology of Jeremy Taylor: Has there been a development in or a modification of his views, and if so, is this due, as Dugmore believes, to the influence of his partner William Nicholson?[40] Certainly their association in partnership at Newton Hall over a period of years was a close one. The fact that his partner's *Exposition of the Catechism* was published in 1655, the year after Taylor's *Real Presence* and five years after *Holy Living*, may well raise the question in the form 'Who influenced whom?' This would not be to deny the very likely probability that Taylor and Nicholson must often in their situation have discussed the subject thus influencing one another, nor is it to pre-empt the question concerning

Taylor's High Church views yielding with time to a form of Central Churchmanship.

William Nicholson was the dispossessed Archdeacon of Brecon when the two men met and it was his suggestion that they should set up their school in Wales. It was Taylor who brought in an Oxford undergraduate friend, William Wyatt, to act as their assistant. Like Taylor, Nicholson's living had been sequestrated in 1643 and he speaks of himself as 'being ejected and silenced'. The book is dedicated to his parishioners of Llandeilo Vawr, Carmarthenshire, and in the dedicatory epistle he speaks of the Church being so persecuted that 'the precious Body and Blood of our Lord and Saviour Jesus Christ, exhibited in the Sacrament, hath been prohibited to be administered in public assemblies'.[41]

The full title of his book is *A Plain but Full Exposition of the Catechism of the Church of England* and it profits in clarity by reason of the format imposed on it by its subject. For Nicholson, the eucharist is always 'these holy mysteries'.[42] At its centre is the memorial, the remembrance of Christ's sacrifice depicted with that vivid concentration on the Sacred Humanity which is now His glorified humanity, as it is in *The Great Exemplar* and *Holy Living*: 'For here we have Christ crucified before our eyes, represented lively before us as upon the cross: while as the signs of His blessed Body and Blood being sundered the one of them from the other, the one is broken and the other poured out; remembering us how His sacred body was broken with the crown of thorns, the scourges, the nails, the spear; how out of his wounded hands, feet, head, and side, there issued a stream of blood. This he intended by his institution that we should first remember. The other is (the benefits which we receive thereby).'[43] Throughout the *Exposition* he keeps returning to the sacrificial aspect of the eucharist. It was instituted 'to represent, exhibit, and seal the passion of Christ and the benefits thereof to a worthy communicant'.[44] The true causes of eternal life are Christ's flesh and blood 'which yet they are not by the bare force of their own substance, but *through the dignity and worth of His person*, which offered them up by way of sacrifice, for the life of the whole world; of which sacrifice we have in this Sacrament a lively representation and memorial'.[45] The gift of salvation through the Cross is a 'strange, unexpected, unheard of mercy, (which) it pleased him to represent, exhibit, and secure to us by His institution of this Sacrament; and to command that it be continued in His church *in perpetuam rei memoriam* . . . to all which, faith alone can give life and an interest'.[46] Nicholson does not carry the concept of sacramental representation through to the intercessory representation by Christ of His one sacrifice at the heavenly altar, but it has to be borne in mind that his exposition is held to the contents of the Catechism.

Proportionately, he has much more to say on the theme of the Presence than on that of Sacrifice, central though he regards the latter to the understanding of the meaning of the Eucharist, and it is under the former heading that we must seek a comparison with Taylor's teaching.

With a combination of realism and the effectual sign, Nicholson affirms the reception of 'the whole Christ' by the faithful communicant: 'For this we believe too, and in confidence thereof approach and take this Body and this Blood, being assured that by these symbols *we receive all Christ* . . . unbelievers may receive *panem Domini*, the bread of the Lord: believers only *panem Dominum*, that bread which is the Lord'.[47] This is not as Taylor would say, by way of 'metaphor or preternatural signification'. It is mystery but it is also real: 'for what is here represented, is verily and indeed taken and received. It is on all hands confessed that in this Sacrament there is a true and real participation of Christ, who thereby imparts Himself, *even His whole entire Person*, as a mystical head. . . . This though mystically, yet it is truly; though invisibly, yet it is really done'.[48]

He quickly gets to the root of the problem—the nature of the Presence and the relation of Christ's Body and Blood to the elements. As to the presence, 'such a real presence must be admitted, or else the communicant *receives nothing*'.[49] With regard to the elements 'That which is more material to know, is the *change* of these, which is *wholly sacramental, not in substance but in use*. For they remain bread and wine still, such as before in nature: but consecrate and set apart to represent our Saviour's passion, and exhibit and seal to a worthy receiver the benefits of that passion'.[50] Here Nicholson seems to be saying that the sacramental change in the elements consists solely in the sacramental use, a view associated with

early Central Churchmen, and this, in Dugmore's view, is a
point at which Taylor was influenced by his partner. We can
certainly find in the *Real Presence* and *Holy Living* an emphasis on sacramental use being involved in the sacramental
change, but there is more to it for Taylor than Nicholson's
blunt statement that the change is simply in the use. 'The great
mysteriousness of the change' cannot so easily be understood:
'the change is not natural and proper, but figurative, sacramental, and spiritual; exhibiting what it signifies'; 'the
conversion is figurative, mysterious, and sacramental'.[51]
Moreover, when speaking of the change of use specifically,
Taylor always associates with this 'a change of condition'.
Thus in the *Real Presence* he writes of the patristic terminology
'These and the like sayings are no more than the words of
Christ, "This is my body"; and are only true in the same sense,
of which I have all this while been giving an account: that is, by
a change of condition, of sanctification, and usage'.[52] Similarly, arguing that the words of Christ cannot be true in a
natural sense he notes 'But if the bread does not remain bread,
but be changed by blessing into our Lord's body; this also is
impossible to be in any sense true, but by affirming the change
to be only in use, virtue, and condition, with which change the
natural being of bread may remain'.[53] We recall also the
description of the consecrated elements in *Holy Living* (1650)
—'not . . . common bread and wine, but *holy in their use*, holy
in their signification, *holy in their change*, and holy in their
effect'.[54] Cosin, whose early associations could be described as
Laudian, maintained a true, real and spiritual presence and
made the same distinction as Taylor did; 'the bread is wholly
changed in condition, use and office; that is, of ordinary and
common, it becomes our mystical and sacramental food'.
Despite many similarities in their views (given the very different formats and objectives of their books), there is a subtle
difference between Taylor and Nicholson in their respective
theology of the elements, and of the relation of the elements to
the person of Christ. Both are affirming the real, spiritual
presence, but while Nicholson asserts 'Christ to be present in
the Eucharist . . . sacramentally or relatively in the elements',
Taylor claims that '*the symbols become changed* into the body
and blood of Christ, after a sacramental, that is, in a spiritual,
real manner'.[55] In other words, Taylor is saying that there is a

mysterious change in the elements or in their 'condition', apart from the change of sacramental usage. Is he nearer here to Laud's 'mysterious and, indeed, ineffable manner' (a phrase he himself uses in the *Great Exemplar*) and to Andrewes, 'we allow that the elements are changed', but with his added emphasis on the change involved in use? As well as this emphasis there are of course other developments in his thought such as the analysis of the meaning of the reality of the presence, and the evolving of a theology of the elements. There is also the appearance of what we have termed a dualist interpretation—'It is bread and Christ's body too'. Yet there is a sense in which he has not moved from the position taken in his early booklet where the Eucharist is 'mystery' and 'Christ is there really present in the Sacrament, there is the body and blood of Christ which are "verely, and indeed" taken and received by the faithful, saith our Church in her Catechisme'.[56] Taylor returns to the Catechism wording in the *Real Presence* but now it is an examination in depth of meanings.

Nicholson however is also insisting on the real, spiritual presence, and with a clarity and economy of exposition he explains the catechism questions and answers attributed to Overall in a manner which accords with the spirit and the letter of Overall's *Praelectiones*. He leads in by noting the great disputes as to 'how Christ is in the sacrament' and he comments favourably on Hooker's judgment in the matter: 'Shall I wish' wrote Hooker 'that men would give themselves more to meditate with silence what we have by the sacrament, and less to dispute of the manner How?' He had also written 'this bread hath in it more than the substance which our eyes behold . . . what these elements are in themselves it skilleth not, it is enough that to me which take them they are the body of Christ'.[57] This sounds more like Taylor's view of the elements than Nicholson's, but Nicholson desires 'to bring my pitcher, and try if cool water' may not take the heat out of the disputes and 'so reconcile exasperated brethren'. In a concise paragraph he summarises the various interpretations: 'Some conceive, that for His presence there, it is necessary that Christ be incorporated with the sacramental elements. Others, that the bread and wine are changed into His very body. Others, who deny the substantial change, yet acknowledge His presence, express their meaning in different terms, thus: corporally and substantially, say some; sacramentally, say others; typically and figuratively, say a third; spiritually, say a fourth; really, say the last'.[58] He then embarks on an exercise in logic designed to demonstrate in respect of 'the *relatum*, that respect Christ's body hath to the bread: and the *correlatum*, that respect that the bread hath again to Christ's body', that all the various terms used by theologians 'in the explication of this mystery may receive a candid interpretation, except that of Rome'.[59] Here we meet again this suspect interpretation of transubstantiation in which its cruder form is equated with official teaching. Nicholson, like Taylor and others before them, excludes transubstantiation since the doctrine 'clearly takes away the relation, and the essence of a Sacrament. For upon this *corporal* change, what becomes of the sign?'[60]

With an admirable and clinical precision so unlike the more lavish style of his famous partner, he then sets out in easily assimilated terms his understanding of the real spiritual presence: 'Christ is said to be present four manner of ways.

1. Divinely, as God, and so He is present in all places . . .
2. Spiritually, and so He is present in the hearts of true believers . . .
3. Sacramentally, and so He is present in the Sacrament . . .
4. Corporally; so present in Judea in the days of His flesh.

And as the word presence, so the word really, is diversely taken; for sometimes,

1. It is opposed to that which is feigned, and is but imaginary, and imports as much as truly.
2. It is opposed to that which is merely figurative, and barely representative, and imports as much as effectually.
3. It is opposed to that which is spiritual, and imports as much as corporally or bodily'.[61]

Taylor in the *Real Presence* devoted much space to an analysis of terms but Nicholson's almost mathematical condensing of material enables him to build the terms into an easily understood definition of the real spiritual presence as he sees it: 'We then believe Christ to be present in the Eucharist divinely after a special manner, spiritually in the heart of the communicants, sacramentally or relatively in the elements. And this presence of His is real, in the two former acceptions of real; but not in the last, for He is truly and effectually there present though not corporally, bodily, casually, locally'.[62] Nicholson's use, more than once, of the adjective 'effectual' recalls the language of Article XXV concerning sacraments, that they are 'efficacia signa gratiae', conveying the blessing symbolized. They are the instrumental causes 'per quae invisibiliter ipse in nos operatur' and this is brought out by Nicholson in his description of how 'by these symbols we receive all Christ'.[63] Thus he concludes 'If it be demanded how so small a piece of bread, or a spoonful of wine can produce this effect? the answer is easy, that it proceeds not from the elements, but from the will and power of Christ, who ordained these to be means and instruments for that end. *They remain in substance what they were; but in relation to Him are more.* It is spiritual bread and spiritual wine, so called, not so much because spiritually received, but because being so received, it causes us to receive the Spirit . . .'[64] The closeness to aspects of Taylor's teaching is observable and the last sentence is similar in content to passages in the *Great Exemplar* and the *Real Presence*.[65] Nevertheless, what Nicholson says about the elements is not *precisely* what Taylor says. For Taylor there is a change in condition as well as in use and the context of the change is *the mystery which is the eucharistic action in its entirety*.[66] Interestingly, Nicholson refers to the Mozarabic liturgy and to the liturgies of St. James and St. Basil. Taylor's knowledge of liturgies can be seen as far back as *On the Reverence due to the Altar* in which he refers among others to the Mozarabic rite and to the liturgy of St. John Chrysostom. Elsewhere there are further instances and we have noted his borrowings from the liturgy of St. James and others in his *Collection of Offices*. Possibly, here is a point at which Nicholson came under the influence of his friend.

In view of the publication dates of the *Real Presence* and the *Exposition* and in the light of the long and close association of both men with their shared experience in a persecuted Church and their shared and active defence of the Church's theological position, it is likely to remain an open question as to who influenced whom. Probably, the truth is that each had a lot to give to the other and they must obviously have been aware of one another's developing work. The balance is likely to be tilted or inclined by how 'Laudian' we think the young Taylor was and how much his eucharistic theology altered as it developed. The eucharistic material in his first publication is slight and therefore inadequate for a full evaluation but it certainly fits into the Laudian mould of the real presence and mystery. He followed the same line in *The Great Exemplar*, rejecting both the 'material' and the figurative interpretations. A good case can be made out for suggesting that throughout his writings he held on to the concepts of mystery and sacramentality, *but thought them through*. Apart from possible outside influences on his thinking, one can never discount Taylor's originality or the factor of his own personal developing in his understanding of the eucharistic presence within his evolving theology. Similarly, it would be foolish to discount the possible influence of William Nicholson with his clear-eyed approach to the question counterbalancing the more diffuse but deeper line of thought followed by Jeremy Taylor with his active, erudite and enquiring spirit. One ought also to note that while Taylor was Laudian more by his associations than by his written eucharistic theology—the Laudian strain being more marked in his two books on the ministry—he had other associations too. These were with the Oxford moderates, 'rational theologians' such as Chillingworth, Hales and More. Their influence can be seen in Taylor's *Liberty of Prophesying* (1647) and in his attitude to the faith and reason debate as well as in the controversy about original sin. Just as Taylor, student of the Fathers and the liturgies, responded to the appeal of Catholicity, continuity and historicity, so what Rust called 'the largeness of his spirit' found an echo in the openness and the enquiring quality of the Oxford theologians. Half-Laudian and half-'liberal', there remains the irreducible element of personality, and Taylor obstinately resists neat classification or labelling. This is true of his eucharistic theology, particularly in the theme of Sacrifice, as it is true of much in his general theological position. That his friend Nicholson influenced him in some respects is possible but in the last analysis Taylor speaks with his own voice, believing, as he states, that he too is faithfully interpreting the eucharistic teaching of his Church. Their views have much in common and it is no facile criticism of Nicholson to say that Taylor goes deeper since the format and purpose of their respective books largely dictate the manner and extent of their treatment of the real spiritual presence. That there is development in his eucharistic theology seems clear but it is also a natural and inevitable development as he probes further into meanings. Looking back over the range of his work, one wonders if Dugmore is putting quite the right question when he asks whether Taylor's views changed from High to Central in respect of the eucharist. Rather, it could be that as Taylor thought and wrote, he built on his basic themes of mystery and sacramentality, deepening and widening them as he took account of aspects of the eucharistic action which revealed themselves as he worked and learned from other schools of thought and other writers. This process would surely include Nicholson's hitherto unpublished views but would also account for the subtle difference with regard to the use and the condition of the elements and for the fact that later generations have found him elusive and even self-contradictory in his statements: 'It may be doubted whether in his own mind Taylor ever committed himself to any one school of thought about the Eucharist'.[67] This is one of the impressions which would appear to be emerging from this study of the eucharistic theology of Jeremy Taylor.

III

In spite of this characteristic of individuality in the expression of some of his views, Taylor not only affirmed that his teaching was loyally Anglican but he also held it to be consonant with the teaching of the primitive Church. The Fathers use eucharistic language that is often rhetorical and terminology that is symbolical and figurative or realist by turns and even occasionally both together. Not surprisingly all sides down to and through the seventeenth century appealed to them in support of their own positions. The varied nature of the material tended to make the exercise difficult. Lampe comments that 'If the Early Fathers are treated as an ammunition dump for later eucharistic controversies . . . the conclusion must be either that "all must have prizes" or that the writers were extraordinarily vague and even self-contradictory. In fact, what might appear to be vagueness is an indication of a richness of understanding'.[68]

The appeal to antiquity has been and remains an essential element in classical Anglican theology as well as being firmly

embedded in Anglican formularies both official and semi-
official. However, in the seventeenth century the matter was
far from clear-cut as a new factor had entered in which
demonstrated the difficulties involved in treating the Fathers as
an ammunition dump. Taylor found himself confronting some
of these difficulties. Right from the beginning of his writing
career he draws on the Fathers to support the thesis of *On the
Reverence due to the Altar* but with the appearance of two of
his major works, separated by five years, the problem surfaced.
Of the Sacred Order and Offices of Episcopacy was published
in 1642 and *A Discourse of the Liberty of Prophesying* five
years later. Both works were reissued in one volume with *An
Apology for Authorized and Set Forms of Liturgie* (1649) in
the year 1657. Taylor seems to have had something of a guilty
conscience or at least a feeling of uneasiness about the different
weight given to the Fathers in the two books because, in a
second dedication (to his friend Sir Christopher Hatton) to
Episcopacy Asserted, he goes to some lengths to explain his
position. In the *Liberty of Prophesying* he was advancing the
claim for toleration, maintaining that there was no absolute
and infallible guide to truth, neither Scripture, Councils,
Fathers nor Pope, and that a man's reason 'guided . . . by
divine revelation' was surest. He would then find support and
corroborative evidence in the Fathers though these were not an
absolute authority in themselves. As he points out in the
second dedicatory epistle, his purpose was to plead liberty
from the Presbyterians for the persecuted Church of England
—'I intended to make a defensative for my brethren and
myself'.[69] Nevertheless, and inevitably, it was seen as claiming
the sort of universal toleration for which many on both sides
were not ready at this stage in the seventeenth century. The
King was said to be displeased and Milton was rumoured to
have admired Taylor. The King however had liked *Episcopacy
Asserted* and a D.D. had been conferred on the author by royal
command. In this work, Taylor had grounded episcopacy on
divine institution, apostolic tradition, and Catholic practice.
Obviously, the patristic writings and the various Councils are
enlisted to support his case. In other words, more weight was
given to them in one book than in the other and Taylor's critics
were not slow to comment: 'I have been told, that my discourse
of episcopacy, relying so much upon the authority of fathers

and councils, whose authority I so much diminish in my liberty of prophesying, I seem to pull down with one hand what I build with the other'.[70]

Four matters seem to require examination at this point: Taylor's reply to the charge of self-contradiction; his view of the function of the appeal to antiquity and his method of using it; the influence of Daillé and a new kind of historical criticism, and then, how all this bears on Taylor's eucharistic theology.

As to the first, he asks in effect, how tolerant should toleration be? To those who complained that 'I had made the roof of the sanctuary so wide that more might be sheltered under it than they had a mind should be saved harmless', the moral theologian replies that equality is the great instrument of justice: 'If we would not do to others as we desired should be done to us, we were no more to pretend religion, because we destroy the law and the prophets'.[71] Most people complained, says Taylor, 'that in my ways to persuade a toleration, I helped some men too far, and that I armed the anabaptists with swords instead of shields'. His response is that it is their teaching not their persons to which he objects and those who thought this too much could have little confidence of 'the goodness of their own cause'. If anyone makes ill use of this tolerance 'it was more than I allowed or intended to him; but so all kindness may be abused.' What would we think of a criminal who claims that his lawyer consents to his crime because he was engaged to plead his case? Taylor will make no apology for speaking truth or acting with charity, nor for defending his brethren 'when the loins of the presbytery did lie heavy upon us'.[72] As to episcopacy, he claims that it relies not on the authority of fathers and councils but on 'the institution of Christ, on the institution of the apostles, upon an universal tradition, and an universal practice'. There is, of course, a degree of simplification here of the New Testament evidence, common enough in the seventeenth-century defence of episcopacy, but unacceptable today. For example, the Council of Trent claims that the three-fold ministry was established 'by divine ordinance' while Vatican II claims that this ministry was exercised 'ab antiquo', that is, not from the beginning, which agrees with historical realities.[73] The point which Taylor makes—and this is relevant to the way in which he uses the appeal to antiquity—is that the Fathers are 'excellent corroboratives in a question already determined'.[74] It can hardly be emphasised too strongly that the Anglican appeal to antiquity is to tradition as conformable to Scripture and to the Fathers as confirming the centrality and primary rôle of Scripture. This was the position set out in detail by Laud and Andrewes, and the main function of the appeal to antiquity was seen as corroborative and its secondary purpose was to show that there was an identity of approach as between the Church of England and the early Church.[75] In Stillingfleet's *Rational Account*, published by the Latitudinarian in 1664 as a defence of Laud's *Conference*, we can find the same line that 'the practice of the Church from apostolical times is a great confirmation'.[76] At the same time, there are the reservations and criticisms of the Fathers which one met with earlier in the Tew Circle and which help to produce an attitude of independence in assessing their value as we have already encountered it in Taylor's criticism of St. Augustine's views on original sin. Thus, Stillingfleet notes that 'nothing ought to be looked on as an article of faith among the Fathers but what they declare that they believe on account of Divine revelation'.[77] He is, in fact, much more interested in establishing the theological method of the Fathers as being by way of Scripture and reason than in treating them as an antiquarian storehouse from which to draw suitable items. He notes too that the Fathers differ on various questions but the value of their concurrence is great and patristic evidence is corroborative and complementary.

This is the way in which Jeremy Taylor saw and used the Fathers and the immediate influence on his thought was that of Daillé and the Tew Circle. Daillé's book was concerned with showing by evidence from the patristic period that doctrinal corruptions had set in so early and differences among the Fathers had appeared so soon that antiquity could provide no settled criterion, and that this was provided by Scripture only. Daillé was anxious to show that the Reformers were far more reliable than the Fathers. Unquestionably, the Tew group received an impetus from the book and this can be seen reflected in Chillingworth's work, but their objective was different. They had no particular interest in any century, and Hyde, for example, felt that the only use of antiquity was to consult it in order to discover 'matter of fact'. Hales regarded 'the circumstance ... of time ... as merely impertinent'.[78]

Nevertheless, the emergence of this new historical criticism had less effect than might have been at first sight anticipated as far as the general Anglican appeal to antiquity is concerned. The reason for this is that the Anglicans, with varying emphasis, saw its function as largely confirmatory. Laud, in his *Conference*, was writing for a Church when, having made the point that for Fathers and Councils alike Scripture is the foundation of faith, he wrote 'we never did, nor never will refuse any tradition that is universal and apostolic for the better exposition of the Scripture'. The point is made even clearer—'tradition doth but morally and probably confirm the authority of Scripture'.[79]

It was out of this developing understanding, and influenced by Daillé's book, to which he refers, that Taylor made his own use of the Fathers. Daillé's *Traicté de l'employ des saincts pères* had appeared in 1631 and Taylor's line is apparent when in the *Liberty of Prophesying* he comments 'but I will rather choose to show the uncertainty of this topic by such an argument which was not in the Fathers' power to help, such as makes no invasion upon their great reputation, which I desire should be preserved as sacred as it ought. For other things, let who please read Mr. Daillé, *Du vrai usage des Pères*.'[80] While stressing the confirmatory rôle of the Fathers who themselves stressed the centrality of Scripture he insisted that confusion exists as to the scope and function of the appeal to antiquity: the only tradition commanding universal assent is 'in the canon of Scripture itself' and 'therefore there is wholly a mistake in this business; for when the Fathers appeal to tradition . . . it is such a tradition as delivers the fundamental points of Christianity, which were also recorded in Scripture'. The consequence for us of appealing to the Fathers is that they acquit us 'from any other necessity of believing than of such articles as are recorded in Scripture'.[81] The true function of the appeal is therefore the confirmatory one. The Fathers are not an ultimate authority in themselves though 'there are some that think they can determine all questions in the world by two or three sayings of the Fathers, or by the consent of so many as they will please to call a concurrent testimony'.[82] This is the use of the Fathers which Taylor firmly rejects and his critical modernity in the use of antiquity is apparent in the prolonged comment in the epistle dedicatory: 'He that says that we may dissent from the fathers, when we have a reason greater than that authority, does no way oppose him that says, you ought not to dissent from what they say, when you have no reason great enough to outweigh it. He that says the words of the fathers are not sufficient to determine a nice question, stands not against him, who says they are excellent corroboratives in a question already determined and practised accordingly. He that says, the sayings of fathers are no demonstration in a question, may say true; and yet he that says, it is a degree of probability, may say true too. He that says they are not our masters, speaks consonantly to the words of Christ; but he that denies them to be good instructors, does not speak agreeably to reason or to the sense of the Church. Sometimes they are excellent arbitrators, but not always good judges: in matters of fact they are excellent witnesses; in matters of right or question they are rare doctors, and because they bring good arguments, are to be valued accordingly'. This is Taylor's use of antiquity in his general theology, and possibly with a certain degree of optimism, he concludes 'I, therefore, have joined these two books in one volume, because they differ not at all in their design, nor in the real purposes, to which, by their variety, they minister'.[83]

Within this setting, he utilises patristic sources to substantiate his understanding and exposition of the real spiritual presence and it is declarative both of his objective and his view of the importance of the Fathers that when he turns from the arguments about transubstantiation to an investigation of the Fathers he writes 'it is time to be weary of all this, and inquire after the doctrine of the church'.[84]

Section XII of the *Real Presence* is an extensive survey of the writings of a very considerable number of patristic authors. Some of them are closely examined, even to a manuscript in All Souls College library, 'of which I had the honour sometime to be a fellow'. This was falsely attributed to St. Cyprian but is written in very poor 'friar's Latin'. Taylor regrets that it cannot be claimed as St. Cyprian's sermons because the author, whoever he is—'the greater the better—gives us great advantage'.[85] He handles all this material by a double approach. In the first place, the rule of Vincent of Lérins applied to the doctrine of transubstantiation means that 'because although no argument can prove it catholic, but a consent; yet if some, as learned, as holy, as orthodox, do dissent, it is enough to prove it not to be catholic'.[86] Behind this, of course, lies a further point, namely, the admissions by such as Suarez that neither Scripture nor the Fathers use the concept of 'the conversion of the whole substance into the whole substance' and that the variety of patristic terms 'are either general . . . or . . . more accommodated to an accidental change'. Taylor concludes from this that we are consequently made free from the pressure of all those authorities of the fathers which speak of the 'mutation, conversion, transition, or passage, or transelementation, transfiguration, and the like', of the bread into the body of Christ; those *do*, *or may*, only signify an accidental change; and come not home to their purpose of transubstantiation'.[87] In the background, both here and in *The Dissuasive*, where it is spelt out in detail, a controlling element of the appeal to antiquity is the affirmation by the Fathers of the absolute sufficiency of Scripture to authenticate doctrine and practice.[88]

In the second place, there is the question of patristic terminology, the words used by the Fathers to describe what happens to the elements in the eucharistic action. There is diversity of opinion and phrasing among them but the weight of the implications is in favour of the real spiritual presence: 'None of the fathers *speak words exclusive of our way, because our way contains a spiritual sense*; which, to be true, our adversaries deny not, but say, *it is not sufficient*, but there ought to be more. But their words do *often* exclude the way of the Church of Rome, and are *not so capable* of an answer for them'.[89] This is his line in approaching the patristic evidence supporting his position, and the qualifications indicate the fairness of Taylor's assessment. He presses the matter of terminology further, claiming that for the Fathers the conversion of the elements is sacramental, not substantial; 'When the fathers, in this question, speak of the change of the symbols in the holy sacrament, they sometimes use the words . . . "conversion, mutation, transition, migration, transfiguration", and the like . . . ; but they by these do understand accidental and sacramental conversions, not proper, natural, and substantial'.[90] He brings Blondel and Suarez from both sides of the debate to support this, adding that even if the Fathers had unanimously affirmed the conversion and 'had not explicated their meaning as they have done indeed', it would still not have helped the case for transubstantiation. The reason is that by 'conversion' the Fathers did not mean 'a proper substantial change', 'a local succession of Christ's body into the place of bread'. 'There is a vast difference between conversion and transubstantiation; the first is not denied; meaning by it *a change of use, of condition, of sanctification;* . . . but this is not any thing of transubstantiation'.[91] What this means for Taylor's thesis is that when the Fathers speak of 'mere bread' before consecration and 'verily the body of Christ' after consecration, this is saying no more than the words of Christ 'and are only true in the same sense, of which I have all this while been giving an account: that is, by *a change of condition, of sanctification, and usage'.* But this is what the Catechism and Article 28 maintain, so to allege these patristic expressions against us is pointless, 'For we speak their sense, and in their own words—the Church of England expressing this mystery frequently in the same form of words; and we are so certain that *to eat Christ's body spiritually is to eat him really,* that there is no other way for Him to be eaten really, than by spiritual manducation'.[92]

Some further comments on his methodology emerge in the course of the section which accord with the overall view of the use of the Fathers set out in the dedication of *The Liberty of Prophesying.* For example, if the sense of a Father's words has to be extracted by argument and 'remote, uneasy consequences; I do not think it fit to take notice of those words, either for or against us'. Similarly, if both sides claim the quotation, it indicates that his meaning is unclear and 'the doctor . . . is not fit, in those words, to be an umpire'.[93] Caution is necessary in interpreting terms since there are differences among the Fathers: 'When the fathers use the word "nature" in this question, sometimes saying the "nature is changed", sometimes that "the nature remains", it is evident that they either contradicted each other, or that the word "nature" hath, amongst them, diverse significations'.[94] He deals very reasonably with the use of 'hyperbolical expressions' in the patristic texts, taking the line of St. Augustine and St. Cyprian, 'the same words represent the sign and the thing signified'. Both Fathers and Scriptures 'call the figure by the name of the thing figurated'.[95]

For Taylor, the conclusion based on these considerations is

that 'upon the account of these premises we may be secured against all the objections, or the greatest part of those testimonies from antiquity, which are pretended for transubstantiation; for either they speak that which we acknowledge, or that "it is Christ's body", that it is "not common bread", that "it is a divine thing", that "we eat Christ's flesh", that "we drink his blood", and the like; all which we acknowledge and explicate, as we do the words of institution; or else they speak more than both sides allow to be literally true; or speak as great things of other mysteries which must not, cannot be expounded literally; that is, they speak more, or less, or diverse from them, or the same with us'. Taylor maintains that 'there is hardly one testimony in Bellarmine, in Coccius, and Perron, that is pertinent to this question, but may be made invalid by one or more of the former considerations'.[96] So much then for Taylor's methodology which is in a sense quite different from that of Andrewes though both lean heavily on the great value of the Fathers in their corroborative and identity-confirming rôle. Taylor however is modern in his use of antiquity, for, with Daillé and the Tew Circle, historical and even textual evaluation and criticism enter into the appeal to antiquity, and both the book and the group influenced Jeremy Taylor. He uses precisely the same approach in the *Dissuasive*, examining the opinions of various Fathers and concluding that 'For when (the fathers) affirm, that in this sacrament is offered the figure, the image, the antitype of Christ's body and blood, although they speak perfectly against transubstantiation, yet they do not deny the real and spiritual presence of Christ's body and blood; which we all believe as certainly, as that it is not transubstantiated or present in a natural and carnal manner'.[97]

The remainder of the section in the *Real Presence* is his 'entry upon the testimonies of fathers' and the objective is restated: 'I am very certain, I can make it appear, not to have been the doctrine of the church, not of any church whose records we have, for above a thousand years together', and 'it is certain that not one, nor two, but very many of the fathers, taught our doctrine most expressly in this article, and against theirs'.[98] Thus the double rôle of the Anglican appeal to antiquity comes into play, the corroborative and the identity-affirming functions working together. More than a score of Fathers is cited but perhaps the most interesting and illuminative aspect here is that this is no mere *catena* designed to impress by weight of names and numbers. Passages from different authors are evaluated and terms analysed and the kind of textual criticism brought forward from time to time demonstrates that Taylor is no florilegist but—within the limitations of contemporary scholarship—a genuine and authoritative exponent of patristic studies. He reminds us, as he gets down to specifics, of the rubric he has established to the effect that much of the polemical use of these writings is invalidated by the methodological considerations ('the premises') already advanced and that, all the time, one has to take account of mere singularity and of contradiction existing in the material.[99] Examples of his critical familiarity with the texts and the controversial use made of them are worth noting: 'if these words had been against us, it had signified nothing; because these words are not in St. Ignatius; they are in no Greek copy of him; but they are reported by Theodoret'.[100] On St. Cyprian's explanation of the presence, he comments 'Bellarmine cites but half of these words, and leaves out that which gives him an answer'.[101] Discussing St. Ambrose's description of the oblation as 'the figure of the body and blood' and of the bread 'remaining what it is, and yet be changed into another thing', Taylor notes 'because these words pinch severely, they have retrenched the decisive words, and leave out "et sint", and make them to run thus, "that the things be—changed into another", which corruption is discovered by the citation of these words in Paschasius, Guitmond, Bertram, Algerus, Ivo Carnotensis, Gratian and Lombard'.[102] Against the claim that certain passages in St. Chrysostom's works supporting Taylor's understanding of the real sacramental presence are 'corrupted ... by some one of Berengarius's scholars', he retorts 'This kind of talk is a resolution not to yield, but to proceed against all the evidence; for that this place is not corrupted, but was originally the sense of the author of the homilies, is highly credible by the faith of all the old manuscripts; and there is in the public library of Oxford an excellent manuscript, very ancient, that makes faith in this particular'.[103] Taylor cannot resist the opportunity of underlining the shakiness of building too much on this sort of handling of the Fathers: 'But, upon this account, nothing can be proved from sayings of fathers. For either they are not their own works, but made by another; or, they are capable of another sense; or, the places are corrupted by heretics; or, it is not in some old copies; which pretences I am content to let alone, if they, upon this account, will but transact the question wholly by Scripture and common sense'.[104] He is quick to notice change in the use of terms during the early centuries, instancing a growing unease concerning the words 'image', 'type', and 'antitype' as applied to the elements after consecration: 'For Christ said not, This is the type of my body, but it is it. But, however, this new question began to brangle the words of type and antitype, and the manner of speaking began to be changed, yet the article, as yet, was not changed. For the fathers used the words of type, and antitype, and image, to exclude the natural sense of the sacramental body: and Damascene, and Anastasius Sinaita, and some others of that age, began to refuse those words, lest the sacrament be thought to be nothing of reality, nothing but an image'.[105] This is perceptive criticism as in his assessment of Theodoret and Gelasius on the meaning of *ousia* and *substantia* in their explications of how the elements being 'a divine thing' do not cease to be of 'the substance or nature of bread and wine'.[106]

The patristic authors are fairly treated and if there is a trace at all of selectivity this is surely inevitable considering that the book is contrasting two opposed understandings of the eucharistic presence. Thus, Tertullian is 'on our side' and Ephrem and Eusebius 'teach our doctrine',[107] and so on. Occasionally there are attractive touches of academic humour such as 'St. Austin . . . was a protestant in this article' and 'St. Chrysostom's rhetoric hath cast him on the Roman side . . . and his divinity and sober opinions have fixed him on ours'.[108] In fairness to Taylor, he substantiates these asides by quotations and extracts. Finally, in assessing his use of antiquity it is worthy of observation that, while Daillé and the Tew Circle were an immediate influence, a distinct trend in respect of the handling of patristics had already been developing among Anglican scholars. The critical study of the Fathers had been early established in the seventeenth century with Henry Savile's edition of St. John Chrysostom's works (referred to in Evelyn's *Diary*) and which just predates Taylor's birth in 1613. Patrick Young published I and II Clement in 1633 and Ussher's rescue of the genuine Ignatian

Epistles appeared in 1644. Taylor's frequent use of these Fathers may fairly be taken to imply his acquaintance with these editions and with this critical and scholarly approach to the patristic tradition, one from which in general terms his own method obviously benefited and with which he clearly identifies.

The Real Presence, not much known today, was in fact one of his major works both positively as a statement of belief and negatively as a doctrinal defence, and the strengths and weaknesses of his eucharistic theology are apparent in a book into which its author put much of himself. As one turns its pages, one is left with the continuing impression of a mind richly-stored and complex, acute and imaginative, deeply and seriously devout; 'what I cannot be of myself, let me be made by Thee'.[109]

Notes

1. *Real Presence*, Section V (10), ib. Vol. IX, pp. 476–477.
2. *An Exposition of the Catechism of The Church of England* (1655), Parker ed. (1842), p. 188.
3. *Real Presence*, Section V (10), ib. Vol. IX, pp. 472–3.
4. J. Armitage Robinson, *Giving and Receiving* (1928), pp. 24–5, 84–5.
5. Stranks, loc. cit., p. 137; Stone, loc. cit., Vol. II, p. 334.
6. *Real Presence*, Section I (4), ib. Vol. IX, p. 424.
7. ib. Section IV (9), ib. Vol. IX, p. 464.
8. *The Great Exemplar*, Discourse IX (2–4), ib. Vol. III, pp. 290–294.
9. cp. *Holy Living*, Ch. IV, Section X (5), ib. Vol. IV, p. 266.
10. *Real Presence*, Section I (4), ib. Vol. IX, p. 424.
11. ib. Section IV (7), ib. Vol. IX, p. 461.
12. *Clerus Domini*, Section VII (10), ib. Vol. XIV, p. 473 and cp. Section V (4).
13. *Real Presence*, Section IV (8), ib. Vol. IX, p. 462 and J. E. L. Oulton, *Holy Communion and Holy Spirit*, p. 37.
14. cp. *Holy Living*, Ch. IV, Section X (6) and *Clerus Domini*, Section V (1).
15. *Real Presence*, Section I (2), ib. Vol. IX, p. 422.
16. cp. H. E. W. Turner in *Thinking about the Eucharist* (1972), p. 103.
17. *Real Presence*, Section IV (9), ib. Vol. IX, p. 462.
18. ib. Section I (13), ib. Vol. IX, p. 432.
19. *The Great Exemplar*, Discourse XIX (2), ib. Vol. III, p. 290.
20. ib.
21. *Real Presence*, Section V (3), ib. Vol. IX, p. 467.
22. *Holy Living*, Ch. IV, Section X (9), ib. Vol. IV, p. 270.

23. *Real Presence*, Section I (4), ib. Vol. IX, p. 424.

24. *Great Exemplar*, Discourse XIX (2), ib. Vol. III, p. 290.

25. ib. Discourse XIX (8), ib. Vol. III, p. 298 and cp. *The Worthy Communicant*, Ch. VII, Section I (14).

26. ib. Discourse XIX (1), ib. Vol. III, p. 289.

27. *Holy Living*, Ch. IV, Section X (5), ib. Vol. IV, p. 266.

28. *Holy Living*, Ch. IV, Section X (8), ib. Vol. IV, p. 269.

29. *Clerus Domini*, Section V (6), ib. Vol. XIV, p. 455. The phrase is an echo of Justin Martyr.

30. *The Worthy Communicant*, Ch. VII, Section I (12), ib. Vol. XV, p. 673.

31. *Real Presence*, Section I (13), ib. Vol. IX, p. 432.

32. ib. Section VII (7), ib. Vol. IX, pp. 493–4.

33. ib. Section I (4) and Section XI (17).

34. *The Great Exemplar*, Part III, Section XV, Discourse XIX (3)–(4), ib. Vol. III, pp. 291–4.

35. *Real Presence*, Section I (5)–(6), ib. Vol. IX, pp. 424–5.

36. *The Great Exemplar*, Discourse XIX (9), ib. Vol. III, p. 300.

37. *The Real Presence*, Section I, (8)–(11), ib. Vol. IX, pp. 427–431.

38. ib. Section VI (1), ib. Vol. IX, p. 481.

39. ib. Section I (13), ib. Vol. IX, p. 432 and Section IV (9), ib. Vol. IX, p. 464.

40. C. W. Dugmore, loc. cit., p. 90–101.

41. *An Exposition of the Catechism of The Church of England* (1655), Parker ed., pp. xiii–xiv.

42. e.g., pp. 178, 186, 194, 198.

43. *Exposition*, p. 176.

44. ib. p. 178.

45. ib. p. 183.

46. ib. p. 185.

47. ib. p. 185.

48. ib. p. 183.

49. ib. p. 179.

50. ib. p. 177.

51. *Real Presence*, Section IV (9) and Section I (13).

52. ib. Section XII (4), ib. Vol. X, p. 60.

53. ib. Section V (10), ib. Vol. IX, p. 480.

54. *Holy Living*, Ch. IV, Section X (10), ib. Vol. IV, p. 271.

55. *Exposition*, p. 179 and *Real Presence*, Section I (4); Cosin, *Works*, Vol. IV, p. 46.

56. Heber & Eden ed., Vol. V, p. 330.

57. *Ecclesiastical Polity*, V, lxvii, 3, 12.

58. *Exposition*, p. 177.

59. ib. p. 178.

60. ib. p. 180.

61. ib. p. 179.

62. ib. p. 179.

63. ib. p. 185.

64. ib. p. 188.

65. *The Great Exemplar*, Discourse XIX (9) and *The Real Presence* Section I (8).

66. *Clerus Domini*, Section VII (10), ib. Vol. XIV, p. 473 and *Real Presence*, Section IV (8), ib. Vol. X, p. 462.

67. Stranks, loc. cit., p. 137.

68. G. W. H. Lampe in *Eucharistic Theology Then and Now* (1968), p. 37.

69. *Episcopacy Asserted*, Dedication, ib. Vol. VII, p. xiii.

70. *Dedication*, ib. Vol. VII, p. xvi.

71. ib. pp. xiii–xiv.

72. ib. pp. xv–xvi.

73. cp. Hans Küng *The Church* (1967), p. 418.

74. loc. cit., p. xviii.

75. For a fuller treatment of the Anglican appeal to antiquity, see H. R. McAdoo *The Spirit of Anglicanism* (1965), Chs. IX and X.

76. *Rational Account*, Ch. IV, p. 101, (1681 ed.).

77. ib. Ch. V, p. 595.

78. See *The Spirit of Anglicanism*, Chs. IX and X.

79. *Conference* (3rd ed.), pp. 34, 63.

80. *Liberty of Prophesying*, Section VIII (4), ib. Vol. VIII, p. 84.

81. ib. Section V (8) and (11), ib. Vol. VIII, pp. 18, 24.

82. ib. Section VIII (1), ib. Vol. VIII, p. 78.

83. *Dedication*, ib. Vol. VII, pp. xviii–xix.

84. *Real Presence*, Section XI (38), ib. Vol. X, p. 59.

85. ib. Section XII (22), ib. Vol. X, pp. 81–2.

86. ib. Section XII (1), ib. Vol. X, p. 60.

87. ib. Section XII (5), ib. Vol. X, pp. 61–2.

88. *Dissuasive*, Part I, Preface, ib. Vol. X, pp. cxv–cxviii.

89. *Real Presence*, Section XII (2), ib. Vol. X, p. 60.

90. ib. Section XII (5), ib. Vol. X, p. 61.

91. ib. Section XII (5)–(6), ib. Vol. X, pp. 61–63.

92. ib. Section XII (4), ib. Vol. X, pp. 60–61.

93. ib. Section XII (3), ib. Vol. X, p. 60.

94. ib. Section XII (7), ib. Vol. X, p. 63.

95. ib. Section XII (9)–(10), ib. Vol. X, pp. 64–5.

96. ib. Section XII (13), ib. Vol. X, pp. 67–8.

97. *Dissuasive*, Ch. I, Section V, ib. Vol. X, p. 159.

98. *Real Presence*, Section XII (15)–(16), ib. Vol. X, pp. 70–71.

99. ib. Section XII (18), ib. Vol. X, p. 74.

100. ib. Section XII (18), ib. Vol. X, p. 74.

101. ib. Section XII (22), ib. Vol. X, p. 81.

102. ib. Section XII (26), ib. Vol. X, p. 84.

103. ib. Section XII (27), ib. Vol. X, p. 85.

104. ib. Section XII (27), ib. Vol. X, p. 86.

105. ib. Section XII (28), ib. Vol. X, p. 89.

106. ib. Section XII (31), ib. Vol. X, pp. 94–5.

107. ib. Section XII (21) and (24)–(25).

108. ib. Section XII (27)–(28), ib. Vol. X, pp. 84–86.

109. *The Worthy Communicant*, Ch. VI, Section IV (5), ib. Vol. XV, p. 665.

VIII Holy Spirit and Holy Communion

It was the first and the only book to bear his new episcopal title, 'Jeremy Dunensis', with which he signed the epistle dedicatory to the Princess Mary, 'a daughter to such a glorious saint and martyr'.[1] *The Worthy Communicant* was given to the printer just before Taylor departed for Ireland to take up his new appointment and it was published late in 1660. He was not consecrated until 27th January 1661 so the signature was a proleptic gesture in tribute to one whose religious practice he held in esteem and 'because I have received the great honour of your reading and using divers of my books'.

There is evidence to suggest that it is a composite book, partly put together from previously existing papers. Stranks notes, as does Taylor himself, that it contains a brief résumé of the argument followed in the *Real Presence* and possibly contains some material used for sermons and for the compilation of cases in *Ductor Dubitantium*.[2] Porter has remarked that *The Worthy Communicant* is an expansion of 'the material from the latter part of *Holy Living*', paragraphs in the latter becoming chapters or sections in the former, both showing the influence, significantly, of St. John Chrysostom.[3] In any event, the result is a devotional book of some beauty and depth which in spite of its length became a popular manual in its day. At first sight, the work would seem to set so high a standard of preparation and devotion as to put people off. However, this would be to use the manual not as its author intended and to lose sight of the fact that much of what he is writing about is the 'remote' preparation of applying Christ's standards to ordinary daily life and relationships. Acts of repentance and amendment and devotional exercises are made available for use by different people in different situations and are not supposed to be worked through in their entirety by every communicant preparing to receive the blessed sacrament. Yet withal it is a solemn and profound manual full of the spirit of thanksgiving and with an undercurrent of joyfulness.

From the point of view of its eucharistic theology, not a great deal of notice has been taken of it today. C. W. Dugmore comments very briefly that the book has 'a strongly mystical note' and that 'Taylor also gives us here his later doctrine of the eucharistic sacrifice',[4] though, in fact, this is identical with what he had written in earlier works. Stranks describes the content and style of the book but never comes to grips with its eucharistic theology. In fact, nobody seems to have remarked what Taylor is doing in *The Worthy Communicant*, and I would suggest that it is here, if anywhere in his work, that we can detect a shift of emphasis in his teaching. It is not that he has gone back on any of his views as formerly stated. Rather is it that the weight of emphasis is differently distributed, and new facets of 'the nature and purpose of this great mystery' are put before the communicant. Always the objective is that 'we must have him within us, and we must be in him'.[5]

What then is Taylor about from the theological angle and where is the redistributed weight of emphasis being placed? First of all, he is developing an emphasis already existing in his work on the Holy Spirit in the Holy Communion and doing this by way of the teaching of Fathers such as Clement, Origen, Tertullian and Chrysostom. Only Darwell Stone has noticed the Alexandrian influence.[6] Taylor connects this with what he understands John 6 to be saying, a subject which he has already opened up in the *Real Presence*. As a moral theologian, it is natural and inevitable that, arising out of this, he will go on to the respective rôles of the sacramental and the non-sacramental in the economy of grace. In point of fact, it is worthy of comment that just as *The Great Exemplar* is a melding of a *Life* of Christ with a related exposition of moral/ascetic theology, so we find in *The Worthy Communicant* that Taylor merges eucharistic theology and moral theology in one book of preparation for receiving the sacrament: 'Every worthy communicant must prepare himself by a holy life, by mortification of all his sins, by the acquisition of all Christian graces; *and this is not the work of a day, or a week*'. This is a recurring aspect of how Taylor structures his eucharistic work and one which has not been sufficiently recognized. Yet it is integral to his theology as a whole and to his understanding of religion and of the working of the Faith in real life: 'Every time we receive the holy sacrament . . . we mend our pace'.[7] It is the central element around which *Holy Living* and *Holy Dying* are built, the totality of the working of grace, sacramental and non-sacramental, in the members of the mystical body, through which they 'fully grow up into Christ'. Taylor links this growth specifically with the reception of the Sacrament: 'Because, in the holy communion, we are growing up to the measures of the fulness of Christ, we can no otherwise be fitted to it, but by the progressions and increase of a man, that is, by habits of grace and states and permanencies of religion'. It is the Spirit at work through the word and sacraments which 'are a jewel enchased in gold when they are together'. Taylor insists that 'the ministries of the Gospel are all of a piece; they, though in several manners, work the same salvation by the conduct of the same Spirit'. The sacrament is 'the more eminent' and he stresses 'that if the word ministered by the Spirit is so mighty, it must be more, when the word and the Spirit join with the sacrament, which is their proper significatory'.[8] Here, Taylor's main theological theme in *The Worthy Communicant*, the Spirit and the Eucharist, joins with the theme of the rest of the book, the Spirit and membership in the Spirit-filled Body, the Church. The life of the Christian is life in the Spirit, a life of grace. Thus, three of the six chapters are concerned with faith and charity, repentance and forgiveness, as necessary dispositions and actions 'preparatory to the blessed sacrament' and the last chapter deals with examination of conscience, the manner and frame of mind suitable to such a holy encounter, and devotional exercises, for 'the receiving of the blessed sacrament is a receiving Christ'.[9] These chapters are liberally sprinkled with those characteristic apophthegms which are as attractive as they are indicative of Taylor's insight as a moral theologian. Examples are numerous and we catch the flavour from such as 'revenge is the disease of honour'; 'Love . . . is the excellency and perfection of a man'; 'If it be not in hands to do well, it must be in our hearts; and the contrary never be upon our tongues'; 'true Christian faith must have in it something of obscurity, something that must be made up of duty and by obedience'.[10]

Ought we not also at this point to call to mind that repentance, charity and faith, are the three prerequisites for

communicating worthily as set out by the short Invitation in
the Holy Communion Service of the Book of Common Prayer?
Liturgy, theology and devotion are mutually supportive components in the whole and this is particularly evident in Taylor's
last chapter on behaviour and devotional practices at 'the reception of the Divine Mysteries'.[11] At all events, like the Prayer
Book, he lays it down that without these three; Faith, Charity,
Repentance . . . 'we can never approach to these divine mysteries with worthiness, or depart with joy'.[12] Incidentally, the
constant use of the term 'divine mysteries' in the book is a
reminder, not that the argument allows one for a moment to
forget it, that the concept of mystery is as central to Taylor's
eucharistic theology in this his last work on the subject as it
was when as a young man he wrote 'there we commemorate
His death and passion in the dreadful and mysterious way that
himself with great mysteriousness appointed'.[13]

II

On Holy Spirit and Holy Communion, Taylor sets out the
schema for the opening part of his book when, commenting on
the words 'I am the bread of life' and 'He that eats my flesh
hath life abiding in him', he writes; 'The plain consequent of
which words is this, that, therefore, this eating and drinking of
Christ's flesh and blood, can only be done by the ministries of
life and of the Spirit'.[14] There is nothing new in his insistence
on the rôle of the Spirit in the total eucharistic action. Already
in *Clerus Domini* he asserts that 'the Holy Spirit is the consecrator' and 'the glory of the change', 'the divine alteration',
'that great mysteriousness, which is the sacramental change', is
effected by Him in response to 'the prayers of the church,
presented by the priests'. In the *Real Presence* the mystery of
the eucharist is part and parcel of the essentially mysterious
manner of the Spirit's working. Liturgical expression is given
to this in the *Collection of Offices* with the epiclesis in which
the Father is prayed to send His Spirit on hearts and gifts alike
for blessing and sanctifying so that the gifts 'may become' the
holy body of Christ and His life-giving blood. The constant in
Taylor's many-faceted understanding and exposition of the

eucharist is mystery. 'To consecrate the sacramental symbols into the mysteriousness of Christ's body and blood' is the inestimable privilege of priesthood.[15] The appropriation of the elements by the Spirit is such that 'Christ's body is truly there, and there is *a conversion of the elements* into Christ's body; for what before the consecration *in all senses* was bread, is, after consecration, *in some sense*, Christ's body'.[16] This is from the *Dissuasive*, the last of his major works, and he claims that this is Anglican teaching and that many earlier theologians such as Lombard, Scotus and Durand 'more agreed with it' than with 'the present Church of Rome'. Be that as it may, here is that quality of reverent agnosticism which is wholly consistent with Taylor's doctrine of the mystery of the eucharist and of the change in the elements. Consistently, he has insisted that, because the eucharist is mystery, to define how or in what way this alteration takes place is a contradiction in terms and he reiterates this later on in *The Worthy Communicant*: 'In the holy communion, we must retain an undoubted faith, but not inquire after what manner the secrets of God are appointed. Whether it be or no, that is the object of faith to inquire, and to accept accordingly. What it is, he that is to teach others, and speak mysteries, may modestly dispute; but how it is, nothing but curiosity will look after'—an echo of St. Bernard.[17] The concept of mystery as being at the heart of the eucharist dominates the short Introduction to the book and is the key to all that follows: 'Christ comes to meet us, clothed with a mystery'.[18]

What Taylor now adds to his teaching on Holy Spirit and Holy Communion is a deep personalising of the Spirit's action in the eucharist through which the worthy communicant lives 'the life of the Spirit' and receives 'the fruits of the Spirit and the joy of the Spirit'.[19] Furthermore, there is a developing of the relation of the Spirit to the real spiritual presence of Christ in the eucharist so that there is a theological and devotional enrichment of our understanding of 'the greatness and excellency of the mystery'. Yet that enlightenment is inseparable from its effects in the life of the Christian: 'we cannot discourse of the secret, but by describing our duty; and we cannot draw all the lines of duty, but so much duty must needs open a cabinet of mysteries'.[20] Truly, it is quite inadequate simply to describe *The Worthy Communicant* as 'mystical' for Taylor is always a moral/ascetical theologian even when expounding his doctrine of the eucharist as mystery.

He is in the process of adding another dimension to his exposition that 'as the sacrament operates only by virtue of the Spirit of God, so the Spirit ordinarily works by the in-strumentality of the sacraments'.[21] Into this enlargement come the marked influence of the Alexandrians, the concept of the *verbum visibile*, the interpretation of St. John 6 and the relation of sacramental to non-sacramental grace, the rôle and function of faith in the eucharistic mystery, and, once again, the relation of the great High Priest to the members and ministers of His Church, 'the holy table being a copy of the celestial altar'.[22] There is development here, but development onwards from what is already there, a deepening and a widening which makes Taylor's views even less open to a ready and convenient classification.

The Introduction sets the tone by its double emphasis on worthy reception and on the mystery of the eucharist. Those who wish to share in God's secrets, says Taylor, must first look into their own 'by the rules of the Spirit', for 'the sacraments are mysteries, and to be handled by mystic persons'. As our spiritual life begins to develop, 'Christ comes alone and offers his grace, and enlivens us by his Spirit, and makes us begin to live . . . yet this great mysterious feast, and magazine of grace . . . is for those only that are worthy'. Accordingly, more than half of *The Worthy Communicant* is devoted to faith, hope and love, to repentance and amendment, and to the graces and responsibilities of the good life which is the only real preparation for worthy reception of the sacrament: 'the holy communion . . . is the most sacred, mysterious, and useful conjugation of secret and holy things and duties in religion'. Its essential nature is mystery, the mystery of the Spirit: 'It is not easy to be understood; it is not lightly to be received: it is not much opened in the writings of the New Testament, but still left in its mysterious nature'. Yet at once, the mystery leads the Christian to the practicality of life for both are bound together inextricably: 'I find it engages us upon matters of duty, and inquiries practical: if I describe our duty, it plainly signifies the greatness and excellency of the mystery'. Here, as elsewhere in his work, Taylor's very modern view that moral theology is all about our life as it is lived in union with Christ merges with his strong sacramentalism in the total picture of grace and response.[23] His purpose in this book is 'not to dispute' but to understand 'what it is that we go about'. He is only too well aware of the range of differences and of 'seemingly opposed doctrines' which separate 'good men'. But since all Christians greatly esteem the eucharist 'all speak honourable things of it' and all the differences in faith and practice 'proceed from some common truths'. We may therefore find that the purposes of the Spirit may be served by 'the differing opinions and several understandings of this mystery, which (it may be) no human understanding can comprehend'.[24] This is Taylor at his most irenic. At several points in his career we have seen him reluctantly forced into the lists, either by the historical weight of Christian divisions or by the pressures of his own immediate situation, but here he can be true to the best inclinations of his own temperament. He was not to know that very shortly and towards the end of his life, his fellow-bishops would find it necessary to oblige him once again to engage in what he called 'the worst part of learning'.

In New Testament phrasing, life in Christ does not differ from life in the Spirit. This new life in the *koinonia*, the fellowship of the Spirit and of the family of Christ, is imparted by baptism and nourished by eucharist. Because it is this totality of the Christian's life which is his main concern, Taylor's opening sentence in *The Worthy Communicant* reads 'When our blessed Lord was to nail the hand-writing of ordinances to his cross, he was pleased to retain two ceremonies, baptism and the holy supper'.[25] As the book progresses, he will develop further the relation of the two sacraments which 'Christ was pleased . . . to assist . . . with the presence of his Spirit'.[26] At the same time, the communicant is being reminded that this new life is the life of Christ continuing, through His Spirit, in the lives of the members of His mystical Body: 'By Christ we live and move, and have our spiritual being in the life of grace. . . . He took our life, that we might partake of his; He gave his life for us, that he might give life to us . . . every good word we speak it is by his Spirit'.[27] In the living of this new life after baptism there will be, as Hooker observed, daily hindrances and the life begun in baptism needs the eucharist 'for continuance of life'.[28] Taylor says the same, that 'by these it is that we have and preserve life',[29] but he develops this more widely and deeply to take in not only the relationship between the two sacraments but that between sacramental grace and grace 'out of the Sacrament', non-sacramental grace. As his theme develops, there is revealed by turns or together an evangelical simplicity, a richly complex eucharistic theology and an unchanging awareness of mystery in the eucharist and in all the Spirit's working. It is in this area that Taylor is adding a fresh dimension to his theology of the eucharist.

He begins his chapter on the nature and intention of the sacrament with an analysis of current understandings of the sacrament and a striking list of traditional descriptions of it. He calls these 'excellent appellatives' and comments that 'if the explications and consequent propositions were as justifiable' the result could be nothing but increased devotion.[30] There are three types of view, the first being that of a bare symbolical commemoration—'we receive nothing in the blessed euchar-ist'. Taylor regards this as quite inadequate: 'This, indeed is something, but very much too little'. On the other hand, there is the 'natural' view of the presence and his criticism is to be noted in that he clearly wishes to maintain the real and spiritual presence but rejects the implications of this approach: 'They who teach this doctrine, call the holy sacrament, "The host; the unbloody sacrifice; the flesh of God; the body of Christ; God himself; the mass; the sacrament of the altar". *I cannot say that this is too much, but that these things are not true; and although all that is here said, that is of any material benefit and real blessing, is true, yet the blessing is not so conferred, it is not so produced*'. His third type of believers and his assessment of their view are interesting: 'A third sort of Christians speak indefinitely and gloriously of this divine mystery'. The problem is that they work by emotion and experience but with an imperfect comprehension of the sacra-ment. His analysis is as understanding as it is acute: 'they speak enough, but they cannot tell what; they publish great and glorious effects . . . such which they desire, but cannot prove; which indeed they feel, but know not whence they do derive them'. Their intentions are admirable, says Taylor, and he handles them gently; 'they mean well, but do not always understand that part of Christian philosophy which explicates the secret nature of this divine sacrament'. He is anxious for them because 'They sometimes put too great confidence in the mystery . . . and are sometimes troubled that their experience does not answer to their sermons'. The result is scruples instead of comfort and doubts and anxiety instead of a peaceful conscience. Taylor's experience as counsellor and casuist is always there near the surface as his theme unfolds. He concludes that those who are of this mind 'both in their right and in their wrong, enumerate many glories of the holy sacrament'. His design therefore must be 'to represent the true, and proper and mysterious nature of this divine nutriment of our souls'.[31] Accordingly, the question to be put is the fundamental one 'What is it which we receive in the holy sacrament?' At once, he sets about sketching a fresh perspective which will enable the worthy communicant to apprehend the mystery for 'we have two lives, a natural and a spiritual; and both must have bread for their support'.[32]

The perspective is that of grace in and through the Spirit. Just as in a picture the perspective gives light, depth and proportions, so it is here for the spiritual life of men and women: 'All our prayers are by the aids and communications of the Spirit of Christ. . . . In fine, all the principles and parts, all the actions and progressions of our spiritual life, are derivations from the Son of God, by whom we are born and nourished up to life eternal'.[33] 'Christ is our life', Taylor reminds us, and Christ is 'the food of our souls'. It is thus that He presents Himself to us in the blessed sacrament 'in a way that was nearest to our capacity'. The very ordinariness of the means, bread and wine, makes His coming more intelligible but always mysterious. Taylor seeks for words to convey the paradox of the presence and concludes that 'I am the bread of life' is Christ 'representing' himself 'in a more intelligible manner, not further from a mystery, but nearer to our manner of understanding; and yet so involved in a figure, that *it is never to be drawn nearer than a mystery*, till it comes to experience and spiritual relish and perception'. Here is Taylor striving to go as deep as he can into the mystery of the eucharist and of what happens in Holy Communion, knowing that the mystery both illuminates and limits enquiry by its very nature. The search, he writes, is 'within the fringes and circles of a bright cloud' and can only end in worship.[34] The longer Taylor studies and writes about the eucharist (and this is his last work devoted to the subject) the more he appears to be convinced that it is a mystery of light and that human understanding can only go so far and, in a phrase of his own, 'leave the rest for wonder'.

At once, he introduces the teaching of Clement of Alexandria and Origen and Tertullian that 'The flesh of Christ is his word: the blood of Christ is his Spirit', a view to which he has more than once referred in *The Real Presence*, particularly in his examination of St. John 6.[35] In this latter connection he cites numerous patristic writers and it is a point to which we must return. The Alexandrians were reacting against materialism and consequently laid the emphasis on the spiritual meaning of the elements and of the Gospel and of its teaching on salvation. The snag here, as Heron indicates in his chapter on early eucharistic theology, is that Origen (and others), by sharply distinguishing between the material elements and the spiritual reality of Christ the Word of God, and by insisting that what matters is not simply the physical eating, but the reception of the Word, of Christ, in faith, were actually driving 'a wedge between the physical and the spiritual (so) that they can no longer really be held and seen together'.[36] What then is the real value of the Eucharist? What grace can it convey which is not already available through hearing and receiving the proclaimed Word? *We are left with a gap* and Heron suggests that this was filled by St. Augustine's concept of a sacrament.

Taylor was alive to the difficulty and aware of the existence of the gap. He too turns to St. Augustine and to his definition of a sacrament; 'when the word and the element are joined, then it is a perfect sacrament'.[37] In effect, Taylor bridges the gap by his insistence on a change of condition in the elements, remaining outwardly the same as before but 'changed inwardly by the powerful virtue of the Holy Spirit'.[38] The Ante-Nicene Fathers have however left a marked impression both on Taylor's understanding of Holy Spirit and Holy Communion and on his interpretation of the sixth chapter of the Fourth Gospel. The influence of Clement and Origen in particular is notable in *The Worthy Communicant* and in *The Real Presence*, as is also that of Tertullian. In the latter work, he refers to Tertullian's discussion of our Lord's teaching at Capernaum—'these words are spirit and life'—and he quotes

Theophylact on the same point in a collection from the Fathers designed to demonstrate 'the spiritual sense' of John 6: 'To warrant the spiritual sense of these words against the natural, it were easy to bring down a traditive interpretation of them by the fathers, *at least a great consent*'.[39]

In *The Worthy Communicant* he develops the same theme in a more personalised way for the communicant, using the Epistle to the Hebrews (9: 14, 10: 29, 13: 20) to show the unity of 'the blood of the eternal covenant' and the work of 'the eternal Spirit': 'for, by the blood of Christ we are sanctified; and yet that which sanctifies us is the Spirit of grace, and both these are one'. The point here in respect of the eucharist, says Taylor, is that by these 'expressions we are taught to distinguish the natural blood of Christ from the spiritual; the blood that he gave for us from the blood which he gives for us: that was indeed by the Spirit; but was not the same thing, but this is the Spirit of grace, and the Spirit of wisdom'. To receive the sacrament is to 'partake of the Spirit' for by Christ we live spiritually in this world and eternally hereafter: 'Thus are sensible things the sacrament and representation of the spiritual and eternal, and spiritual things are the fulfillings of the sensible'. He is striving to underline the essential connection between the elements and their reception on the one hand and the reception of Christ and life through Him on the other. Eating and drinking is 'the symbol and the sacrament of a new life by Christ'. The physical and the spiritual are purposefully and indissolubly linked in the sacrament, 'the growth in grace being expressed by the natural instruments of nutrition . . . and the graces of God by the blessings of nature'. The physical elements are essential 'for these we know, and we know nothing else; and but by fantasms and ideas of what we see and feel, we understand nothing at all'. The spiritual is sacramentally expressed by the physical and the physical achieves the fulfilment of its divinely ordained purpose through the spiritual. Taylor affirms, perhaps rather optimistically, that 'this is not done to make this mystery obscure, but intelligible and easy'.[40] Behind all this, of course, there stands firmly his central assertion concerning the presence of Christ in the sacrament that it is both real and spiritual: 'the symbols become changed into the body and blood of Christ, after a sacramental, that is in a spiritual real manner . . . the result of which doctrine is: It is bread, and it is Christ's body. It is bread in substance, Christ in the sacrament . . . and Christ does as really nourish and sanctify the soul, as the elements do the body'.[41] What is newly entered into the exposition of the real spiritual presence is the Alexandrian theme and Taylor's interpretation of St. John 6. The effect of this is to redistribute the emphasis in the light of deeper understanding of the Spirit's action in the eucharist. There is the unspoken suggestion that Taylor may have felt at this stage that some people might have regarded him as falling into the trap of so over-spiritualizing his interpretation that he makes sacraments merely marginal exercises. He insists that, *on the contrary*, 'this is so far from being a diminution of the glorious mystery of our communion, that the changing of all into spirituality is the greatest increase of blessing in the world'. When we receive Christ's body and blood, he continues, we do not receive simply sacral entities, 'not his lifeless body, but his flesh with life in it; that is, his doctrine and his Spirit to imprint it, so to beget a living faith'.[42] In his view, St. John 6 is speaking of the general mystery and communion with Christ of which sacraments are 'but particular instances'. Accordingly, he must enquire as to the advantage that 'we receive by the sacraments, besides that which we get by the other and distinct ministries of faith'.

Taylor's strong sacramentalism is not weakened by importing into his exposition this interpretation of the Johannine material and the Alexandrian presentation of the flesh and blood of Christ as the word and the Spirit. In fact, because both emphases aimed at countering a 'materialist' view of religion and the 'natural' view of the presence, he obviously thinks that his sacramental theology is reinforced rather than weakened. So, he launches into an exposition of sacramentality, of the nature of a sacrament, the manner in which the eucharist works in the life of grace, and how the sacrament is also a sacrifice, and how the Spirit effects His purposes in the lives of faithful communicants. He leads in with a phrase, 'The word and the Spirit are the flesh and the blood of Christ, that is the ground of all', which is pure Clement of Alexandria.[43] The Gospel, says Taylor, can be summed up by two words 'believe and repent' and Christ invested these two words with two sacraments which are assisted 'with the presence of his Spirit, that in them we might do more signally and solemnly what was in the ordinary ministrations done plainly and without extra-ordinary regards'. When we receive the word and the Spirit illuminates us 'in our first conversion', this is to be nourished by the flesh and blood of Christ, but 'much more in baptism'. Here, following St. Paul, St. Augustine and Tertullian, it can be said that 'the flesh and blood of Christ crucified are, in baptism, reached to us by the hand of God, by his Holy Spirit, and received by the hand of man, the ministry of a holy faith'. The difference is that 'out of the sacrament' the Spirit operates with the word in the ministry of man, but 'in baptism, the Spirit operates with the word in the ministry of God. For here God is the preacher, the sacrament is God's sign'. Precisely the same applies to the eucharist and 'in the same divine method the word and the Spirit are ministered to us in the sacrament of the Lord's supper'. If the word in baptism is 'believe and repent', the word here is that by communicating we proclaim the saving Cross: 'This is *verbum visibile*; the same word read to the eye and to the ear'. The word of God is made to be our food so that 'our tongues and palates feel the metaphor and the sacramental signification'. The reception of the sacrament is both an exercise of and an advancement of our faith: 'it is faith in mystery, and faith in ceremony; it is faith in act, and faith in habit: it is exercised and advanced'. Yet Taylor never appears to deviate from the position that 'the elements . . . are changed, translated, and turned into the substance of Christ's Body and Blood; though as in a sacrament, mystically. Yet, therefore, *by virtue of the consecration, not of his faith that receives*',[44] to quote his elder contemporary Thorndike.

What is coming through here as a result of this developing emphasis on the nature of the Holy Spirit's working in the Holy Communion, is a heightening of the concept of the dynamism of a presence which is personalist. This has already appeared as something central to Taylor's understanding of the eucharist. Now he presents this dynamic presence in terms of Christ continuing through the sacrament the life-imparting work which was the purpose of the Incarnation so that, says Taylor, the sacrament is rightly seen as an extension of the Incarnation. This presence is not a passive one, but active and dynamic and the mode of it is unique for the working of the Spirit in the sacrament is mystery. All this suddenly comes together in a passage where Taylor is taking stock of the material so far displayed in *The Worthy Communicant*. He writes: 'The sum is this: Christ's body, his flesh and blood, are, therefore, called our meat and drink, because by his incarnation and manifestation in the flesh *he became life unto us*: so that it is mysterious, indeed, in the expression, but very proper and intelligible in the event, to say that we eat his flesh and drink his blood, since by these it is that *we have and preserve life*. But because what Christ *began* in his incarnation, he *finished* in his body on the cross, and all the *whole progression* of mysteries in his body, was *still an operatory of life and spiritual being to us*—the sacrament of the Lord's supper being a commemoration and exhibition of this death, which was the consummation of our redemption by his body and blood, does contain in it a *visible word, the word in symbol and visibility*, and special manifestation. Consonant to which doctrine, the fathers, by an elegant expression, call the blessed sacrament, "the extension of the incarnation"'.[45]

III

The position which Taylor is advancing is that Christ always comes to the faithful believer through the same grace of the same Spirit. This can be sacramental or non-sacramental as to the means, but the former, where 'the Spirit is the teacher' is better and more sure, though both are effective: 'that spiritual eating of Christ, which, as it is done out of the sacrament very well, so in it and with it, much better'. The sacrament is a sign of His own appointing and so through it we receive 'bread and drink, flesh and blood, the word and the spirit, *Christ in all his effects*'. The real presence of Christ, in other words, is to be understood dynamically and as a personalist and not as an entitative presence: 'Christ is their life . . . and Christ is to them all in all, for we must put on Christ, and we must eat Christ, and we must drink Christ: we must have him within us, and we must be in him . . . but these things are not consequent to the reception of the natural body of Christ, *which is now in heaven*; but of his word and his Spirit, which are, therefore, indeed his body and his blood, because by these we feed on him to life eternal'.[46]

Taylor is next at pains to explain the true nature of the

sacrament to people who 'speak things too contemptible of these holy mysteries' and dismiss the eucharist merely as 'a ceremony of memorial, but of no spiritual effect'. He is saying in effect that neither Zwinglianism nor transubstantiation is an adequate or true presentation of the mystery of the euchar- ist. Like Article XXVIII which rejects both these views he is affirming the real spiritual presence but in a markedly indi- vidual form and mode of expression unusual in the seven- teenth century and deriving in part from the third century. He believes that he has sufficiently 'explicated the secret' for his third kind of Christians by giving substance to their 'con- jecture and zeal' but the position of the bare memorialists requires that sacramentality itself should be expounded. Im- mediately he tackles the relation of the Christ of history to the Christ of the sacraments. To understand what he calls 'this economy and dispensation . . . we are to consider, that Christ, besides his spiritual body and blood, did also give his natural, and we receive that by means of this'. His natural body died but once and 'heaven was the place appointed for it'. Through the Cross, Christ is the author of our salvation and 'our hope depends upon this death' and the word preached is nothing but Jesus Christ crucified, 'and the sacraments are the most emi- nent way of declaring this word: for by baptism we are buried into his death and by the Lord's supper we are partakers of his death'. From this reconciliation flows the heavenly inter- cession and the sending of the Spirit which are linked with the operation of the sacraments. The word of salvation is pro- claimed in the eucharist 'much more clearly than in baptism, much more effectually than in simple enunciation, or preaching and declaration by words'. The sacramental prin- ciple means that it is the real Christ Himself who through the Spirit gives Himself to the worthy communicant because He has first given Himself on the Cross. Taylor is striving to show that the reality of the eucharist and of its blessings depends on the reality of the Atonement in history which in the sacrament is perpetually represented because the crucified and glorified Christ lives to make intercession for us: 'therefore we eat Christ's spiritual body, *because* he hath given us his natural body to be broken, and his natural blood to be shed, for the remission of our sins, and for the obtaining the grace and acceptability of repentance'.[4] Discussion as to whether grace is conferred by the sacraments *per se* or whether their effect comes from the moral disposition of the receiver is pointless: 'Neither one nor the other say true: for neither the external act, nor the internal grace and morality, does effect our pardon and salvation, *but the Spirit of God*, who blesses the symbols, and assists the duty, makes them holy, and this acceptable'. The work of the Spirit is for Taylor's exposition the heart of sacramentality. God is not bound by His own ordinances and 'the Holy Ghost sometimes comes like lightning' but always 'by the hand of faith' through the ministry of the Word and Sacraments. Without 'the impresses of the Holy Spirit of God ... all preaching and all sacraments are ineffectual'. The sacramental principle does 'not work by the methods of nature'. Rather it means that external and internal are inter-dependent in the sacraments but together are still only the channel through which, as Article XXV puts it, 'He doth work invisibly in us'. Holy Communion and Holy Spirit: 'neither the outward nor the inward part does effect it, neither the sacra-ment nor the moral disposition; only the Spirit operates by the sacrament, and the communicant receives it by his moral dispositions, by the hand of faith'.[48]

It is inevitable and it is proper that the eucharistic symbolism and the historical associations of the eucharist with our re-demption through the Paschal Mystery, should concentrate the communicant's mind on Christ's glorified humanity made available to men in and through the sacrament. Perhaps this was stressed, particularly in the seventeenth and the late nineteenth centuries, almost to the exclusion of the obvious, that all this is the work of the Spirit. Taylor, in *The Worthy Communicant* more than redresses the balance. So do the Lima and ARCIC I Reports in our own time. 'The whole action of the eucharist has an epikletic character because it depends upon the work of the Holy Spirit' who 'makes the crucified and risen Christ really present to us in the eucharistic meal'.[49] So goes the Lima Report and ARCIC I ten years earlier spoke of 'the transforming action of the Spirit of God' in the elements when 'the bread and wine become the body and blood of Christ by the action of the Holy Spirit' a phrase paralleled in Lima, 'by the power of the Holy Spirit the bread and wine become the sacramental signs of Christ's body and blood'. The Holy Spirit 'appropriates' bread and wine, says ARCIC I, so

that 'it is the glorified Lord himself whom the community of
the faithful encounters in the eucharistic celebration through
the preaching of the word, in the fellowship of the Lord's
Supper, in the heart of the believer, and, *in a sacramental way*,
through the gifts of his body and blood already given on the
cross for their salvation'. Our generation needed this reminder
as did Taylor's, and the modern affirmations, especially the
last passage quoted, chime with much in *The Worthy
Communicant*.[50] Indeed Taylor could readily make his own
the affirmations of Lima that in the *anamnesis* 'the Church,
united with its great High Priest and Intercessor' is offering its
prayer in union 'with the continual intercession of the risen
Lord'; that the work of the Spirit 'is not to spiritualize the
eucharistic presence of Christ but to affirm the indissoluble
union between the Son and the Spirit. This union makes it clear
that the eucharist is not a magical or mechanical action but a
prayer addressed to the Father, one which emphasizes the
Church's utter dependence. There is an intrinsic relationship
between the words of institution, Christ's promise, and the
epiklesis, the invocation of the Spirit, in the liturgy'.[51] What
we have seen of Taylor's eucharistic theology confirms the
similarities which have their reflections liturgically in his
Collection of Offices and devotionally in many prayers such as
that provided in *The Worthy Communicant* for the moment of
reception: 'I hear thy voice blessing these symbols . . . thy Holy
Spirit sanctifying my spirit, thy blessed self making
intercession for me at the eternal altar in the heavens . . .
this is thy body, O blessed Saviour Jesus, and this is thy
blood'.[52]

Constantly in this book Taylor is declaring mystery, even
praying 'that I may not search into the secret of nature, but
inquire after the miracles of grace', and at the same time
endeavouring to make the mystery of sacramentality something which, paradoxically, can be grasped. The 'sacraments
evangelical' are a mystery but 'even signs of secret graces do
exhibit as well as signify'. The sign and the thing signified are
so inextricably linked that St. Paul could say 'he hath saved us
by the laver of regeneration, and that the grace of God is given
by the imposition of hands'. This is so 'because both the
sacrament and the grace are joined in the lawful and holy use
of them, by sacramental union'. But always it is the Spirit in the

sacrament who confers the grace. So Taylor takes St. Augustine's definition, '*accedit verbum ad elementum et tum fit sacramentum*' as the best way of understanding the meaning and purpose of a sacrament. He reminds the reader of St. Chrysostom's point that sacraments would have been unnecessary only 'if we were wholly incorporeal'. The Spirit ordinarily works by the instrumentality of the sacraments, the elements being the means of grace 'with the Spirit'. The sacrament 'operates both as word and sign . . . and is the conduct of the Spirit'. Taylor is going deep, to the roots of the Christian experience, when he affirms that 'justification and sanctification are continued acts' because God is always giving and we are always receiving. There is a constant traffic of grace and response in which the sacraments both proclaim and channel this grace. His conclusion is that 'the sacraments and symbols, if they be considered in their own nature, are just such as they seem, water, and bread, and wine; they retain the names proper to their own natures: but because they are made to be signs of a secret mystery . . . therefore the symbols and sacraments receive the names of what themselves do sign; they are the body and they are the blood of Christ: they are metonymically such. But because, yet further, they are instruments of grace in the hand of God, and by these his Holy Spirit changes our hearts, and translates us into a divine nature —therefore the whole work is attributed to them by a synecdoche: that is, they do in their manner the work for which God ordained them, and they are placed there for our sakes, and speak God's language in our accent'.[53]

As the book develops, Taylor gets deeper and deeper into the progressions of the spiritual life and the mystery of sacramentality as he enlarges on what has become a central theme, 'receiving Christ', 'eating Christ's body in a spiritual sense', and the rôle of the eucharist in which the sign and the signification are joined and 'we conjoin the word and the spirit'. Faith and charity are self-multiplying by their exercise and move in ever-increasing concentric circles: 'To eat the flesh and to drink the blood of Christ *sacramentally*, is an act of faith; and every act of faith, *joined with the sacrament*, does grow by the nature of grace . . . and therefore is eating of Christ spiritually; and this reflection of acts, like circles of a glorious and eternal fire, passes on in the univocal production of its own parts, till it pass from grace to glory'. Christ is the head of the Body and the members 'are united to him in this mystical union by the holy sacrament'. This is the operation 'of the Holy Spirit in the sacrament' who works as a reconciler so that we may be one body because we partake of one bread: 'This bread is the body of Christ, and the church is Christ's body too; for by the communion of this bread, all faithful people are confederated into . . . the body of the Lord'. This is stated in a figurative way, says Taylor, 'yet that spiritual sense means the *most real event in the world*: we are really joined to one common divine principle, Jesus Christ our Lord'.[54] Taylor is saying in effect that Christ, the head of the Church, the law and the life of Christians, is the great *mustērion*, and that it is in Him, through the Spirit's action, that all sacramentality is grounded and has its purpose and meaning. 'Now, then,' he asks 'what can any man suppose a sacrament to be, and what can be meant by sacramental participation? For unless the sacraments do communicate what they relate to, they are no communion or communication at all.' We eat the elements, but faith eats too by partaking 'of the thing signified . . . (and) . . . feeds upon the mystery itself; it entertains the grace, and enters into that secret, which the Spirit of God conveys under that signature'.[55] 'The sum of all I represent in these few words of St. Hilary "These holy mysteries, being taken, cause that Christ shall be in us, and we in Christ".'[56]

What we are seeing here is a personalist concept of the presence mediated sacramentally and in a mystery through the agency of the Spirit. Taylor has already gone on record that he believes that his use of the concept of the word and the spirit as the flesh and blood of Christ and his sapiential interpretation of John 6 have not in any way watered down his concept of the real spiritual presence in the eucharist. Now, in support of the position taken earlier in his works, he can still quote approvingly 'the change is made by grace' and he will try to elaborate further on this. In the course of developing the theme he analyses the meaning of the mysterious presence and it is at this stage that, in a phrase we used earlier, Taylor appears to skim the cream off virtualism. Yet at the same time, as we have seen in the *Dissuasive* at the end of his life, he holds on to a mysterious change in the elements which while remaining in all senses bread and wine become 'in some sense' Christ's body and blood. The mystery of sacramentality positively demands the reverent admission that we do not know *how*. In *The Worthy Communicant*, he reiterates this both in respect of the elements, the meaning of sacramentality, and with regard to how Christ is united to us in the eucharist. The passage merits quotation, taking up and linking as it does the concept of 'present in reality' with the same admission that the sacramental change in the elements and their function in relation to Christ and to reception in faith are mystery:

'Our faith in this sacrament is not obliged to inquire or to tell how the holy bread can feed the soul . . . how Christ is united to us, and yet we remain imperfect even then, when we are all one with him that is perfect: there is no want of faith, though we do not understand the secret manner how Christ is really present, and yet this reality be no other but a reality of event and positive effect; *though we know not that sacramental is more than figurative, and yet not so much as natural, but greater in another kind.* . . . We need not be amazed concerning our faith . . . though we cannot apprehend how the symbols should make the grace presential, and yet that the grace of God in the receiver can make the symbols operative and energetical'.[57]

Taylor is posing the question, What specifically is the work and the rôle of faith in the reception of Holy Communion? It cannot engage us to believe something contrary to our senses —Christ 'wrought faith in St. Thomas by his fingers' ends'. This is true of the elements handled by priest and communicants which our senses tell us are bread and wine, but 'faith sees more in the sacrament than the eye does . . . but nothing against it'.[58] Neither can faith oblige us to believe anything which is against right reason. Here, the substance of Taylor's eucharistic theology fits into the setting of his general theology and he reproduces the argument concerning faith and reason more fully developed in the *Ductor Dubitantium* published in the same year as *The Worthy Communicant*. Reason is not the positive measure of our faith and yet 'in all our creed there can be nothing against reason'. We must take care, however, that what we call reason is really reason and not something else. Reason is a right judge but it ought not to pass sentence in matters of faith 'until all the information be brought in'. Unless this is done, we 'may conclude well in logic, and yet infer a false proposition in theology'. Our experience and observation enter into the assessment as well as what is revealed. The 'natural' interpretation of the eucharistic presence cannot pass these tests. Likewise, faith must eschew mere curiosity and he returns to the familiar emphasis on mystery, quoting St. Cyril of Alexandria 'Believe firmly in the mysteries, and consent to the words of Christ; but never so much as speak or think, How this is done'. Taylor agrees, and in this at least he never parts company with the Laudians; 'He hath told us, "This is his body", "This is his blood": believe it, and so receive it: but he hath not told us how it is so'. The relation of faith to the elements is controlled, so to speak, by the fact that 'they are sacramental'. As we contemplate 'this mysterious sacrament and its symbols, we are more to regard their signification than their matter; their holy employment than their natural usage; *what they are by grace*, than what they are by nature'. We are to remember that 'they are made holy to purposes of religion' and what is important is 'what they are to the spirit, not what they are to sense and disputation'.

In other words, there is a real, spiritual presence, to be apprehended by faith, not created by it: 'The change is made by grace'; 'It remains after consecration the same it did before, but it is changed *inwardly* by the powerful virtue of the Holy Spirit'; 'by sensible things, he gives us insensible or spiritual'. The quotations from the Fathers pile up and Tertullian's 'the figure of my body' and Gregory of Nazianzen's 'figure of a figure' are brought into play with St. Augustine's 'The body of Christ is truth and figure too'. Taylor gathers up all this and more in a highly nuanced exposition of the real, spiritual presence in which, more than anywhere else in his work, he takes the best from virtualism but contains it by asserting that in the sacrament Christ's body and blood are really exhibited: 'The holy sacrament is *not only called* the Lord's body and blood, for the figure, similitude and sacramentally; but for *the real exhibition* and ministration of it. For it is truly called the body of Christ, because there is joined with it the vital power, virtue and efficacy of the body: and, therefore, it is called by St. Austin, 'The intelligential, the invisible, the spiritual body' . . . 'the spiritual food, and the body of the Divine Spirit', by St. Ambrose. For, by these means, it can very properly be called 'the body and blood of Christ': since it hath not only the figure of his death externally, but internally it hath hidden and secret, the proper and divine effect, the life-giving power of his body: so that, though it be a figure, *yet it is not merely so: not only the sign and memorial of him that is absent, but it bears along with it the very body of the Lord, that is, the efficacy and divine virtue of it*'. One might compare *The New Week's Preparation* (1749) for a late example of a somewhat similar stance: 'the real presence of Christ's invisible power and grace, so *in* and *with* the elements of bread and wine, as to convey spiritual and real effects'. The prepositions used would suggest more than Waterland's 'relative holiness' and 'new relation' and 'change of use' and seem to imply something like Taylor's change of condition.[59]

This is in any case the nearest Taylor comes to a virtualist position but he claims to affirm it 'in the words of the fathers of the Church, rather than mine own', and goes on to quote St. Epiphanius, 'The bread indeed is our food, but the virtue which is in it, is that which gives us life'.[60] If we take this in conjunction with Taylor's frequent assertion of a 'divine alteration' in the condition of the elements we have a rich doctrine of the eucharist which is individual if at times elusive. Its basis is the affirmation of the real spiritual presence but Taylor belongs completely to no school possibly because he believes that none can adequately describe 'the chief of all the Christian mysteries and the union of all Christian blessings'.[61] One can easily see how, by isolating passages like that just quoted from his over-arching concept of 'the real presence and spiritual', Taylor could be ranked among the virtualists, as Stranks reckons him. On the contrary, I would suggest, Taylor is here once again anticipating in his own way a theological trend which would make its appearance at a later date. He is in effect formulating a doctrine of the real presence in terms of 'the vital power, virtue and efficacy' of the body of Christ 'joined with' the elements to effect 'the real exhibition and ministration of the body and blood of the Lord'. The thrust of this is to express the real presence in a way which safeguards the two realities in the eucharist, that of Christ's body and blood and that of the bread and wine. We recall his phrases, 'It is bread and it is Christ's body' (*Real Presence*) and 'The sacrament is life: the bread of the sacrament is the life of our soul, and the body of our Lord is now conveyed to us, by being

the bread of the sacrament' (*Great Exemplar*). Earlier I referred to this as a dualist interpretation and one is reminded
of Temple's term 'convaluation' by means of which two sets of
value are held together in relation to one object. Fifty years
ago, the report *Doctrine in the Church of England* (Temple
was Chairman of the Commission) discerned among 'some
Anglican theologians today' a fresh and tentative restatement
of the doctrine of the Real Presence in terms of value. The
effect of this, the report held, was to destroy 'the boundary-line
between the older doctrine of the Real Presence and that of
Virtualism' (p. 175).

Has Jeremy Taylor been there before them? This looks very
like the point he has reached; not using the actual term 'value'
but the sense and content of it, he combines this with those
elements in his teaching which we have been analysing. The
effect of this is designed to undergird a doctrine of the real
presence which is personalist and through which the whole
Christ, the life of Christ, divine and human, is made available
and accessible by means of the effectual signs which, in this
mystery, become his body and blood—to quote the Windsor
Statement. Taylor's exposition calls to mind a definition of the
real presence by Will Spens, lay-theologian of the nineteen
twenties and thirties—'accessibility dependent on material
objects'. Bearing in mind his emphasis on the rôle of faith, one
may think that Taylor would not have quarrelled with this.

At all events, 'to this spiritual food must be fitted a spiritual
manner of reception; and this is the work of faith'. There are
two complementary movements, says ARCIC I, within the
unity of the eucharistic mystery, 'Christ giving his body and
blood, and the communicants feeding upon them in their
hearts by faith' and both must be held together in the doctrine
of the Eucharist. Similarly, Lima affirms that Christ's mode of
presence in the eucharist is unique and that 'While Christ's real
presence in the eucharist does not depend on the faith of the
individual, all agree that to discern the body and blood of
Christ, faith is required'.[62] Taylor concurs that it is through
faith that 'a life-giving encounter results'. Faith is 'the great
instrument' but the cause is the Holy Spirit—'it is effected by
the Spirit'. Nor is this faith simply 'believing the articles but the
dedication of our persons'. It is the faith which 'makes a new
creature', and it is most particularly exercised in the reception

of 'this divine sacrament . . . for here we come to Christ, and Christ comes to us; here we represent the death of Christ as he would have us represent it . . . and hither we come to be invested with a robe of light'.[63] The eucharist is the sacrament of life in Christ and the representment of His life-giving sacrifice.

Already in *The Worthy Communicant* Taylor has devoted space to the other great theme, that of sacrifice, which he has been developing since 1649 in *The Great Exemplar* and during the following two years in *Holy Living* and *Clerus Domini*. Here he sets it out once more, the theme of the great High Priest and Intercessor representing His one complete sacrifice on our behalf and mirrored in the Church's offering, 'the holy table being a copy of the celestial altar'. He sees his own thinking perfectly summarised by a quotation from St. Augustine, 'By this he is the priest and the oblation, the sacrament of which he would have the daily sacrifice of the church to be: which because it is the body of that head, she learns from him to offer herself to God by him, who offered himself to God for her'. This teaching and the emphasis laid on it is a characteristic of Taylor's very individual theology of the mystery of the eucharist.

The exposition here is even richer and stronger than in the earlier books but the substance is the same.[64] Christ became our High Priest, being consecrated on the Cross through which He reconciled us to God 'and was admitted to the celestial and eternal priesthood in heaven; where, in virtue of the cross, he intercedes for us and represents an eternal sacrifice in the heavens on our behalf'. We see from Hebrews that He is a priest in heaven and because there is no other sacrifice but that of the Cross, this perfect sacrifice is what He 'perpetually offers and represents . . . to his heavenly Father'. What He does in heaven, He commands us to do on earth, 'that is, to represent his death, to commemorate this sacrifice, by humble prayer and thankful record; and by faithful manifestation and joyful eucharist, to lay it before the eyes of our heavenly Father, *so ministering in his priesthood*, and doing according to his commandment and example; the church being the image of heaven; the priest, the minister of Christ; the holy table being a copy of the celestial altar; and the eternal sacrifice of the Lamb slain from the beginning of the world, being always the same;

it bleeds no more after the finishing of it on the cross; but it is wonderfully represented in heaven, and graciously represented here; by Christ's action there, by his commandment here'. The passage is a beautiful condensation of Taylor's theology of representment, of the unbloody sacrifice and of the heavenly altar. At first sight, one might think from the words underlined and from similar phrasing which follows, that either the richness of the vision or a deliberate change of mind has caused Taylor to abandon his earlier position and to believe now that we share in the High Priesthood of Jesus. However, the use of the word 'imitating' on five successive occasions and the phrase 'he as High Priest, and we as his servants, his ministers', would suggest that, not for the first time, the beauty of concept and the flow of words have run away with Taylor the poet and that Taylor the divine has had to set the theology aright. For, as Rust put it, 'he had the fancy of a poet and the acuteness of a school-man'. But the reader must judge for himself as Taylor depicts the 'external' ministry of the priest as an imitation of the priesthood of Melchisidec who 'brought forth bread and wine, and was the priest of the most high God'. The concept of imitation is then applied to the 'internal' priestly ministry after the pattern of Christ's self-offering. There is also the qualification of officiating in His priesthood 'after the manner of Christ himself'. Taylor is returning to the way of expressing himself which he used in *Holy Living*. There, the ministers of the sacrament present to God the sacrifice of the Cross 'by being imitators of Christ's intercession'. This representation in the eucharist is only 'so far as his glorious priesthood is imitable by his ministers on earth'.

Thus, in the liturgy 'we minister in the priesthood of Christ, who is a priest for ever after the order of Melchisidec; that is, we are ministers in that unchangeable priesthood, *imitating*, in the external ministry, the *prototype* Melchisidec . . . and, in the internal, *imitating the antitype*, or the substance, Christ himself; who offered up his body and blood for atonement for us—and, by the sacraments of bread and wine, and the prayers of oblation and intercession, commands us to officiate in his priesthood, in the external ministering like Melchisidec, in the internal, *after the manner* of Christ himself'.[65] In a following passage, he makes the same point twice and the closing sentence reminds us that nowhere does Taylor say plainly that

Christians or the ministerial priesthood share in the unique High priesthood of Jesus. The eucharist, he writes, is '*in our manner* a representation of that eternal sacrifice—*an imitation* of Christ's intercession in heaven . . . (it) . . . is so excellent a representation of Christ's death, by Christ's commandment; and *so glorious an imitation* of that intercession, which Christ makes in heaven for us all; it is all but the representation of his death, in the way of prayer and interpellation; Christ as head, and we as members; *he as High Priest, and we as servants, his ministers*'. Doubtless, what Taylor is attempting to convey is that the celebrant of the holy mysteries exercises a priesthood of like pattern, analogically the kind of priesthood of which Melchisidec is a type and Christ's priesthood the reality. The stress on imitation clearly implies that there is a similarity of form and function but not a shared identity: 'See Christ doing, in his glorious manner, this very thing which thou seest ministered and *imitated* upon the table of the Lord'.[66]

The practical conclusion from the examination of the rôle of faith in the reception, is like that of Lima—'to discern the body and blood of Christ, faith is required'—and Taylor writes; 'For Christ in the sacrament is Christ under a veil: as without the hand of faith, we cannot take Christ, so we must be sure to look here with an eye of faith; and whatsoever glorious thing is said of the holy sacrament, *it must be understood of the whole sacrament, body and spirit, that is, the sacramental and spiritual communion*'.[67]

IV

The influence of his interpretation of John 6 has been apparent as Taylor treats of the work of the Holy Spirit in the Holy Communion for the same Spirit works through all the ministrations of the Gospel. Grace is both sacramental and non-sacramental and the believer also 'feeds on Christ' through His word and teaching. 'To believe in Him' says St. Augustine 'this is to eat the living bread', and 'Believe and you have eaten'. This *Treatise on the Gospel of St. John* has certainly influenced Taylor in the interpretation of John 6 and in the exposition of the eucharist, and he quotes it more than once. His general position is that 'receiving Christ by faith includes any way of communicating with his body: by baptism, by holy desires, by obedience, by love, by worthy receiving the sacrament'.[68] In *The Real Presence* he devotes an entire section to John 6 which includes a wide range of patristic extracts. He is well aware that even in antiquity there was difference of opinion and his own view is 'That Christ did speak of the sacrament as well as of any other mystery, of this amongst others; that is, of all the ways of taking him, is to me highly probable'.[69] From the earliest times there have been two interpretations of the chapter. There is the 'sapiential' view which understands the bread from heaven or the bread of life of which Jesus spoke as the divine revelation in the Person and teaching of Jesus. This view is complicated by vv. 51–8 in which the bread of life is clearly identified with the flesh of Jesus and the words appear to apply to eucharistic bread. The second interpretation views the whole discourse as referring to eucharistic bread. Raymond Brown notes that Clement of Alexandria, Origen and Eusebius took the whole discourse spiritually, the first interpretation. The other view was favoured by Chrysostom, Gregory of Nyssa and the Cyrils' of Jerusalem and Alexandria. Many of the Reformers did not accept the eucharistic interpretation but then neither did Cajetan. The Council of Trent sat on the fence 'largely lest it give ammunition to the Hussites, who used John 6: 53 to demand communion under both species'.[70]

Remarkably, all these points are commented on by Jeremy Taylor. He claims that 'many of the most learned Roman Catholics affirm that, in this chapter, Christ does not speak of sacramental or oral manducation, or of the sacrament at all', and he lists Cajetan with Biel and others. He then comments that Bellarmine tries to excuse them saying 'that they did it, that they might confute the Hussites and the Lutherans about the communion under both kinds'.[71] In the same way, amongst many other Fathers, he quotes Clement of Alexandria, Origen and Eusebius. He even finds a passage in St. Chrysostom's homily on John 6 which supports his view though he is aware that the same writer uses 'metaphors . . . in the height of his rhetoric' which are used by the upholders of transubstantiation.[72]

Modern exegetes propose a range of interpretations. C. H. Dodd says that the main theme is Christ as the Bread of Life and He is contrasted with the manna, which is not the 'real' bread: 'If Christ is both Bread and the Giver of bread, then what he gives is Himself—His flesh and blood . . . the instructed Christian reader cannot miss the reference to the sacrament of the Eucharist' (vv. 51–54).[73] Oscar Cullmann believes that the Fourth Gospel 'treats the two sacraments as expressions of the whole worship-life of the early community and correspondingly sets forth the relation between the Lord of the community present especially in these two sacraments and the life of Jesus'.[74] Rudolph Bultmann, on the other hand, rejects any connexion with the sacraments and regards as interpolations such passages as 6.52–58, holding that what is solely at issue is revelation through the Word.[75] Raymond Brown furnishes further contemporary names, categorising their views as (a) The whole discourse is 'sapiential' (b) This applies only to the first part, vv. 51–8 being a eucharistic reference (c) The entire discourse refers to eucharistic bread (d) 'Bread' in the discourse refers to both revelation and the eucharistic flesh of Jesus. Brown himself 'sees the two themes in the first part of the discourse (vv. 35–50) which refers primarily to revelation but secondarily the Eucharist; the second part (vv. 51–58) refers only to the Eucharist'[76] One should also add to the list the work of J. E. L. Oulton who shares the view of Lightfoot and of Westcott that the discourse is about 'feeding on Christ in general, of which the eucharist is a special means'. He regards the discourse as being based on teaching given by Christ on the occasion to which it is attached in the Gospel. This teaching was assimilated by the Evangelist and given 'in a form of words in which it is impossible to distinguish between what the Holy Spirit has taught him concerning the inner meaning of the teaching and the original teaching itself. In the particular instance of the discourse on the bread of life this inner meaning has been deepened for the Evangelist through eucharistic worship'.[77] It is noteworthy that Oulton cites passages from *The Worthy Communicant* to show how Jeremy Taylor perceived the relationship between Holy Baptism and Holy Communion on the one hand, and between sacramental and non-sacramental grace on the other, a matter to which we have already drawn attention.

Taylor's handling of John 6 in respect of the eucharist is geared in *The Real Presence* to showing that the discourse does nothing to support the doctrine of transubstantiation but the treatment is far from being negatively confined to this. In *The Worthy Communicant* he is concerned with the relationship of sacramental grace and grace 'out of the sacrament', with the rôle of the Spirit in the two sacraments, with the emphasis on the word and the spirit being the flesh and the blood of Christ, and with the impact of John 6 on 'this mystery in general'. Where then does he stand in respect of this division of interpretation lasting from the third to the twentieth century and how does it bear on his theology of the eucharist?

The section in *The Real Presence* rejects the claim that in 'the whole sermon' or in vv. 51–58 'our blessed Saviour taught the mystery of transubstantiation'.[78] The positive thrust however is the conviction that the words of Christ 'were to be understood in a spiritual sense' and 'that Christ here spake of spiritual manducations, not of sacramental'.[79] 'A great consent' of the fathers uphold 'the spiritual sense of these words against the natural'.[80] Quotations follow from Tertullian, 'Athanasius, or who is the author of the tractate', Origen, Ambrose, Eusebius, Jerome, Clement of Alexandria, a goodly roll-call of those favouring the sapiential interpretation as Taylor sees it. He then comments 'yet after all this, suppose that Christ, in these words, did speak of the sacramental manducation . . . what is this to transubstantiation?' Taylor thinks it 'highly probable' that Christ spoke of the sacrament 'amongst others, that is, of all the ways of taking him'. This receiving of Christ 'comes in only as it is an act of faith . . . now the sacraments of baptism and the eucharist being acts and symbols and consignations of faith . . . may well be meant here, *not by virtue of the words*, for the whole form of expression is metaphorical . . . and from that verse forward (v. 51) he doth more particularly refer to his death; for he speaks of 'bread' only before, or 'meat', but now he speaks of flesh and blood, 'bread and drink'; and therefore, *by analogy*, he may allude to the sacrament, which is his similitude and representation; but this is *but the meaning of the second or third remove*'. He sums up his own position, following on from this, by enlarging on the spiritual eating of the Bread of Life in John 6 as being by the exercise of faith, by hearing the word of God, by submission of the understanding, by the imitation of Christ and by conforming ourselves to His life and teaching 'and as the sacraments are instruments or acts of this manducation, so they come under this discourse, and no otherwise'.[81] He takes the same line in *The Worthy Communicant* that 'St. John having thus explicated this mystery in general, of our eating the flesh and drinking the blood of Christ, added nothing in particular concerning the sacraments, these being but particular instances of the general mystery and communion with Christ'. Taylor's verdict then comes down emphatically on the side of the sapiential interpretation. With his accustomed independence however he adds his own rider. The sacrament is probably included, not by reason of the Johannine text itself but 'by analogy' as being a specific and eminent manner in which the believer feeds on Christ by faith, an extension of the Alexandrian view.

As he develops his doctrine of the real spiritual presence with these redistributed emphases, can we say that Taylor has avoided the Origen-trap? I believe that he has done so with the aid of St. Augustine's sacramental theology and by his own theology of the elements within a personalist concept of the Presence rather than an entitative one. For example, he will cite Augustine that 'in the sacrament there is a verity or truth of Christ's body' and he believes that Augustine teaches the real spiritual presence clearly, 'I have commended a sacrament to you, which, being understood spiritually, will give you life'. The point is, says Taylor, 'besides that he gives testimony to the main question on our behalf, he also makes *sacramentally and spiritually to be all one*'.[82] We have already noted his use of Augustine's definition of a sacrament and how Taylor uses it in *The Worthy Communicant*, and his own comment in the same book on the meaning of sacramentality—'sacramental is more than figurative, and yet not so much as natural, but greater in another kind'.[83] We recall the affirmations in the *Great Exemplar* that spiritual is not only figurative and in *Holy Living* that the elements are holy in their change. By asserting that something happens, that as he puts it in the *Dissuasive*, 'there is a conversion of the elements into Christ's body', or as in *The Real Presence*, that 'the symbols are changed into the body and blood of Christ after a sacramental, i.e. a spiritual, real manner', Taylor is standing clear of the snare of so separating the physical elements and the spiritual reality that they can no longer be seen to have an essential and necessary connexion. Sacramentality is rather the mystery of the unity of the spiritual and the physical as the conduit of grace—'the great mysteriousness which is the sacramental change'. 'It is not bread alone, but *sacramental* bread . . . the bread neither is the natural body of Christ, nor yet is it alone a sufficient symbol of representment of it. But the bread "broken, blessed, given, distributed, taken, eaten"; this is Christ's body, viz., as Origen's expression is, "typicum symbolicumque corpus".' And in fact we can see how he uses Origen to go beyond Origen in the succeeding paragraph by affirming 'it is bread and Christ's body too; that is, it is bread "naturally", and "Christ's body spiritually"'.[84]

Can one summarise Taylor's eucharistic theology? Probably we can, but quite certainly we cannot effectively categorise it. Though it belongs in the main to one school of thought the tenets of that school cannot encompass it, for it is too wide and rich for the valid attaching of labels. His sources are varied and used with individuality and he was alive to and commented on the aspects of truth in the many disparate expositions of the mystery of the eucharist. Yet withal he believed and claimed that he was expounding the eucharistic doctrine of the Church Catechism and the Articles. He did so, but with his own unmistakable stamp and still C. H. Sisson can say that *The Worthy Communicant* should 'be read . . . by anyone who wants to understand the temper of Anglicanism'.[85]

In the previous chapter I suggested that the central elements in Taylor's teaching—a position at once simple and complex —could be found in seven propositions in one paragraph from *The Real Presence* taken together with the rich concept of the eucharistic sacrifice and the heavenly altar which is contained in all his writings on the mystery of the eucharist. What does *The Worthy Communicant*, and for that matter *The Dissuasive*, add to this outline of a doctrine of the real spiritual presence which is personalist, a dynamic presence? The outline is already distinctive by reason of a 'dualist' overtone in its theology of the elements—it is 'bread and Christ's body too'. It is 'bread in substance, Christ in the sacrament'.

The fresh emphasis is that we are now presented with a doctrine of the real spiritual presence in which the work of the Holy Spirit in the sacrament is seen as being of the essence and not just in the comfortably general sense that sacraments are the normal conduits of the Spirit's grace. Whether it is possible to define satisfactorily the characteristics of the eucharistic theology of Central Churchmanship and whether it can be demonstrated that the development of Jeremy Taylor's views tended to shade off in this direction seems to me to be of comparatively little consequence when attempting to assess a theologian who is as naturally resistant to classification as Taylor is.[86] What is really different, a marked development of what was previously there in outline, is this elaboration on Holy Spirit and Holy Communion. The Spirit is the consecrator, the energiser and sacramentality issues from and is effectual only through Him: 'As the sacrament operates only by virtue of the Spirit of God, so the Spirit ordinarily works by the instrumentality of the sacraments'. It is not just that the epikletic quality of the eucharist is efficacious in changing hearts and changing the elements; 'send thy Holy Ghost upon our hearts, and let him descend upon these gifts, that by his good, his holy, his glorious presence, he may sanctify and enlighten our hearts, and he may bless and sanctify these gifts; that this bread may become the holy body of Christ'.[87] The element 'remains after consecration the same it did before; but it is changed inwardly by the powerful virtue of the Holy Spirit'. The personal point for the communicant is that 'in the holy communion we are growing up to the measures of the fulness of Christ'. But the agent is the Spirit—'This eating and drinking of Christ's body and blood, can only be done by the ministries of life and of the Spirit'. In Taylor's thought there is a virtual merging of the receiving of Christ and of the Spirit's working so that he can even say that we 'partake of the Spirit' when we receive the blessed sacrament. What Taylor is saying is that it is the Spirit who through the sacrament perpetually makes effective for us the benefits of the once-for-all perfect sacrifice of Christ: 'By the blood of Christ we are sanctified and yet that which sanctifies us is the Spirit of grace, and both these are one'. By eating and drinking Christ 'we live the life of the Spirit'. At the same time, Taylor does not allow this merging of concepts to cause any 'diminution of the glorious mystery of our communion' by understressing the personalist nature of Christ's presence in the eucharist: 'Christ comes to meet us clothed with a mystery'; 'The receiving of the blessed sacrament is a receiving Christ'; We receive 'Christ in all his effects'; 'the ministry of the Spirit, the sacrament of Christ himself'.

There is a sacramental change, a conversion of the elements into the Body and Blood of Christ. We do not know how this is so, 'how the symbols should make the grace presential', any more than we can understand the Spirit's working by which the symbols are made 'operative and energetical'. The Christian accepts Christ's word 'This is my body . . . but he hath not told us how this is so'. The conclusion for Taylor is simple: 'If Christ be not there *after a peculiar manner*, whom, or whose body do we receive?'[88]

The master-theme in *The Worthy Communicant* is 'The word and the Spirit are the flesh and the blood of Christ, that is the ground of all'.[89] How successful Taylor has been in marrying this concept to his doctrine of the real, spiritual presence of Christ, a presence both personalist and dynamic, must remain a matter for debate. In this evaluation as in the corresponding section in the last chapter, we have tried to come at a resolution by allowing Jeremy Taylor to do his own summarising. At all events, if we put together this summary and that in chapter seven we have a reasonably inclusive picture of his understanding of the eucharist, sacrament and sacrifice, 'queen of the mysteries'. Unshakable at the heart of Taylor's teaching is the paradox that only by accepting its essential mystery can the eucharist, its meaning and purpose be expounded and apprehended. As I have been maintaining throughout, the twin bases of Taylor's eucharistic thinking are mystery and sacramentality which in turn are inseparable from the Holy Spirit's working in Holy Communion. Only one who thought in these terms could lay such stress on the heavenly altar where the sacrifice 'bleeds no more after the finishing of it on the cross; but it is wonderfully represented in heaven, and graciously represented here; by Christ's action there, by his commandment here'.[90] Mystery in the eucharistic theology of Jeremy Taylor is not the last refuge but the first and only starting-point—'the sacraments are mysteries'.

Taylor's eucharistic theology is revealed as subtle and as solidly and profoundly devout. The complexity of his mind and his reflective spirit are seen in the individuality with which he expresses his nuanced doctrine of the real spiritual presence but as one who always submitted 'to the judgment of my afflicted mother the Church of England'.

V

What manner of man evolved this theology? Inevitably, glimpses of Taylor the man, his temperament and mind-set, are vouchsafed to the reader of his books, leaving the clear impression that here is no ordinary mind. 'Not a safe man' is allegedly a characteristic Establishment view of someone who is unusual or brilliant and unconventional, and who does not exemplify 'orthodoxy' at its best and most cautious. In Taylor's case the voice of the Establishment was Gilbert Sheldon, Archbishop of Canterbury after the Restoration, who described his great contemporary as 'a man of dangerous temper, apt to break out into extravagances'. The outcome in 1661 was that Taylor's comparatively unknown friend and colleague, William Nicholson, was chosen for the See of Gloucester while Taylor was appointed to Down and Connor. It was no disgrace to be sent to join John Bramhall (whose funeral sermon Taylor would be called on to preach in a couple of years' time) but one of the best known literary figures among the English clergy might fairly have expected an English bishopric when the Lord turned again the captivity of Zion. A letter from Taylor to Sheldon complains 'I have been informed from a good hand in England that your grace was pleased once to say that I myself was the only hindrance to myself of being removed to an English bishopric'.[91] Without any doubt, England's loss was Ireland's gain but behind this is the poignancy of an uneven relationship. Taylor ingenuously assumed a degree of friendship which was not equally felt on both sides. Sheldon had helped him financially during the lean years (in 1653) but earlier in their acquaintance when he was a Fellow of All Souls he had done his best to block Taylor's appointment to a Fellowship as desired for him by Archbishop Laud. Later, Sheldon's uncompromising spirit was offended by *The Liberty of Prophesying* (1647). When *Unum Necessarium* with Taylor's attack on the currently received doctrine of original sin appeared in 1655, Sheldon failed to understand it and demanded a recantation. 'You would pity and despise my weakness if I should' was Taylor's reply. The upshot was that he was regarded by the most powerful personality in the Restoration Church as not being a safe man.

Sisson could be correct in suggesting that a distrust of

literary ability and fame may have entered into the judgment and certainly Sheldon himself wrote virtually nothing. Sheldon was too big a man and Taylor too good a man for the triviality of professional jealousy to be an element in the situation. The distrust on Sheldon's side went deeper, theologically and temperamentally, and in any event the situation of two dispossessed clergymen of a persecuted Church hardly lent itself to considerations of clerical careerism. On the one hand, we have Taylor so attractive a personality that people like John Evelyn, Christopher Hatton, Lord Conway and Lord Carbery held him as friend and spiritual adviser—'a person of most sweet and obliging humour, of great candour and ingenuity . . . a rare conductor of souls'. His ability and the popularity of some of his writings were accepted in his own time and Warburton would later say of him 'I have no conception of a greater genius on earth than Dr. Jeremy Taylor'.[92] During his lifetime his works were read and valued by royalty. John Evelyn called him 'my ghostly father' and Rust spoke feelingly of his sanctity and the openness and harmonious charm of a personality as cultured as it was theologically learned. On the other hand, there is Gilbert Sheldon, the leader with Henry Hammond of the Laudians under persecution, courageous and indomitable, capable of 'a front of iron' in facing down his King, and winning. Charles II had to yield to him over the Royal Declaration of Indulgence and Sheldon proved as formidable in ascendancy as he was fearless in adversity. Pepys commented on his administrative decisiveness and the Church of England was in many ways fortunate to have him in a position of power during the transitional touch-and-go situation at the Restoration. Though Bishop of London at that time he was the real power even before succeeding to Canterbury for Archbishop Juxon was old and authority was in fact wielded by Sheldon. R. S. Bosher regards him as one of the few post-Reformation primates to stand in the tradition of Langton and Becket: 'His love of princely state and his munificent benefactions were not unparalleled among Stuart and Hanoverian bishops; but in a combination of other qualities—courtliness and political finesse, driving energy and single-minded devotion to the Church, above all, readiness to defy the Royal will—he is reminiscent of the great medieval churchmen'.[93] There was also in Sheldon the 'darker side of the same ecclesiastical tradition', compulsion and authoritarianism. Sheldon insisted on outward conformity and strict ecclesiastical discipline. Relentlessly he enforced uniformity and presided over the exodus of the Presbyterians.

That Taylor did not happen to be Sheldon's sort of safe man is something for which posterity can be grateful while not being unmindful of the worth of Sheldon's courage and leadership. There can hardly be any question that at the Restoration when so much was in the melting-pot he was the man for the hour but Taylor remains a man for all seasons.

'This is the chief of all the Christian mysteries, and the union of all Christian blessings, and the investiture of all Christian rights, and the exhibition of the charter of all Christian promises, and the exercise of all Christian duties . . . although we serve God in every virtue, yet, in the worthy reception of this divine sacrament, there must be a conjugation of virtues, and, therefore, we serve him more.'

(*The Worthy Communicant*
Ch. III, Section V (5)).

Notes

1. *The Worthy Communicant*, Epistle Dedicatory, ib. Vol. XV, pp. cccxcvi.
2. Stranks, loc. cit., p. 225.
3. Porter, loc. cit., pp. 62–4.
4. Dugmore, loc. cit., pp. 103–4.
5. *The Worthy Communicant*, Ch. I, Section II, ib. Vol. XV, p. 420.
6. Stone, loc. cit., Vol. II, p. 331.
7. *The Worthy Communicant*, Ch. V, Section III (1), ib. Vol. XV, p. 590.
8. *The Worthy Communicant*, Ch. I, Section V (7), ib. Vol. XV, pp. 449–450, 493.
9. ib. Ch. VI, Section I (1), iv. Vol. XV, p. 652.
10. ib., pp. 553, 540, 543, 511.
11. ib. Ch. VIII, ib. Vol. XV, pp. 667–688.
12. ib. Ch. III, ib. Vol. XV, p. 498.
13. *On the Reverence due to the Altar*, Works (ed. Heber & Eden), Vol. V, p. 330.
14. *The Worthy Communicant*, Ch. I, Section II (1), ib. Vol. XV, p. 411.
15. *Clerus Domini*, Section V (10), ib. Vol. XIV, p. 459.

16. *Dissuasive*, ib. Vol. XI, p. 99.

17. *The Worthy Communicant*, Ch. III, Section V (3), ib. Vol. XV, p. 526.

18. ib. Introduction, ib. Vol. XV, p. 398.

19. ib. Ch. I, Section II (3), ib. Vol. XV, p. 416.

20. ib. Introduction, ib. Vol. XV, p. 403.

21. ib. Ch. I, Section III, ib. Vol. XV, p. 429.

22. ib. Ch. I, Section IV (4), ib. Vol. XV, p. 438.

23. cp. Bernard Häring, *The Law of Christ*, I, p. vii, and Herbert Waddams, *A New Introduction to Moral Theology*, p. 28, for contemporary Anglican and Roman Catholic assessments of the nature and function of moral theology.

24. Quotations from the Introduction, ib. Vol. XV, pp. 398–403.

25. ib. Ch. I, Section I (1), ib. Vol. XV, p. 404.

26. ib. Ch. I, Section II (4), ib. Vol. XV, p. 418.

27. ib. Ch. I, Section II (1), ib. Vol. XV, p. 412.

28. *Ecclesiastical Polity*, V, lxvii, 1.

29. *The Worthy Communicant*, Ch. I, Section II (4), ib. Vol. XV, p. 419.

30. ib. Ch. I, Section I, ib. Vol. XV, p. 406.

31. Quotations from ib. Ch. I, Section I, ib. Vol. XV, pp. 405–8.

32. ib. Ch. I, Section II (1), ib. Vol. XV, p. 409.

33. ib. Section II (1)–(2), ib. Vol. XV, p. 413.

34. ib. Section II (2), ib. Vol. XV, p. 413.

35. ib. Section II (3), ib. Vol. XV, pp. 413–4.

36. Alasdair Heron, *Table and Tradition*, pp. 68–70.

37. *The Worthy Communicant*, Ch. I, Section III, ib. Vol. XV, p. 429.

38. ib. Ch. III, Section V (4), p. 530.

39. *Real Presence*, Section III (7), ib. Vol. IX, p. 446.

40. *The Worthy Communicant*, Ch. I, Section II (3), ib. Vol. XV, pp. 415–417.

41. *The Real Presence*, Section I (4), ib. Vol. IX, p. 424.

42. *The Worthy Communicant*, Ch. I, Section II (3), ib. Vol. XV, p. 417.

43. ib. Section II (4), ib. Vol. XV, p. 417 and cp. Clement of Alexandria, *Paed.* II, ii, 19, 20 and *Strom.* V, X, 67.

44. Herbert Thorndike (1598–1672), *Works* (L.A.C.T. ed.), Vol. IV, p. 73.

45. *The Worthy Communicant*, Ch. I, Section II (4), ib. Vol. XV, pp. 419–420.

46. ib. Ch. I, Section II (4), ib. Vol. XV, pp. 420–1.

47. ib. Ch. I, Section III, ib. Vol. XV, pp. 421–3.

48. ib. Ch. I, Section III, ib. Vol. XV, pp. 424–5.

49. *Baptism, Eucharist and Ministry* (1982), Eucharist, II (2), (14)–(18).

50. *The Final Report* (*Windsor Statement*, 1971, and *Elucidation*, 1979), pp. 16, 19, 21, 23. The Irish patristic scholar, the late J. E. L. Oulton, repaired the omission for Anglicans by his study of the connection between the doctrine of the Holy Communion and the doctrine of the Holy Spirit, *Holy Communion and Holy Spirit* (1949).

51. loc. cit., Eucharist II, (9), (14), Commentary, (23).

52. *The Worthy Communicant*, Ch. VII, Section II, ib. Vol. XV, p. 679.

53. ib. Ch. I, Section III, ib. Vol. XV, pp. 426–431.
54. ib. Ch. I, Section IV, ib. Vol. XV, pp. 431–4.
55. ib. Ch. I, Section IV, ib. Vol. XV, pp. 435–6.
56. ib. Vol. XV, p. 444.
57. ib. Ch. III, Section V, ib. Vol. XV, p. 524.
58. ib. pp. 522–3.
59. *The New Week's Preparation* (Dublin ed. 1812), Part II, p. 38 and cp. C. W. Dugmore, loc. cit., p. 182, who says that it adopts the doctrinal position of Waterland.
60. ib. pp. 525–530.
61. ib. p. 532.
62. ARCIC, Final Report, p. 22; *Baptism, Eucharist and Ministry*, p. 12.
63. ib. Ch. III, Section V, ib. Vol. XV, pp. 531–3.
64. Ch. I, Section IV, ib. Vol. XV, pp. 437–440.
65. ib. pp. 438–9.
66. ib. p. 440, p. 671.
67. ib. Ch. I, Section V(1), ib. Vol. XV, p. 445.
68. *Real Presence*, Section III (6), ib. Vol. IX, p. 444.
69. ib. Section III (17), ib. Vol. IX, p. 452.
70. *The Gospel According to John* (1966), by Raymond E. Brown, p. 272.
71. *The Real Presence*, Section III (1), ib. Vol. IX, pp. 437–8.
72. ib. (5) and (13), ib. Vol. IX, pp. 442, 450.
73. *The Fourth Gospel* (1953), C. H. Dodd, pp. 333–9.
74. *Early Christian Worship* (1953), p. 58.
75. *Das Evangelium des Johannes* (1941), p. 360.
76. loc. cit., p. 272.
77. *Holy Communion and Holy Spirit* (1951), pp. 78–80, 163.
78. *Real Presence*, Section III (1), ib. Vol. IX, p. 436.
79. ib. Section III (5), (6), ib. Vol. IX, pp. 441, 444.
80. ib. Section III (7), ib. Vol. IX, p. 446.
81. ib. Section III (17), ib. Vol. IX, pp. 451–2.
82. ib. Section III (21), ib. Vol. IX, p. 455.
83. *The Worthy Communicant*, Ch. III, Section V, ib. Vol. XV, p. 524.
84. *Real Presence*, Section V (2)–(3), ib. Vol. IX, pp. 466–7.
85. In a brief biographical note on Taylor in *The English Sermon* (1976), Vol. II, p. 20.
86. C. W. Dugmore, loc. cit., pp. 96–102.
87. *Collection of Offices*, ib. Vol. XV, pp. 299–300.
88. *The Worthy Communicant*, Ch. VII, Section I (10), ib. Vol. XV, pp. 671–2.
89. ib. Ch. I, Section II (4), ib. Vol. XV, p. 417.
90. ib. Ch. I, Section IV (3), ib. Vol. XV, p. 438.
91. Stranks, loc. cit., p. 259.
92. *History of the Church of Ireland* (ed. W. Alison Philips), Vol. 2, p. 124.
93. *The Making of the Restoration Settlement* (1951), pp. 264–5.

Index